Mummy,
All love for Christmas 2016
from Ben, Jess & Beatrix

Dawn of Discovery: The Early British Travellers to Crete

Richard Pococke, Robert Pashley
and Thomas Spratt, and their contribution to the
island's Bronze Age archaeological heritage

Dudley Moore

BAR International Series 2053
2010

This title published by

Archaeopress
Publishers of British Archaeological Reports
Gordon House
276 Banbury Road
Oxford OX2 7ED
England
bar@archaeopress.com
www.archaeopress.com

BAR S2053

The Early British Travellers to Crete: Richard Pococke, Robert Pashley and Thomas Spratt, and their contribution to the island's Bronze Age archaeological heritage

ISBN 978 1 4073 0542 4

Printed in England by CMP (UK) Ltd

All BAR titles are available from:

Hadrian Books Ltd
122 Banbury Road
Oxford
OX2 7BP
England
bar@hadrianbooks.co.uk

The current BAR catalogue with details of all titles in print, prices and means of payment is available free from Hadrian Books or may be downloaded from www.archaeopress.com

CONTENTS

Abstract

It is intended to focus on three important British travellers to Crete during the 18th and 19th centuries to establish whether or not they made any significant contribution to the field of research with regard to the archaeological heritage of Bronze Age Crete. It is an attempt to bring these 'lost pioneers' of antiquity to the fore and to recognize their efforts as part of the foundation of the discovery of the island's Bronze Age archaeology prior to the groundbreaking excavations of Sir Arthur Evans. They are Richard Pococke (1704-65), Robert Pashley (1805-59) and Thomas Spratt (1811-88).

Having dealt with the terms that these travellers used in describing ancient remains, the work will look briefly at the background to Bronze Age Crete itself. Thereafter the development from antiquarianism into archaeology will be followed to establish the motives behind these travellers' wanderings in Crete. This will also involve a discussion of other British travellers to Crete and problems they may have encountered with an island in the throws of Ottoman turbulence.

In order to try and see what Pococke, Pashley and Spratt may have discovered, their footsteps have been followed around the island comparing their written accounts with what is physically there today. Consideration is then given to whether any sites they described might have been of the Bronze Age. This has not always been easy as the landscape of the island has changed over the years. However, in some cases, what has been found was indeed pertinent to the Bronze Age of Crete. In addition, various views of the mythical Labyrinth are looked at in an attempt to compound the theory that there may have been a certain belief in a period prior to the known Classical era (of the 5th century BC Greece) – even if the tales themselves were not accepted as fact. Views of British travellers to mainland Greece are compared to emphasize this belief. Finally, there is a discussion of the theories referred to in the earlier chapters.

Questions raised and, hopefully, answered are: How do the travellers' 'field surveys' and discoveries compare with what is now known today from excavation? Were some of their references to 'Cyclopean' stonework an identification of Bronze Age architecture? Do they deserve recognition for the identification of a prehistory of Crete? Why are their names missing from so many books on the history of archaeology and the discovery of Cretan archaeology?

This work will bring together, for the first time, an understanding of the views and comparative discoveries of three 18th and 19th century travellers of the, then, unknown ancient pre-history of Bronze Age Crete. It will conclude that they did indeed contribute to the realization of an earlier civilization than the Classical period even if it was not an exact knowledge as to what it might have been.

Acknowledgements

During this work I have received much assistance from various people and organizations to whom I am deeply grateful. They may not remember their contributions and I would point out that their inclusion below in no way means that they approve of, or agree with, any of my views and/or conclusions.

For such assistance I thank: David Rudling, Dr Richard Carter, Peter Drewett (Professor Emeritus) and Professor Brian Short, all of Sussex University; Dr Margarita Díaz-Andreu of Durham University; Professor Peter Warren of Bristol University; Dr Nicoletta Momigliano of Bristol University; Dr Elizabeth French of Cambridge University; Dr Sue Sherratt of Sheffield University; Professor John Bennet of Sheffield University; Dr David Gill of Swansea University; Dr Lucilla Burn of the Fitzwilliam Museum at Cambridge University; Professor Gerald MacLean of Wayne State University, Detroit; Dr Don Evely, Curator at Knossos; Lt Cdr Henry Lehmann RN rtd; Lt Cdr David Harries RN rtd; Cdr Andrew David RN rtd; Capt Christopher Page RN; Professor John Bartlett of Trinity College, Dublin; Caoimhe Ni Ghormain of Trinity College Library, Dublin; Lucia Nixon of St Hilda's College, Oxford; Julian Reid of Corpus Christi College, Oxford; Adam Green of Trinity College Library, Cambridge; Vanna Niniou-Kindell of the Ephoreia of Classical Antiquities in Chania in Crete; Dr Krystof Nowicki; Dr Elpida Hadjidaki; Dr Yiannis Papadatos; Dr Eleni Hatzaki; Dr Adonis Vasilakis; Don Tumasonis; Jason Thompson; Stelios Jackson; Efstathios Tamviskos, Edward Rowland and Hannah Cunliffe.

I also wish to thank the following institutions for allowing me to search through their records and archives for material used in this work: British School at Athens (in both Athens and Knossos); museums at Heraklion, Aghios Nicholias, Sitia and Hierapetra in Crete; National Maritime Museum at Greenwich; Fitzwilliam Museum at Cambridge; Society of Antiquaries in London; Royal Geological Society; Royal Geographical Society; British Museum; British Library; University of Edinburgh Library; Sackler and Bodleian Libraries at the University of Oxford; University of Sussex Library; University of Southampton Library; National Library of Scotland (John Murray Archive); Bartlett Library at the National Maritime Museum in Cornwall; UK Hydrographic Office at Taunton (MOD); Honourable Societies of Middle Temple, Inner Temple and Lincoln's Inn; School of Advanced Studies and Institute of Historical Research of University of London and the Institute of Classical Studies.

Appreciation is given to the various unnamed Cretans who helpfully gave directions to some of the more obscure locations during my approximate 3000 miles of travel around Crete.

Finally, I would like to express my special thanks to Sarah Green for her continued support, particularly on our visits to Crete.

The author

Dudley Moore is a barrister (member of Middle Temple) and a lecturer in both Law and Aegean Archaeology. He studied Law as an undergraduate at Sussex University and Aegean Archaeology as a postgraduate at Oxford University (Brasenose). He returned to Sussex University for his DPhil in Archaeology, on which this work is based.

Abbreviations

BSA	British School [of archaeology] at Athens
HO	Hydrographic Office
	LB: Letter Book
	IL: Incoming Letters prior to 1857
NLS	National Library of Scotland *Robert Pashley Correspondence*
NMM	National Maritime Museum, Greenwich
Pck	Pococke, R. (1745) *A Description of the East and some other Countries* Vol. II. Part I, Fourth Book: 'Of the island of Candia'
Psh I	Pashley, R. (1837) *Travels in Crete*, Vol. I
Psh II	Pashley, R. (1837) *Travels in Crete*, Vol. II
RGS	Royal Geographical Society
Sp I	Spratt, T.A.B. (1865) *Travels and Researches in Crete*, Vol. I
Sp II	Spratt, T.A.B. (1865) *Travels and Researches in Crete*, Vol. II

Minoan chronology

EM	Early Minoan
MM	Middle Minoan
LM	Late Minoan

1. Introduction

The island of Crete (Map 1, Appendix A – see Appendix A for all maps) is situated in the Aegean, southeast of mainland Greece. Ancient Bronze Age 'Minoan' Crete (*c*.3000–1450 BC) was one of the most important and earliest sophisticated civilizations of Europe and it formed part of the origins of European civilization itself. It was lost for centuries and Sir Arthur Evans has been given the credit for its rediscovery at the beginning of the 1900s.

In 1734, some 160 years earlier than the first explorations of Evans, Richard Pococke too travelled to Crete in search of its history. Almost a hundred years later Robert Pashley was reporting back to the hydrographer, Francis Beaufort, about his finds of ancient sites on the island. Then in the 1850s, still fifty years before Evans put a spade in the ground in Crete, Thomas Abel Brimage Spratt chose to travel the island to observe its topography and ruins which he believed held secrets to an ancient past.

Pococke was a member of the clergy with a passion for travel. His visit to Crete was not extensive but sufficient to reveal an island of antiquity awaiting discovery. Pashley was a barrister seeking knowledge and with the encouragement of the Admiralty was able to pursue his interest in antiquities on Crete. Captain Spratt was a Royal Naval hydrographer and followed Pashley's lead with a further and more detailed investigation of the island's ancient past. His initial task was to survey the seas of the Mediterranean and the Aegean, but he considered it necessary to review the geological status of the island of Crete to assist with this commission.

The three of them did not limit their studies to ancient history. They were all curious about how the Cretan people lived during the 18th and 19th centuries and how they coped with the oppressive Ottoman rule. They were interested in the natural history of the island and Spratt went to great lengths to report his findings to his old friend the naturalist Edward Forbes. Spratt looked at the island's geology and established that it had tilted during its ancient period and wrote to the eminent geologist Sir Charles Lyell with his discovery. Spratt also corresponded with Charles Darwin and sent him a copy of his book to see if it was of interest to him.

All three travellers recorded their discoveries in books[1] which have long since been forgotten following the revelations of Arthur Evans regarding his 'Minoans'

of Crete. Sadly Evans' publications[2] overshadowed Pococke's, Pashley's and Spratt's work.

Sir Arthur Evans' achievements on Crete are without doubt of immense value, but some credit is due to these earlier travellers. Evans must have known of these early forages into the island's history, yet his otherwise detailed accounts and reports are surprisingly sparse when it comes to mention of Pococke, Pashley or Spratt. These three were pioneers of the exploration of Crete and its antiquity, yet their names are all but absent from the history and archaeology of the island. They set the scene for those such as Evans to follow.

In a consideration of the achievements of Pococke, Pashley and Spratt with regard to the discovery of the Bronze Age of Crete, it is necessary to first look briefly at the island itself and how it developed during the Bronze Age and how the chronology of that period has subsequently been reported.

The motives behind travelling abroad during the 18th and 19th centuries form an important part of a social history of that period, and how those motives changed during the latter part of the 19th century is also of interest. This was an era that saw fundamental changes to the discipline of archaeology and its development through to the end of the 19th century is exactly the period when Pococke, Pashley and Spratt were making their investigations. Were they simply travellers, collectors or antiquarians, or could they be termed archaeologists as we would use the title today? Do the terms they used to describe and record ancient remains give insights into a phase of activity on the island that took place earlier to the Classical period of the 5th century BC? Is it relevant whether or not they knew of the Bronze Age, or is it enough that they believed in a Cretan civilization earlier than the known Classical period? These are questions that will be addressed in this work.

In order to investigate the significant contribution made by Pococke, Pashley and Spratt, it is necessary to 'follow their footsteps' around the island using their published guides in an attempt to establish that what they saw was either of the Bronze Age or, at least, of an earlier age than the Classical era which was already well known to the scholars of the 18th and 19th centuries. Comparisons of these three travellers will be made with other British travellers to the island to show that the three were distinct

---

[1] Pococke, 1745; Pashley, 1837; Spratt, 1865.

[2] Evans, 1921, 1928, 1930, 1935.

in their search for ancient knowledge. Spratt's intrigue with the 'Labyrinth' at Gortyns is of much interest as it gives a further indication of his highly inquisitive nature and therefore requires investigation. There will be a general discussion of earlier points raised to see if they have been answered following the research. A summary and conclusion will complete the work.

It cannot be denied that Evans' excavation of Knossos and other sites brought the Bronze Age civilization on Crete back to life and led the way for research which still continues today. However, he was not the first to understand that the history of Crete stretched back way beyond the Classical period. That honour should go to travellers, explorers and early archaeologists such as Richard Pococke, Robert Pashley and Thomas Abel Brimage Spratt.

Terminology
Part of the basis of this work relates to an interpretation of Pashley's and Spratt's use of the word 'Cyclopean' when describing ancient walls of Crete seen by them. Dating ancient sites is no easy task without some factor to link it with a known datable similarity such as pottery by way of typology. In the 19th century, Cretan datable pottery was not available and the main source of identification was architecture.[3] Pashley and Spratt were able to relate to the architecture of the ancient Classical period from the 5th century BC and the Hellenistic period from the 4th century BC, which they both called 'Hellenic'.[4] However, they did mention, and Pashley drew, various walls that did not seem to fit these styles. These are the 'Cyclopean' walls to which the two travellers referred, and these walls need to be considered as a possible identification of an earlier period, perhaps as early as the Bronze Age. It is necessary to consider the meaning of 'cyclopean' and whether or not there is any evidence that it should be distinguished from Pashley and Spratt's 'Hellenic'.

References
Pococke, Pashley and Spratt were primarily of the 'classical text in hand' type of travellers. Such texts included Homer's *Iliad* (composed 8th century BC) for 'historical' references, Strabo (1st century BC/1st century AD) and Pausanias (2nd century AD) for geographical references, to name but three.[5] Pococke, Pashley and Spratt were mainly interested in identifying sites of the Classical and Hellenistic 5th and 4th century BC periods because they were known to them. However, this does not mean to say that what they saw with respect to archaeological ruins was all of the Classical or Hellenistic eras. Not all of the many Bronze Age sites

of Crete were built over by later Classical or Hellenistic or Roman buildings, and so some would still have been visible to the traveller in the 18th and 19th centuries.

Interpretations
It is worth remembering that archaeology, like any science, is merely a body of arguments advanced to make sense of observations about the world. Consideration must always be given to the fact that there is often more than one acceptable way of interpreting archaeological finds and sites. This is something which is even more important when there are no contemporary written records to collaborate the evidence which is therefore subject entirely to the interpretation of the excavator. Subsequent re-examination of excavation/ travel reports may produce a different interpretation from that initially proposed. Parts of both Pashley's and Spratt's assumptions were criticized by later writers, and Spratt himself queried some of Pashley's observations.

The reference to Cyclopean was based on the size and style of the stones which have been defined as 'thick walls built of cyclopean blocks, barely hewn yet cunningly assembled'[6] (see Figs. 1.1 and 1.2 in Appendix B – see Appendix B for all figures). This definition may be somewhat of a generalization as certainly not all 'Cyclopean' blocks of the Bronze Age were 'barely hewn' as can be seen from the Mycenaean Treasury of Atreus (Fig. 1.3).

Cyclopean was a name used by the ancient geographers/ historians Strabo and Pausanias in their own descriptions of Homeric/Mycenaean architecture. Strabo mentioned the Cyclopean-built walls of Mycenaean Tiryns, 'Prœtus seems to have used Tiryns as a stronghold, and to have fortified it by means of the Cyclopes.'[7] Pausanias said of Mycenae, 'They say this is the work of Cyclopes …',[8] but he was a little more descriptive as to what the name may imply when he mentioned the walls of Tiryns (Fig. 1.2), '… built by Cyclopes with natural rocks, all so huge that a pair of mules would not even lift the smallest'.[9] The term was borrowed/used by Pashley and Spratt to supposedly differentiate it from the neat uniform 'Hellenic' style of the 5th century BC[10] (Fig. 1.4).

Although this cyclopean style of architecture was a trademark of 13th century BC Bronze Age Mycenaeans, it must be remembered that it is likely that the Mycenaeans took control of Crete during the middle of the 15th century BC[11] and would have imposed their own architectural styles onto the island. Even so, some of the 15th century BC Minoan 'palaces' were made up from very large stone walls equal to the Mycenaean 'Cyclopean' mainland examples. One such example is Malia (Figs. 1.5a and b). The American archaeologist Harriet Boyd Hawes described

---

[3] Flinders Petrie provided the basis for establishing a chronology of Aegean prehistory of mainland. Greece in 1893 by finding Mycenaean sherds at Tell el-Armana (Medwin, 2000: 241; Farnoux (1996: 66) and thereafter John Myers linked Petrie's finds at Kahun in Egypt with Middle Minoan kamares ware in Crete (Cadogan, 2000: 20).

[4] 'Hellenic' simply means 'Greek'.

[5] Eisner commented, 'Of course one reason early travelers packed their accounts with learned references was because it was only in the texts that many of the classical places existed as sites' (Eisner, 1993: 67), and this included the 'Homeric classical' sites (incorporating Idomeneus' Crete).

[6] Martin, 1988: 33.

[7] Strabo, 8.6.11.

[8] Pausanias, II.16.4.

[9] Pausanias, II.25.7.

[10] '[In] the mid-fifth century [BC], however, Greek masonry attained a finesse hitherto unparallel … blocks were fitted together with extraordinary precision' (Copplestone, 1966: 47).

[11] See Wace, 1949, and the next chapter.

the various Bronze Age styles of construction in her work on Gournia in Crete:

> During the Town period (L.M. I, c. 1700-1500 B.C.) larger stones were used; the clay mortar was inconspicuous and small stones were wedged into interstices of the walls. One style of building ... employs stones of moderate size, flat-faced and roughly oblong in shape, wedged by small stones which are sharp-edged. Probably chips from the rude trimming of larger blocks ... Another style uses small boulders, similar to those that pave roads, roughly aligned in courses, with small round stones between them ... Certain walls built in this fashion are sufficiently massive to deserve the name 'Cyclopean' ... the impulse to this heavy form of construction [Cyclopean masonry] appears to have come from the mainland and journeyed slowly southward ... The usual dimensions of these blocks are c. 1.40 m long, 90 cm. wide, and 60 cm high, but one block attains the length of 2.10 m. Even this good ashlar masonry ... was overlaid with brick-clay ...[12]

It has been suggested that although some ten cyclopean walls had been reported in Crete, none were cyclopean based on the considered construction style of cyclopean walls to which five types and an unclassified type were identified.[13] These proposed different types rather complicates the idea of Cyclopean.

Mention was made of the tholos tomb at Akhladia, Sitia in Crete, 'Although the blocks in the chamber are large and unhewn, and wedged with a great deal of interstice stones, the term Cyclopean refers to nothing more than the size of the stones.'[14] It does relate, and always has related, to size and the definition need not be any more specific. As mentioned above, reference to walls as 'Cyclopean' is an ancient epithet from Strabo and Pausanias whose ideas of its meaning simply related to the size of the stones and it is not necessary to take this definition much further.

The Classical/Hellenistic architects did not attempt to copy the Mycenaeans and so it is difficult to mistake the styles, or so one might imagine. However, care must be taken in assuming that all references by Pashley and Spratt to 'Cyclopean' remains automatically mean the Bronze Age. Some of them may not, but at least both travellers are considering an earlier period than the Classical and of an existence of some civilization when using the term. Although they may also have called later buildings cyclopean, this must not detract from the fact that some of their discoveries may have been of the Bronze Age.

So who were these ancient Cretans of the Bronze Age? Where did they come from and how did they create such a sophisticated and wealthy civilization so as to be able to construct buildings of such immense structure?

[12] Hawes, 1908: 21 and her Figs. 4, 5, 6 and 7.
[13] Loader, 1998: 124.
[14] Loader, 1998; 126.

2. Background To Bronze Age Crete

Ancient Crete

Crete is around 8000 sq km and about 250 km east to west, and is the largest of the Aegean islands. Crete's mountains emerged from the sea around 135-65 million years ago, and following a re-submergence 25-5 million years ago the island began to acquire its present form around 1.6-0.7 million years ago.[1] Settlement is first believed to have taken place at the beginning of the Neolithic period, roughly 7000-3000 BC,[2] although sites during this period are somewhat limited. Knossos was the first known settlement area during the initial Neolithic aceramic period of c.7000-6500 BC.[3]

The Bronze Age of Crete, c.3000 BC–c.1100 BC, was comprised of two 'civilizations', the 'Minoans' from about 3000 BC to about 1450 BC, and the 'Mycenaeans'[4] from about 1450 BC to 1100 BC. Both these civilizations had similarities, mainly due to the fact that the Mycenaean's culture and ideals included many elements which they had already copied from those of the Minoans.

Chronology of Bronze Age Crete

Unlike the Egyptians, the Babylonians and the Hittites, the Cretans of the second millennium BC left little written history. What they did leave were inscriptions on clay which have become known as Linear A and Linear B. Linear A is as yet undeciphered, but probably developed around the 18th century BC until 1450 BC from Cretan hieroglyphics (c.1900-1600 BC) and possibly a form of the Cretan/Minoan language, whereafter Linear B evolved probably from Linear A.[5] Linear B was deciphered by Michael Ventris in 1952 as an early form of ancient Greek and of Mycenaean origin rather than Minoan.[6] It does not help with the historical background of Crete as it is administrative by nature which does give an insight into the island's commercial activities.

When Pococke, Pashley and Spratt made their way around Crete the word 'Minoan' did not exist as a name for the island's early occupants. It was a name given to the ancient islanders by Arthur Evans simply based on the myth of their ancestor and founder, King Minos:

> The Golden Age of Crete lies far beyond the limits of the historical period … the great days of Crete [were] those of which we still find a reflection in the Homeric poems – the period of Mycenaean culture, to which here at least we would fain to attach the name 'Minoan'.[7]

In the first of his books on his excavations at Kephala Hill, Knossos, Evans wrote, 'To this early civilization of Crete as a whole I have proposed – and the suggestion has been generally adopted by the archaeologists of this and other countries – to apply the name 'Minoan'.'[8] This had not been his original theory as he first considered that the Minoans were simply part of the Mycenaean culture, but this was to change once he had started excavating. He was to banish the word 'Mycenaean' as a generic description of the early civilization of Crete, insisting that his 'Minoans' were quite a different race, even suggesting that they were the creators of the Mycenaeans.[9] The discovery of an ancient civilization was the agenda referred to by Papadopoulos when he described Evans' revealing of his so-called Minoans, 'Behind the romantic and idealistic vision of an invented society lay a very real agenda.'[10]

It was Evans who first used the pottery styles found at Knossos to divide the Minoan civilization into three phases: Early, Middle and Late Minoan (EM, MM, LM respectively). The phases run nearly parallel to the tripartite division of Egyptian history into Old, Middle and New Kingdoms. Evans' tripartite system is drawn from, and has parallels in, both biological science and art history. The system introduced by Evans was expanded to include the Bronze Age cultures within the central and western Aegean islands and termed 'Cycladic', as well as those on the mainland of 'Greece', termed 'Helladic'.[11] These too have been divided in terms of relative chronology into Early, Middle and Late phases. Thus Early Minoan, Early Cycladic and Early Helladic are all roughly contemporary, as are the Middle and Late references.

The basic tripartite scheme was further subdivided, based on pottery styles and stratigraphy, such that each of the three periods contained three or more divisions (EM I, II, III). These were then further subdivided into units indicated by

---

[1] Rackham & Moody, 1996: xv.
[2] Sherratt & Sherratt, 2008: 291.
[3] See papers in Isaakidou & Tomkins (eds.), 2008, particularly Broodbank's (273-90).
[4] The term 'Mycenaean' was used in the 19th century as describing all the peoples of the Aegean from the Neolithic to the beginnings of 5th century BC Classical Greece (Burrows, 1907: 40), but more specifically, from the Argolid in the eastern Peloponnese on mainland Greece.
[5] Chadwick, 2001: 43-4.
[6] Ventris & Chadwick, 1958.

[7] Evans, 1896a: 512.
[8] Evans, 1921: 1.
[9] A view later disputed with some zeal by Alan Wace (1949).
[10] Papadopoulos, 2005: 106.
[11] After the Greeks' own word for Greece, 'Hellas'.

letters of the alphabet (for example, LM IB). As additional excavations and studies have been undertaken this system has come under criticism for being too inflexible and partly inaccurate.[12] A system that seems less confusing and better reflects cultural developments is the one that revolves around the building and destruction of the major architectural complexes. The reference to 'palatial' periods is based around the so-called Minoan 'palaces'[13] of Knossos, Phaistos, Malia and Kato Zakros. This system also has a tripartite division: pre-palatial, palatial and post-palatial, with the palatial period being subdivided into proto- (old) and neo- (new)[14] and the post-palatial which is the Mycenaean phase. The divisions are based on the belief that most of the palaces suffered major damage and were then rebuilt in a more magnificent style. The exact chronological sequence is still uncertain but, nonetheless, it is useful to classify the phases architecturally, although the original Early, Middle and Late classifications are often still used when speaking of pottery styles. For clarification the dating of Bronze Age 'Minoan' Crete looks like this:[15]

	circa BC	
EM I	3000-2700	pre-palatial
EM IIA	2700-2400	
EM IIB	2400-2200	
EM III	2200-2000	
MM IA	2000-1900	
MM IB	1900-1800	proto-palatial
MM II	1800-1700	
MM III	1700-1600	neo-palatial
LM IA	1600-1500	
LM IB	1500-1450	
LM II	1450-1400	post-palatial (Mycenaean)
LM IIIA1	1400-1370	
LM IIIA2	1370-1300	
LM IIIB	1300-1200	end of Mycenaean palatial period
LM IIIC	1200-1100	end of Mycenaean Age

The quest for an *absolute* chronology of the Aegean Bronze Age has centred both on the use of Egyptian and Mesopotamian chronologies and on the scientific methods of radio-carbon dating and dendrochronology. However, absolute dates are not yet completely reliable and different sets of dates are often in use for one and the same phase or period. In recent years doubts have been cast on the value or significance of the use of the historical chronologies of Egypt and Mesopotamia, while radiocarbon dating too

has proved not to be as reliable as once thought due to difficulties with correlation and various climatic changes that may affect calibration.[16] Recent developments in dendrochronology may ultimately help to resolve the various issues. Of particular interest is the 'Aegean Dendrochronology Project' whose long-range goal is to build a single master tree-ring chronology for the Aegean and Near East that will extend from the present to the seventh millennium BC.

Settlement of ancient Crete

There does not appear to be any evidence in Crete for permanent settlement in either the Palaeolithic or Mesolithic periods, but there may have been a pre-Neolithic culture on the island. 'Culture' does not necessarily mean permanent settlement. The existence of humans on Crete in the Mesolithic period of 9000-7000 BC is evidenced by finds of large numbers of obsidian flakes from the island of Melos, north of Crete, together with indications of Mesolithic huts at the sites of Trypiti and Rouses and rock-paintings at Asphendos near Sphaka, which suggest the existence of a society of hunter-gatherers.[17]

With regard to settlement, the island was an obvious choice due to its climate, rainfall and fertility, making it good for agriculture. An abundance of ovicaprines, cattle, pig, bread wheat and other flora has been found at Knossos.[18] The bread wheat is not of a natural growth, it is a hybrid of domesticated *tetraploid* wheat and wild wheat.[19] This implies that their existence must be from a planned external origin. In support of this there has been a suggestion that the island was colonized in one or more deliberate acts.[20] So where did these settlers come from? 'Knossian' bread wheat has been found on the Anatolian coast at Can Hasan III and Catal Huyuk,[21] indicating possible connections between the two and Crete. Although the first settlers were aceramic, Early Neolithic pottery seemed to be inspired by ceramic traditions in West Anatolia.[22] African-Egyptian and Aegean mainland origins have been eliminated as no relevant domesticates were found in Crete for that early period.

At the beginning of the Early Minoan period the main areas of settlement was Knossos with its port at Poros-Katambas. Cycladic style pottery found at this port indicates it to have been an important trading port at this time.[23] There were also early settlements in the Mesara at Phaistos and Ayia Triadha.

---

[12] Biers, 1996: 23; but see also Dickinson (1999: 8ff) for a discussion of how Evans himself could not adhere to the system he suggested.

[13] If 'palaces' are what they were. There is a view that they may have been temples (Castleden, 1990) or perhaps a combination.

[14] But see also Dickinson (1999: 11-13), who divided the palatial period into first, second and third, making five divisions in all (including pre- and post-palatial).

[15] Adapted from Shelmerdine, 2008: 4 (Fig. 1.1) but open to variations (e.g. EM I may have commenced 3300, but I have tried to give a simple 'generalization' of dates); see also Huxley, 2000: xxi, and Dickinson, 1999: 19.

[16] Dickinson, 1999: 17.

[17] Vasilakis,1999: 70, also Rackham & Moody, 1996: 1.

[18] Evans, 1971: 99, but this does not mean Knossos was the only early Neolithic settlement site (see Macdonald, 2005: 6).

[19] Zohany & Hopf, 1998.

[20] Manning, 2008: 107.

[21] Renfrew, 1972: 203.

[22] Evans, 1971:115, although he added that in Early Neolithic II, the coloured pottery indicates links with the Aegean mainland.

[23] Wilson, 2008: 82.

Emergence of palaces

The Middle Minoan civilization has become known as a highly developed hierarchal society culminating in 'palace' buildings. But how did this come about? What must first be considered is what is meant by the word 'palace' in relation to the Middle and Late Minoan periods of Crete. A modern day understanding of the word is a large and impressive residential building for a wealthy royal family. Minoan 'palaces' were certainly large and for the wealthy, but not necessarily royalty, as it is not known who lived in them other than that they must have had some authority. They may have been Priests or Priest Kings if the 'palaces' were of a religious nature (they appear to have been involved in cult practices). However, for convenience sake these Minoan buildings will be referred to as 'palaces' as their architectural design warrants the word. As mentioned above, the place sites (in order of size) were Knossos, Phaistos, Malia and Kato Zakros. Also, recent discoveries at Galatas indicate a palatial residence. There are possibly more, as yet, undiscovered.

The old palaces or proto-palatial, may have incorporated nearly all the basic features and infra-structures of the new palace or neo-palatial period. These 'features' being a central court, west court, storage magazines, residential quarters, banquet hall, public/administrative apartments, cult rooms, theatral area and workshops. It is difficult to be certain due to the destruction of most the old palaces to make way for the new. Little of the old sites remain in evidence other than the foundation to the west façade of Phaistos, as here the new palace was not built immediately above it. After the destruction of the old palaces the neo-palatial sites, particularly at Knossos, Phaistos and Malia, were all enlarged with grander and more imposing styles.[24]

The building of palaces required larges surpluses of wealth, and it is this emergence of wealth that must account for the emergence of palaces. 'Wealth' may be defined as possession of goods for their desirability and not for their usefulness.[25] For example, gold is desirable but not always of great use compared with practical or domestic items of bronze or ceramics. But how was this wealth obtained?

When land no longer becomes readily available to all due to an increase in population, inequalities develop and those with no land become labourers. This leads to the possibility of the beginning of a hierarchy. As time goes on, specific individuals who are able to best exploit the 'inequalities' become the elite. These elite then compete within themselves for power and one way to exercise power is to display wealth by way of hospitality through dinner parties or gift-giving (*xenia*). So the elite needed investment and this leads to a revolution in agricultural products, centralization, movement of surplus, redistribution, rapid population growth and a more organized/controlled settlement.[26]

Initially farmers only needed to grow only enough to keep the immediate family alive from year to year which may assume some surplus to ensure survival. Also the family produced domestic goods such as pots and utensils for their own use and essential to their own needs. This would extend to less domesticated luxury goods. As farms increased in size, both in acreage and population, so too did the community, and distribution of excess produce and luxury goods led to wealth.

Due to its position in the Mediterranean, Crete would have had some contact with overseas travellers from the surrounding continents, Asia, Africa and Europe, and there is evidence of trade connections with other regions during this EM period.[27] There must be a close link between social and commercial progress: trade in various products with other countries brought in new ideas which led to more trade, both within Crete and outside, which led to an increase in wealth for the traders. The finding of sealstones on some sites[28] indicated movement and identification of goods, which required development of administration in a land becoming more organized. Such development would require employment of labourers and craftsmen to keep up with the volume of demand. Larger houses would have been built to accommodate the wealthy.

As pottery production was on the increase, the need to cope with it would result in a change from solely agricultural activity to a new ceramic industry which would lead to a new social culture incorporating wealth and the building of palaces.[29]

Destruction and coming of the Mycenaeans

It is not known for certain what caused the demise of the Minoan civilization. All that is known is that around 1450 BC a disaster struck the island of Crete and its civilization came to an end and the Mycenaeans from the Argolid of the eastern Peloponnese on mainland 'Greece' appeared to have taken control of Knossos. Whether the Mycenaeans were a part of this destruction is not clear[30] but they may well have been covetous of the Minoan wealth and trade links.

These Mycenaeans were a rich community by the 17th century BC, as Heinrich Schliemann discovered golden treasures in Grave Circle A within the walls of the city of Mycenae on the mainland[31] which were later dated to this period. Homer referred to the city of Mycenae as 'deep golden Mykenai'[32] and must have had his own good reasons for such an epithet. The main Mycenaean cities within the

[24] See Fitton, 2002; also Younger & Rehak, 2008: 140-64 on material culture of the new palaces.
[25] Renfrew, 1972: 370.
[26] See Renfrew, 1972; but also see Hamilakis' criticism of Renfrew's
redistribution theory, 2002: 2-28; also Manning, 2008: 106-7; and Strasser considered that the kouloures at Knossos and Phaistos were not for grain storage which would affect the redistribution theory (1997: 73-100) but Halstead disagreed (1997: 103-7).
[27] Branigan, 1970: Egypt (180), Levant (182), within the Aegean (184), Cyprus and Syria (187).
[28] See Evans, 1909.
[29] See Manning, 2008: 105-20 on the formation of palaces.
[30] See Manning, 1999a; also Macdonald, 2005: 197ff
[31] Schliemann, 1878.
[32] Homer's *Iliad*, 11:47.

Argolid consisted of Mycenae itself, Tiryns, Midea and Argos. Based on the goods in the aforementioned Grave Circle A, and from the immenseness of their fortifications, these cities were possibly warrior communities capable of pillaging other areas, including Crete, for an increase in wealth. The Mycenaeans remained in Knossos for around 200 years before another unknown disaster brought an end to the island's civilized world.

The known myth

Spratt said of Crete, 'A charming land without legend, some may feel, is like a bird of bright plumes without song.'[33] Legend or myth would be used to explain the unexplainable but it might be said that anthropologists would now consider that myth holds some information relating to fact. To some extent such recognition owes its credence to the likes of Schliemann with his discovery/ publication of Troy and Mycenae,[34] giving a 'ring of truth' to the Homeric poems, and Evans for the discovery/ publication[35] of the 'Minoan civilization of King Minos'.

Was it King Minos who colonized Crete and built up a supreme navy, the Minoan thalassocracy, clearing the Aegean of pirates,[36] or was it all myth? We have no evidence to say he did, but also we have no evidence to say that he did not. However, behind these myths may lay elements of truth, particularly as it is now known that Crete was a wealthy and powerful kingdom in the Bronze Age and one of the great civilizations at that time.

According to mythology, King Minos built a labyrinth as a lair for his Minotaur, which was the off-spring of his wife's dalliance with a bull. This beast was later to be slain by the equally mythological Theseus of Athens. However, such tales were not considered mythological by the Classical 5th century BC ancient Greeks, they were their history.

Pococke, Pashley and Spratt were interested in and made reference to King Minos because he appeared in the old texts. Ancient poets, commentators, historians, geographers and travellers such as Homer, Hesiod, Herodotus, Thucydides, Appollodorus, Diodorus Siculus, Pliny, Pausanias, Strabo, Pindar, Appian and Ptolemy all made reference to King Minos and to his Crete as a very real civilization. The earliest of these individuals, the 8th century BC poet Homer,[37] said/sang of Crete:

There is a land called Crete in the middle of the wine-blue water, a handsome country and fertile, seagirt, and there are many peoples in it, innumerable; there are ninety cities. Language with language mix there together. There are Achaians, there are great-hearted Eteokretans, there are Kydonians, and Dorians in three divisions, and noble Pelasgians; and there is Knossos, the great city, and the place where Minos was king for nine-year periods, and conversed with great Zeus.[38]

So were Homer's 'great-hearted Eteokretans'[39] actually Evans' 'Minoans', and was Homer 'singing' of the Bronze Age? Although there is some conflicting evidence in Homer's *Iliad* about the time period, as some references to armour are of Homer's own 8th century BC Archaic period and some of the earlier 14th century BC Bronze Age, it is generally presumed that he was reflecting the heroes of the latter.[40]

Many scholars in the 19th century treated both the Homeric poems (*Iliad* and *Odyssey*) as myths, firstly because of their fanciful content, and secondly because no civilizations involving such characters were known to exist. The idea was that this whole early age of the Aegean was simply a figment of a poet's imagination. However, in 1858 William Gladstone, then MP for the University of Oxford prior to becoming Prime Minister, wrote a three-volume discussion of the possible accuracy of Homer as history, observing, '… the earliest Greek history should be founded on the text of Homer, and not merely on its surface, but on its depths.'[41] Gladstone's books are based on a literal belief in Homer's world and therefore have not gone uncriticized, but what is relevant is this consideration, during the middle of the 19th century, of an earlier pre-Classical period.

Were the Cretan myths behind the purposes of Pococke, Pashley and Spratt's travels? When Cyriac of Ancone(a), in the 15th century AD, was asked why he went to such a horrible country as Greece, he replied, 'I go to wake the dead.'[42] This may have been one of the reasons why Pococke, Pashley and Spratt went to Crete. In this respect, it is worth considering the motives behind early travellers to the ancient lands.

---

[33] Spratt, 1865, Vol. II: 134.

[34] 1875 and 1878 respectively.

[35] I use 'discovery and publication' as, although Evans may not have been the first to discover 'Minoan' archaeology (being the purpose of this research), he was the first to publicize his findings theorizing on the civilization.

[36] Thucydides, in the 5th century BC, said that this was so 'according to tradition' (1.4).

[37] If, indeed, he actually existed as an individual, but see Manning, 1996: 118-20 on a discussion of the date of Homer.

[38] Homer's *Odyssey* XIX: 172-9.

[39] Eteo-Cretans: Ετεο: true or genuine: the 'old-stock' Cretans; see reference to 'Eteocretans' by Diodorus Siculus, v.64.1; see also Sherratt, 1996: 90 (and whole article for observations on Homer and Crete).

[40] Manning, 1996: 121-42.

[41] Gladstone, 1858: 81, Vol. I.

[42] From Eisner, 1993: 13.

3. Early Travellers And Archaeology

Travellers' motives

The Grand Tour

The Grand Tour began around the 16th century, with Fynes Moryson being one of the first Grand Tourists in 1591. However, it was not until the 18th century that it became fashionable. By this latter date such travel had become part of the elite youth's education and social image. It was a fusion of tourism and social status. The popular countries to visit were France and Italy, travelling via Germany, Switzerland and Austria. Paris was fashionable, but Rome was warm and cultural. Italy was in the Mediterranean, which was the centre of four great empires, Assyrian, Persian, Greek and Roman, which made Italy a more popular venue for the Oxbridge and classically educated aristocrats.

The tutors that accompanied these young gentlemen had little control over them and, although the initial idea behind the Grand Tour was education, some aristocrats focused more on simple enjoyment. This meant few made records of their travels. The more committed traveller did publish reports but these were more on the lines of advice in travelling rather than educational information about the particular country. As far as education was concerned, the Grand Tourers devoted more time to the art than to the politics, society and economy of the cities that they visited.[1]

Some of the less youthful Grand Tourers were more interested in acquisitions. Wealthy aristocrats who had both the time and finance to travel to the exotic ancient world gathered up remains of the past. They were the gentlemen collectors and Thomas Bruce, the Earl of Elgin (1766-1841), fits into this loose category.[2] Some intended to collect ancient memorabilia to show off in their stately residences, and they are not to be confused with scholarly researchers of the 18th and 19th century. Others were happy to donate their collections to museums in exchange for some recognition, such as Edward Daniel Clarke (1769-1822) and John Marten Cripps (1780-1853).[3] Clarke in particular was held in high regard for his donations and

was awarded an LL.D from Cambridge University and thereafter a Professorship. There was also Charles Wateron (1782-1865), an expert in taxidermy, who returned from South America in 1802 with his tropical animals, not just for the benefit of future generations but also for political satire.

Learned travellers, such as Pashley and Spratt, although not interested in treasures as such, were not averse to removing the occasional item. Pashley brought back to England a sarcophagus and Spratt an altar, a lid to a sarcophagus and various small engravings which were donated to the Fitzwilliam Museum in Cambridge and the British Museum. Pashley and Spratt's motives were of a scholarly interest, and it could be said that anyone with an interest in antiquity is acquisitive by nature. Certainly Pashley and Spratt's values would not be in question as they did not keep their acquisitions but allowed them to be preserved for public viewing and future prosperity.

The Grand Tour was in decline by the beginning of the 19th century, mainly due to the French Revolution (1792) and Britain's subsequent war with France (1793-1815). It was between the deaths of Samuel Johnson in 1784 and Sir William Hamilton in 1803 that the Grand Tour came to an end. However, the Grand Tourers were not all decadent aristocrats and some were looking to Classical Greece for inspiration.

The Enlightenment

It was in the early 18th century that a group of Grand Tourers set up the Society of Dilettanti (see below), which instigated its 'Greek Project', which was a 'quintessential Enlightenment enterprise in search of antiquity'.[4] The project involved three major expeditions to Greece by prominent architects for the purpose of drawing and recording the classical buildings. The first expedition was led by James Stuart (1713-88) and Nicholas Revett (1720-1804) between 1750-3, the second by Richard Chandler (1738-1810) and William Pars (1742-82) in 1764, and the third led by William Gell (1777-1836 – see chapter 12) in 1812. Others travelled overseas to find answers to ancient languages, and William Warburton (1698-1779) travelled to Egypt to attempt to decipher the Egyptian hieroglyphs,[5] as did Richard Pococke in the 1730s.

One of the ideas of the Enlightenment was that the present

---

[1] Black, 2003: 14.
[2] Arguably, he was a contributor to the preservation of the heritage of the past rather than knowledge, although Sir Arthur Evans gave some credibility to the wealthy 'traveller' with his intensive excavations and reconstruction work (even though criticized in some quarters) at Knossos.
[3] They brought back from overseas 183 crates in 1802 and the library of Jesus College, Cambridge, benefited from this collection. This library was the 'museum' in Cambridge before the Fitzwilliam Museum was completed in 1840 (Dolan, 2000: 151, 157).

[4] Jenkins, 2004: 173.
[5] See Cheesman, 2004.

should learn from the past. Accordingly some travellers during the 18[6] and 19[6] centuries were investigating the origins of human society, and the modern discipline of anthropology has roots in the 18[6] century.[6] It developed from the study of natural history, which required travelling to other countries for comparisons and learning. As research developed throughout the 19[6] century so too did the sciences of the study of mankind. Interest in fauna and flora led to interest in artefacts and archaeology.

By the end of the 19[6] century Charles Darwin's theories on evolution had taken shape with his publication of *On the Origin of Species* in 1859 and ethnology, anthropology and archaeology became linked. Archaeology was a natural progression from the re-examination of the question of human origins. It was now considered possible to look into the past by studying existing 'primitive' societies. This was a new era of learning with antiquarians, historians and archaeologists working alongside one another.

The 18[6] and 19[6] centuries were part of the period of the Enlightenment involving new ideas in philosophy, art and literature.[7] It also involved exploration and developments in science, and it was a time of changing attitudes to these various topics. Pococke, Pashley and Spratt were in Crete to search for antiquarian knowledge as part of the Age of Enlightenment and not as part of the aristocratic Grand Tour. They were keen travellers with a desire for historical information even though they may not necessarily have fully understood all the information that presented itself to them on the island. To establish whether they had an involvement in archaeology it is necessary to see how the science of archaeology evolved.

Beginnings of archaeology

The term 'archaeology' may be considered a modern (20[6] century) term, but it was known by the ancient civilizations. It comes from the Greek *arkhaeologia*, translated as 'discovery of old things' or 'antiquity in general', and was used by Plato in his *Hippias as Major* in the 4[6] century BC.[8] From the 5[6] century BC, Thucydides' first chapters (2-19) were called the 'Archaeology', although not as we know it today.[9] However, he reported:

> These [Karians and Phoenicians] settled most of the [Aegean] islands, and here is the proof: when Delos was purified by the Athenians in this war and all the burials on the island removed, more than half proved to be Karian, recognizable by the weaponry used as grave furnishings and by the method of burial which is still in use.[10]

He also made an interesting observation about the problem of interpretation of ruins of the past:

> For if the city of the Lacedaemonians were deserted and the shrines and foundations of buildings preserved, I think that after the passage of considerable time there would eventually be widespread doubt that their power measured up to their reputation … but that if the Athenians were to suffer the same fate their power would be estimated, from the city's pure appearance, as twice what it is.[11]

Archaeology developed as a natural progression from the work of antiquarians and there is a distinct similarity between the two roles (see below). Alain Schnapp, a professor of archaeology at the University of Paris, referred to the 2nd century AD Greek geographer and traveller Pausanias as the 'prince of antiquaries',[12] determining that such terminology was nothing new. Robert Eisner, the Professor of Classic and Comparative Literature at San Diego University, remarked, 'Like Herodotus, he [Pausanias] was trying to preserve a memory of the past, the relics of which he saw crumbling all around him.'[13]

In the second millennium AD, western nations had been fascinated by societies of the past, particularly the Classical world of the Greeks and Romans. During the 14th–17th century Renaissance the social elite spent time building up collections of antiquities from these ancient eras. Unfortunately they had little regard for interpretation of their meaning within the culture from which they came. In the 18th century antiquarianism continued to be a leisure activity for the gentry and aristocracy. Schnapp suggested the term had originated in the 17th century,[14] but Piggott referred to John Leland (1503-32) as 'probably' claiming the title in England in the 16th century.[15] However, it was the 19th century that saw the developing disciplines of scientific methodologies of archaeology and historiography and the professionalization of researching.

Most of the interest lay in visible sites of some prominence, and Pompeii in Italy was one of the first that fired the imaginations of the culturally inquisitive. Although it was excavated in the 18th century, it was not properly recorded as an archaeological site until the late 19th century by Guiseppe Fiorelli. As far as Great Britain was concerned, perhaps the first scholar to make systematic archaeological studies was William Stukeley (1687-1765).[16] He made accurate plans, by way of engravings, of sites such as Stonehenge[17] and could be regarded as 'the last of the great English antiquarians and the first of the reliable

---

[6] See Jones, 2004.

[7] See Diaz-Andreu (2007) for an innovative history of archaeology during the 19th century.

[8] Plato's *Hippias*, 285d.

[9] Lattimore, 1998: 3 (fn 1.2-19).

[10] Thucydides, 1.7.

[11] Thucydides, 1.10.

[12] Schnapp, 1996: 46. Although the earliest traveller (and producer of a 'guidebook') of the Mediterranean was Scylax (*c.*350 BC) and thereafter Herakleides Kritikos (2nd or 1st century BC) and then Strabo (63/64 BC-AD 24).

[13] Eisner, 1993: 32.

[14] Schnapp, 1996: 179. As far as Britain is concerned, Robert Plot (1640-96), the first Keeper of the Ashmolean Museum, Oxford and/or Peter Mundy (1608-67) are such examples.

[15] Piggott, 1989: 14.

[16] Whom Richard Pococke corresponded with about his own travels (see Kemp, 1887: xl, xlvi-vii).

[17] Stukeley, 1740.

archaeologists'.[18] Although in the 17th century John Aubrey was a pioneer of observation and imagination which led to archaeological reconstruction.

It was in the middle of the 19th century that archaeology became an established discipline following the newly developed science of geology, particularly in regard to stratigraphy, a science advanced by Sir Charles Lyell (1797-1875).[19] Geology, through stratigraphy, was the foundation of archaeology which led to the beginnings of the discovery of the antiquity of mankind. Certainly towards the end of the 19th century the archaeologist was clearly recognized as a methodical collector of evidence rather than a treasure hunter,[20] having taken 'centre stage' from antiquarianism. However, there was still a distinct divide between amateurs and 'professionals'[21] and a concern about allowing amateurs with no training or knowledge to 'tamper with ... the very deeds of our earliest history'.[22]

As far as the earlier prehistorians were concerned the world had been created in 4004 BC, based on the biblical reference to the Flood and Creation in the first chapter of the Book of Genesis. However, a Frenchman, Jacques Boucher de Perthes (1788-1868), in his excavations in northern France, discovered human artefacts of chipped stone (hand axes) and bones of extinct animals of a time long before this presumed biblical Creation. His colleagues frowned upon his theory until it was considered and endorsed by two Englishmen, John Evans (1823-1908, father of Sir Arthur Evans) and Joseph Prestwich (1812-96).[23] The quest was on for the history of mankind to be unravelled and archaeology was part of the process.

De Perthes was not the first to consider stratification. In 1800 *Archaeologia*[24] published a letter article by an Englishman, John Frere, which mentioned his findings of flint weapons in a twelve foot layer of a gravel pit, overlaid by a level of sand containing bones of extinct animals, shells and the remains of marine life. His observation was that the beginning of the world in 4004 BC might not be correct, and that he was looking at a much remoter period for his finds.[25]

This letter was ignored by the academics until referred to by Prestwich in 1860 in a summary of his paper to the Royal Society in London, supporting de Perthes' opinion on the significance of stratification. A new order of chronology was on the horizon.

By 1837 chronology had already taken shape, albeit without specific dating. The Danish scholar C.J. Thomsen produced his *Guide to Northern Antiquities*, and proposed three chronological stages of prehistory, the Three Age System: the Stone Age, the Bronze Age and the Iron Age.[26] He arranged a collection in the National Museum of Copenhagen into these classifications. The Stone Age was later sub-divided into Palaeolithic and Neolithic. It had its critics who believed that it was not possible to neatly arrange objects in such a way.[27] This is true, being far too vague, and it is impossible to ascertain exactly when one finished and the other started, but it was at least a period guideline.

The British influence followed with the likes of General Augustus Pitt Rivers (1827-1900) who, along with John Evans, devised schemes for evolution of artefacts which gave rise to the method of typology which was an arrangement of artefacts in a chronological and a developmental sequence. British archaeologists such as Sir William Flinders Petrie (1853-1942) and Sir Mortimer Wheeler (1890-1976) were not far behind them and were amongst the early researchers to realize that to truly learn how a civilization existed most excavated finds had to be examined and recorded and that nothing should be discarded. These two characters were to lead archaeology into the scientific study of antiquities.

By 1880 the basic ideals of today's archaeology had been established. Prior to this the Bible had been the main inspiration for the search for the lost civilizations of Egypt and the Near East, and Homer, with his *Iliad* and *Odyssey*, the main inspiration for the search for Troy and early Mycenaean Bronze Age Greece.[28]

However, there were some British travellers who discovered various ancient sites and their work contributed to the emergence of ancient civilizations. Crete is one such situation. Sir Arthur Evans is widely referred to as the discoverer of the ancient Cretan civilization of the Minoans,[29] but he was not the first Briton to set foot on the island with an inquisitive nature. There were other individuals that came before him, including the three main characters of this work, Pococke, Pashley and Spratt, who all made their own contribution to the discovery of the island's ancient heritage. However, in what capacity did they make such discoveries? Were they pioneer archaeologists, historians, antiquarians, or simply treasure hunters? The latter can be discounted on the basis that they did not bring back to Britain a vast wealth of finds. It is worth looking at the other three possibilities to establish exactly what they mean and see whether the three travellers fit into any of the categories. It is also of interest to compare them with other British travellers to Crete and

---

[18] Murray (ed), 2001: 39.

[19] Lyell, 1830. He was an esteemed colleague of Thomas Spratt (see chapter 8).

[20] An observation by Hogarth, 1889: x.

[21] See Pitt Rivers, 1887: 272-3.

[22] Holworth, 1892: 141.

[23] See Renfrew & Bahn, 1996: 24. This endorsement coincided with Charles Darwin's publication of his *On the Origin of Species* in 1859, followed by his *Descent of Man* in 1871, both of which addressed the concept of evolution.

[24] The publication of the Society of Antiquaries of London (first publication, 1770).

[25] Frere, 1800, Vol. 13: 205.

[26] Thomsen, 1837, although P.F. Suhm had referred to successive use of such materials in 1776, followed by L.S. Vedel Simonsen between 1813-16 (Daniel, 1967: 90-1).

[27] Wright, 1875: vii; see also Rowley-Conwy, 2007.

[28] See Schliemann, 1875, 1878.

[29] Fitton, 1995: 36.

the difficulties they all may have encountered considering the strife and turbulence the island has endured during the second millennium.

Archaeologists, antiquarians and historians

The fascination with history was to lead to the 'historical revolution' which was soon to be enhanced by the Universities of Oxford and Cambridge offering history courses. There followed the establishment of new universities in the 19th century that also offered history. It was the *English Historical Review* in 1886 that 'marked the academic arrival of the professional historian'.[30]

Most of the prominent historical writers of the 19th century were male, middle class and Oxford or Cambridge educated and/or members of a profession such as clergy, lawyers, bankers, doctors, architects, engineers and military. So too were many antiquarians and archaeologists.[31] The clergy were especially well suited for antiquarian activity, being Oxbridge and classically educated. Also there was a heavy predominance of barristers involved as antiquarians due to their ability to read documents and being London based in the Inns of Court. However, archaeologists and antiquarians were not professionals in either of those fields, although some were able to combine both their professional work with archaeological activity. As mentioned in the Introduction, Pococke was a clergyman, Pashley a barrister and Spratt a naval officer.

How were antiquarians defined in the 18th century? They were collectors who compiled local histories and topographies. In 1771, the first edition of the *Encyclopaedia Britannica* referred to the 'Antiquary' as:

> a person who studies and searches after monuments and remains of antiquity. There were formerly in the chief cities of Greece and Italy, persons of distinction called antiquaries, who made it their business to explain the ancient inscriptions, and give other assistance in their power to strangers who were lovers of that kind of learning. There is a society of antiquaries in London, incorporated by the king's charter.[32]

Borlase described antiquarians in the 18th century:

> The proper business of an Antiquary is to collect what is dispersed, more fully to unfold what is already discovered, to examine controverted point, to settle what is doubtful, and by the authority of Monuments and Histories, to throw light upon the manners, Arts, Languages, Policy and Religion of past Ages.[33]

Then from the antiquarian the science of archaeology developed as an acceptable form of investigation by the mid 19th century by way of an evolutionary product. The 19th century antiquarian Newton said of archaeologists:

> He who would master the manifold subject-matter of Archaeology, and appreciate its whole range and compass, must possess a mind in which the reflective and perceptive faculties are duly balanced; he must combine with the aesthetic culture of the Artist, and the trained judgment of the Historian, not a little of the learning of the Philologer; the plodding drudgery which gathers together his materials must not blunt the critical acuteness required for their classification and interpretation.[34]

The earlier, more renowned archaeologists came from military backgrounds as the nature of their career gave them more scope to visit ancient lands overseas. They include General Pitt Rivers, Capt. (later Col.) William Leake and Capt. (later Vice-Admiral) Thomas Spratt. Some were employed abroad and able to broaden their own interests in the past. One such individual was Henry Creswicke Rawlinson, who was employed by the East India Company and managed to find time to work on Assyrian inscriptions at Nimrud and Nineveh. Others were funded by newspapers in the hope that they may uncover 'headlines'. An example is George Smith, who was employed by the British Museum and received money from the *Daily Mail* to attempt to discover the missing fragment of the Chaldean account of the Deluge.[35] Some were so disillusioned by their own professions that they sought an interest elsewhere. A.H. Layard and Charles Lyell were both lawyers tired of their profession and the former headed for the East and the latter became a prominent geologist (and colleague of Spratt, see chapter 8).[36]

It was their methods that really distinguished these groups and to some extent still does. Historians observed written texts and aimed to convince by historical narrative. Archaeologists excavated and observed artefacts whereas antiquarians combined the two with more emphasis on collecting than excavating. At the end of the 19th century Thomas Hodgkin suggested that archaeologists collect facts from the past whereas historians arrange them.[37]

Historians may have considered themselves a more reliable source of the past based on their work from actual manuscripts, but care must be taken with this assumption. Old documents may be useful to history but they can never be regarded as history. This is reminiscent of Herodotus' comment: 'My business is to record what people say, but I am by no means bound to believe it - and that may be taken to apply to this book [*The Histories*] as a whole'.[38]

[30] Levine, 2002: 164.
[31] See the study by Altick, 1962, vi: 390ff.
[32] Bell & Macfarquhar (& Smellie), 1771: 328.
[33] Borlase, 1769: v.
[34] Newton, 1851: 25-6.
[35] See Lloyd, 1947: vii.165.
[36] For more on the characters in this paragraph, see Searight & Wagstaff, 2001; Lloyd, 1947; Levine, 2002.
[37] Hodgkin, 1891: 267.
[38] Herodotus, 7.152.

In contrast, archaeologists work from finds rather than hearsay. Their usage as evidence of our understanding of the past is dependant upon the particular interpretation. In this sense, neither the archaeologist nor the historian is in any better position than the other to claim superiority in reliability of the conclusions that may be drawn. Certainly the historian is not concerned with a tile, part of a pot or some indication of flooring or wall. Lord Dacre wrote to Philip Morant:

> I wish you joy of your tessellated pavement,
> I know you will value it and step upon it with
> more pleasure than on finest Persian Carpet: as
> it raises … up in your imagination Proconsuls,
> Generals etc in all their glory, who have been
> dead and gone above these sixteen hundred
> years.[39]

With regard to interpretations it is particularly important to take into account writers' motives when looking at journals or autobiographies of historians, travellers and/or archaeologists. How much can they be relied upon? Some of the following factors must be considered:

- The personal significance of the event: when was the recollection made? (memory can sometimes be selective)
- The language and meanings of culture: have they changed since the recollection?
- The motivation: why is the past being recalled?
- The audience: who is the author attempting to appeal to? Is it other academics? Or just ordinary members of the public?[40]
- The purpose: to entertain or to actually mark historical events?[41]
- The genre: are they recollections, conventions or simply anecdotes?
- The medium: what type of recollection is it? Letter? Diary? Who to (as with audience, it may have a different tone)?[42]
- The archival history of the account: were there any survivors? If not, why not?
- Personal opinion: to some extent linked with personal significance but did the author approve of whom he/she was writing about? This may affect the tone, the conclusions and possibly the accuracy

All these factors may have a bearing on how the 'history' is written and the reader must consider in which manner

the writer is biased, for or against, which may be reflected in the report. Letters are sometimes more opinionated, as are diaries, but the latter are generally not for third-party consumption. An archaeologist's journal is perhaps the most reliable, but how long after the event was it written? Has anything happened in between time to affect the memory?[43] Eisner observed of the traveller, 'Journalists should tell the truth, artists should invent the truth – which is he? Which would he like to be? Which is he resigned to be?'[44] It must depend upon his motive.

The reliability of the recorder is always a difficult matter, and with regard to the traveller, this is problematic in many ways. How long has he spent in a particular area on which he is reporting? Has every possibility been explored? To whom has he spoken and is that information reliable? Has he translated the responses correctly?

Regardless of how the past was recorded, as the 19th century progressed, so to did the reputations of the three 'institutions', but not in the same direction. Historians relished in the new-found university historical courses and the archaeologists gained credibility with recognized and more acceptable techniques of excavating.[45] Antiquarians became excess to requirement, being more outdated with the developing professionalism of historian and archaeologists.

Societies
One of the earliest learned societies to be set up was The Royal Society of London for the Improvement of Knowledge (Royal Society) in 1660, supported by the newly crowned Charles II, for the purpose of scientific learning. It still exists today, as does the Society of Antiquaries of London which was set up in 1707 at the Mitre Tavern in Fleet Street with Humphrey Wanly as its first 'chairman'.[46] It received its Royal Charter in 1751. Unfortunately this latter organization, at that time, may have attracted some of those more interested in the fashion of interest in antiquities rather than the study of them. This could be considered a bad sign but at least it encouraged some interest in activities of the past.

The Society of Antiquaries was a 'poor relation' to the Royal Society, which had greater resources of wealth and patronage. The former suffered various set backs, including suggestions that its 'board' intended to subordinate itself to the Royal Society, and its president, the Earl of Leicester, was accused of being a drunkard and a 'brainless caput'.[47]

---

[39] Dacre to Morant, letter, 26th December 1762, British Library, MS 37220, fol. 46v.

[40] Consider the Homeric tales, *Iliad* and *Odyssey*, which were composed for the Greek people. Would they have been different if composed for the Trojans?

[41] The ancient 5th century BC Greek plays of Aeschylus, Sophocles and Euripides were (arguably) both to entertain, as they were part of a competition, and act as history to link the Greeks with the heroic world of Homer, but we cannot rely upon them as history today.

[42] For example, Heinrich Schliemann's diaries differed in content from his letters on the same finds on his excavations at Troy. Which (if either) were more reliable? (see Traill, 1983: 181; and Traill 1995 generally; but see also Easton on this, 1981: 181).

[43] See, again, the criticism of Schliemann (fn. above).

[44] Eisner, 1993: 21.

[45] The Disney Chair in Classical Archaeology was introduced at Cambridge University in 1851 'but poorly supported' (MacEnroe, 1995: 8). The inauguration of a chair of Classical Archaeology at Oxford was in 1884; see Toynbee & Major (2004) on Percy Gardner who struggled to introduce archaeology into Oxford.

[46] In fact, William Camden was a founding member of this Society in 1572 but it was suppressed by the Scottish born king, James I, in 1604, possibly because it encouraged English nationalism (Trigger, 1999: 47).

[47] Douce to Kerrich, letter, 17th April 1792, Parker Library, Corpus Christi

By 1840 its members were deeply concerned about the Society's purpose.

The Society of Dilettanti was set up in London in 1732 by Sir Francis Dashwood. Its intention was to focus on classical antiquities but with its aristocratic and gentlemen Grand Tour members it had an emphasis on dining. Its members were classed as 'quintessential Grand Tourists'[48] but the art historian, writer, antiquarian and politician, Horace Walpole (1717-97) said of its members, '… the nominal qualification is having been in Italy, and the real one, being drunk'.[49] However, the Society did produce some publications with its three volumes of *Antiquities of Athens* and three volumes of *Ionian Antiquities* between 1762 and 1840, and kept alive an interest in classical antiquities.

The Royal Geographical Society was founded in 1830 for the advancement of geographical science under the patronage of King William IV, and it was given a Royal Charter by Queen Victoria in 1859. Although not involved in archaeology as such, some of its members were to take on a keen interest in the topic and equate it to landscape studies. The Royal Geological Society had been set up in 1807.

In 1843 the Archaeological Association was formed but due to internal squabbling it soon split into two organizations: the British Archaeological Society and the Archaeological Institute, producing the *Journal of British Archaeology* and the *Archaeological Journal* respectively.

The publisher George Macmillan was determined to keep up a following for the ancient Greek world and in 1879 set up the Society for the Promotion of Hellenic Studies. Its purpose was to assist and guide English travellers in Greece and encourage exploration and excavation of ancient sites. Thereafter, in 1886, the British School [of archaeology] at Athens (BSA) was established just outside the Greek capital and an annexe was established in Crete at Knossos in 1926,[50] although the BSA had been involved with Knossos since the establishment of the Cretan Excavation Fund in 1899.

Many county-based societies of local history and archaeology appeared during the 19th century. Although these societies were limited in their appeal, they did attract reasonably large memberships and in some cases from elite personnel. The Sussex Archaeological Society (1846) was criticized for snobbism for its open courting of the aristocracy (9.5% of its first year's members were titled).[51]

Regardless of the varying internal politics and, in some cases, external derision of these societies, they gave credence to the new ideal of archaeology which would assist other inquisitive sciences of the natural world and of man, such as geology, palaeontology and anthropology. The other importance of these societies is that, either by way of talks or publications in their journals, they brought to the fore the activities of some of these travellers and publicized their findings which otherwise would have little value. Spratt, in particular, sent reports of his discoveries to both the Royal Geographical Society and the Society of Antiquaries, and they are still of great value and interest.

Early British travellers to Crete

Neither Crete nor Greece was part of the Grand Tour in the 18th century as accessibility was difficult and at that time they were both considered to be in the Orient. However, by the 19th century package tours had taken off with Thomas Cook as one of its major instigators. By the late 1860s he had set up tours to the east, incorporating Egypt, Palestine, Turkey, Greece and Crete.

Despite the difficulties prior to the 19th century, Crete had been visited by several British travellers as part of their pilgrimage route to the Holy Land.[52] Reasons for travel turned to commerce by the 16th century and thereafter some leaning toward an antiquarian interest. The first known map of Crete was by the Alexandrian geographer and cartographer Claudius Ptolemaeus (Ptolemy) in the 2nd century AD and was copied by the Byzantines in the 13th-15th centuries. Another early map was the *Tabula Peutingeriana*, which was a medieval copy of a Roman road map from the 3rd century AD. More distinct maps appeared during the 15th to 17th centuries,[53] but such maps were more often misleading as they were more fanciful than accurate. Also, they may not always show that sites represent an existing state of affairs but a continuing tradition.[54] However, Skelton reported that the French cartographers of the 18th century introduced new standards of accuracy in the preparation of their maps.[55]

In the 16th century, Richard Hakluyt listed mainly trade voyages of the English Nation to the 'Remote and Farthest Distant Quarters of the Earth'.[56] Of those travelling to Crete, in his second volume, he reported one Anthony Jenkinson between 1546 and 1572; and in his third volume, Capt. Richard Gonson on the *Mathew Gonson* in 1534, Capt. Richard Gray again on the *Mathew Gonson* the following year, Roger Bodenham on the *Barke Aucher*

College, Cambridge, MS 606, fol. 608.
[48] Plouviez, 2001: 45
[49] From Michaelis, 1882: 63 (Walpole was also the 4th and last Earl of Oxford).
[50] In 1926 Arthur Evans gifted all his property at Knossos to the BSA, including the Minoan palace, his house (Villa Ariadne, since transferred to the Greek government in 1952) and the curator and student annexe (the Taverna).
[51] Delheim, 1979: 46-7.

[52] See Rice, 1933.
[53] See Sphyroeras, Avramea & Asdrahas, 1985.
[54] Bennet & Voutsaki, 1991: 372 (referring to sites 'other than Chora' in Keos, but the same could apply to Crete).
[55] Skelton, 1952: 68. He also identified the 'beginnings' of medieval map-making: 'The Geographical Renaissance of the 15th century in western Europe was introduced by the discovery and diffusion of Claudius Ptolemy's *Geographia* [the first world atlas] a Greek manual of the construction and drawing of maps written at Alexandria about AD 160' (1952: 35).
[56] Hakluyt, 1598, 8 vols.

in 1550; M. John Locke on the *Mathew Gonson* in 1553 and M. Laurence Aldersey on the *Hercules* in 1586.

Other travellers to Crete[57] include Symon Simeonis (1332), William Wey (1458 and 1462), Sir Richard Guylforde (1506), Sir Richard Torkington (1517), Denis Harrys (first English Consul in 1522), Roger Bodenham (1551), Fynes Moryson (1596), Richard Darson (1596), Sir Anthony Sherley (1599), William Lithgow (1609), George Sandys (1611), Bernard Randolph (1680), Ellis Veryard (1686) and Richard Pococke (1739).[58] These were followed by Robert Pashley, Charles Rochfort Scott and John Gardner Wilkinson, all visiting Crete in the 1830s, with Thomas Spratt in the 1850s. Edward Lear (1864), John Skinner (1867) and Charles Edwardes (1887) wrote of their experiences on the island, but they were not seeking ancient monuments. Finally, in the 19th century (and into the beginning of the 20th century), Sir Arthur Evans and John Myers visited the island.[59] Most of these individuals had relied on mythology to lead them on their quests around the island, but Arthur Evans would have had Pashley and Spratt's books of their travels for some guidance (see below).

Some of these early travellers made mention of antiquarian sites but with no conviction. Others, Randolph in particular, having little interest in ancient history, sought to consider the current state of the island. Pococke was regarded as 'the founder of the English [British] exploration and identification of ancient remains in Crete'.[60] He was followed by Pashley, who Bowman recognized as being one of England's indefatigable scholar-travellers who opened up a new era for Crete with the publication of his *Travels in Crete* in 1837.[61] In Pashley's footsteps came Spratt before the 'Minoan' world was exposed to the general public by Sir Arthur Evan's publications at the beginning of the 20th century. From the beginning of the 19th century, following Pashley's travels, it was only a matter of time before someone would begin excavations of the island. Both Pashley and Spratt speculated about various ancient sites, particularly as mapping of the island had become more comprehensive for both trade and military purposes (see Map 1 which would have been available to Pashley and Spratt to follow).[62]

Archaeologists in Crete
The first 'excavator' in Crete was Minos Kalokairinos. In 1878, whilst digging in an olive grove at Kephala,

just south of Heraklion, he came upon a buried structure which turned out to be extensive walls of ancient Knossos. The walls were of a rectangular building and storeroom containing huge clay pithoi (or jars) five feet in height.[63] An American painter and journalist, W.J. Stillman, joined Kalokairinos but before they could proceed any further they were stopped by the Cretan Assembly for fear the finds would simply be removed to Constantinople by the Turkish/Ottoman authorities.

In 1883 Heinrich Schliemann became interested in Knossos and two years later attempted to buy the land that the ancient city lay beneath. He was not successful as the price was too high. It was the Italians under the guidance of Federico Halbherr who excavated Crete in 1884. By 1900 Halbherr and his team had dug at Gortyns, Eileithyia, Kamares and Makryteichos (the small hamlet of Knossos). He was keen to move onto the main site at Knossos, but his colleague, Professor Comparetti, was not convinced and instructed him to concentrate on Gortyns. Accordingly, Knossos had not yet yielded anything as impressive as what was to be found by Arthur Evans.

Sir Arthur Evans (1851-1941)
It is not intended to go into any great detail on Sir Arthur Evans as much has already been written about him.[64] However, a brief biography is useful. He was educated at Brasenose College, University of Oxford, whereafter he became the keeper/curator of the Ashmolean Museum in Oxford and set about its refurbishment. On completing this task he turned his attention to Crete and the finding of the pre-Hellenic society responsible, or so he thought (incorrectly), for the creation of the Mycenaean civilization on mainland Greece. This lead to his discovery of the 'Minoan' civilization on Crete. He had been inspired by Heinrich Schliemann's uncovering of the Bronze Age world of the mainland Greeks at Mycenae in the 1870s.[65] At Knossos, in 1906, he built his own house, the Villa Ariadne, adding later the Taverna as an annexe, initially for the curators of Knossos and thereafter as student accommodation, as it still is today.

He had taken an interest in Crete after meeting Federico Halbherr in Rome in 1892. Halbherr discussed the antiquities of the island and his discoveries excited Evans. In February 1893, Evans found sealstones engraved with pictographic or hieroglyphic signs in Shoe Lane, a flea market in Athens. The seller had told him that they were from Crete. Previously, in 1888, the Reverend Greville Chester had donated a similar, although not identical, sealstone to the Ashmolean Museum which was supposedly 'Phoenician',[66] but Evans, comparing it with his own finds,

---

[57] See also chapter 12 for more specific details of some of these individuals.
[58] Warren, 1996: 15; 2000: 2; a full catalogue of travellers to Greece & adjacent regions (including Crete) prior to 1801 is held at the Gennadius Library at the American School of Classical Studies at Athens, see Weber, 1953.
[59] See Brown, 1986, 1993, 2000 and 2001.
[60] Warren, 1972a: 86.
[61] Bowman, 1974: 103-4.
[62] But even today inaccuracies remain which make finding the more obscure sites sometimes difficult. When walking Crete in 1999, Somerville observed, 'I had the measure of it [the map] by now with its misplaced villages, non-existent paths and economies on the truth of contours.' (2007: 110).
[63] See Evans, 1935, Vol. IV, Part II, Supplementary Plate LXI.
[64] Full details of his life and work at Knossos can be found in Joan Evans (1943), Horwitz (1981), MacGillivray (2000) and Brown (2001); see also Pendlebury on Crete (1939).
[65] See Schliemann, 1878.
[66] A generic label. The sealstone was more specifically attributed, incorrectly, to Sparta (Brown, 2001: xii); for image see Sherratt, 2000: 2 (original in Ashmolean Museum, 1889.998).

was convinced it originated from Crete.[67] He was certain that these seals were the writings of an earlier Aegean civilization than Heinrich Schliemann's Mycenaeans and that Crete held its secret. He had met Schliemann in Athens and discussed the German's finds. Many more examples of these seals were to appear in subsequent years, having been gathered from bazaars in Greece and the Middle East and from locals in Crete.

John Myres visited Crete in 1893 and wrote to Evans saying that he hoped to dig there the following year[68] but his request was declined by the authorities. However, with more influence and financial backing than Myres, Evans was able to take up where Kalokairinos had left off at Knossos. He first visited the site in March 1894 and with the help of Dr Joseph Hazzidakis, President of the Society for the Promotion of Education, began negotiations to purchase it.

Although Evans spent most of his post-1900 years at Knossos, between 1894 and 1899 he explored as much of the island as he could.[69] Horwitz commented, 'They [Evans and Myres] found their way into odd corners rarely penetrated by foreigners.'[70] This was not the case at all as some of the sites they visited had already been seen by Pashley and Spratt, if not dated (see Appendix C for a list of sites visited by Pococke, Pashley, Spratt and Evans).

Evans must have read Pococke's book and he had certainly read Pashley's[71] and Spratt's books,[72] and they must have had some influence on him, yet his references to them are brief. He was, perhaps, determined to make sure all credit for the discovery of the island's archaeological heritage was directed to himself, and that he was influenced by nothing other than his own instincts. The same applied to his own time at Knossos.

Although Evans was happy to take the credit for the recording of the excavation at Knossos in his volumes of *The Palace of Minos*, a lot of the content was from the notes of his Scottish curator Duncan Mackenzie[73] but not attributed to him. Mackenzie was meticulous in recording,

and his daybooks were the only attempt to maintain a continuous and systematic record, constituting the most important source of the excavations at Knossos.[74] Dr Nicoletta Momigliano, senior lecturer at Bristol University, wrote in 1999, '*The Palace of Minos* … was never intended to be what one would call a site publication. If there is ever a proper excavation report published on Knossos, this will be largely based on Mackenzie's Day-books.'[75]

Evans was his own man and, as far as he was concerned, Crete, especially Knossos, was his domain and his discovery. It was his money and he would take the credit. During the latter part of the 19th century archaeology was very much a closed society. The likes of Pitt-Rivers, Sir John Lubbock, John Evans and Augustus Wollaston Franks 'worked closely, and even conspiratorially, together to promote certain ideas and orientations … and help exclude other, sometimes opposing interests.'[76] This narrow-minded vision is not conducive to the development of ideas and Arthur Evans was even more 'blinded'. He did not appear to want to join any other 'society' other than his own, and was a 'one man show', establishing a Minoan world of his own creation. Likewise, he published very few of his 'Linear B' tablets for others to consider, which is why it took so long to decipher.[77] As far as he was concerned the task of deciphering the tablets was his alone, but it was a task in which he failed.

He was not involved with any excavations in Crete between 1894 and 1899 as he was not able to without permission, but he did find many more sealstones and various early votive figures, giving a further indication of the importance of the island in a pre-Classical age. Hogarth had hoped to direct the work at Knossos with Evans instructing from home, but Evans would have none of it, and Hogarth stood down leaving Duncan Mackenzie to take his place.

By 1900 Crete had gained its independence from the Turks and Evans was able to begin excavations, having purchased the whole of the site for the sum of £435.[78] He set about revealing the foundations of Knossos, and his excavations were, without doubt, impressive. However, there has been some criticism regarding his reconstruction of the 'palace' as his idea of what it may have looked like is very much his own based on his own lifestyle. John C. MacEnroe commented, 'Remarkable similarities in everything from art to plumbing bridge the gap between the Minoan past and the Edwardian present.'[79] It has also been suggested that Evans falsified some of his excavation photographs and changed images of the site and archaeological materials in order to reflect his desired historical interpretations.[80]

---

[67] In fact, he was later shown an impression of it by its original owner in Crete (Evans, 1909: 10); also, in 1883, the art historian Arthur Milchhofer suggested that Crete was the source for the many seals found by Schliemann at Mycenae (MacGillivray, 2000: 74; Brown, 2001: xxii); and Schliemann himself had suggested Crete as the origin of Mycenaean culture (Sayce, 1923: 219).

[68] Myres to Evans, letter, 8th August 1893, Ashmolean Museum, AJ Evans Correspondence, Vol. 3.

[69] See Brown, 2000: 9-14.

[70] Horwitz, 1981: 89.

[71] Evans, 1921: 154, fn. 3; see also chapter 6 re Arvi: Evans referred to the discovery of a sarcophagus at Arvi and its removal to Cambridge. The removal was by Pashley, but Evans did not mention him by name (letter, Evans to the *Academy*, 7th July 1896, Ashmolean Museum, No. 1263).

[72] Evans, 1921: 533, fn. 1; also critical reference to Spratt regarding his confusion of Goulas with Olous (letter, Evans to the *Academy*, 4th July 1896, Ashmolean Museum, No. 1262); also reference to Spratt's map from Evans' diary, 1894: 32 'Inatos' (from Evans archive, Ashmolean museum, Oxford).

[73] Momigliano, 1999: xiii (Preface).

[74] *Ibid*. 42.

[75] *Ibid*. 142.

[76] Chapman, 1989: 154.

[77] Chadwick, 2000: 18.

[78] Macgillivray, 2000: 150, 166.

[79] MacEnroe, 2001: 69.

[80] See German, 2005.

Following his work, the discovery of the island's archaeological heritage thereafter proceeded in 'leaps and bounds'. However, his predecessors' discoveries appear to have dimmed into insignificance.

Why did it take so long for this 'world of King Minos' to be properly explored? Crete has had a turbulent history that had made travel difficult, particularly during the 19th century under the Turkish/Ottoman rule.

Strife and turbulence in 19th century Crete

For centuries Crete has suffered from many invasions by different nations, as evidenced by the historical record. However, Crete's ancient Bronze Age origins are clouded in myth but it served as a minor colony within the Roman Empire from 69 BC under Quintus Metellus and thereafter from AD 395 as part of the Eastern Roman Empire or Roman Byzantium, where it remained until AD 1204. Conflict relating to ownership of the island continued until 1669 when the city was handed over to the Turks after a lengthy siege. The siege had begun in 1648 after the Maltese Knights of St John attacked a Turkish convoy and put into a Cretan harbour which gave the Turks the excuse for an attack on the island. Despite a gallant defence, the 17th century Flemish geographer Olfert Dapper was not very impressed with the Cretans:

> The greater part of the Candiotes or inhabitants of this island are great eaters and great drunkards, devoted to wine and debauchery, to greed and lust, and above all to filthy pleasures of the flesh. In short they lead lazy, idle lives. Moreover, they hate to apply themselves to anything or learn arms, they are effeminate and lack spirit. The Sphakiots [to the southwest], although practically savages, living by brigandage, are firm in battle.[81]

By 1820 the Turks, as part of the Ottoman Empire, had ruled Crete for three hundred and fifty years and the Cretans had been paying homage/tribute to the Sultan in Constantinople. It was particularly difficult for the Cretans as they were Christians and the Turks were Mohammedans and conflict was inevitable. The Ottoman Empire was basically an Islamic war machine which considered itself above trade and just taxed the Christians heavily, so much so that they could barely exist. In 1821 the Great War of Independence on mainland Greece commenced which caused a panic on Crete and the Turks massacred people on the island to show dominance. The islanders rose up in revolt but the insurrection petered out by 1824. The success on the mainland of Greece did not spread to Crete. In fact, an invading mainland force, lead by Hadzi Michali Daliani, was totally destroyed by the Turks in 1828.

In May 1866 the Christian Cretans rose up again. This time the 'revolt' started peacefully. At this stage it was thought that there was no intention of separation from Turkish rule.

A petition was delivered to Ismail Pasha, the Governor General, to forward to Sublime Porte (the Ottoman court in Constantinople). The petition stated that the taxes were too high and the Cretan people, amongst other matters, were being abused and defrauded by the Ottoman Government. The Ottoman Government responded by ordering Ismail Pasha to disperse the assembly with force if need be. Despite intervention from Great Britain, France and Russia, the matter remained unresolved, and by August hostilities broke out between the Cretan Christians (the insurgents) and the Turks (the Mussulmans) when the Cretans decreed a union with the mainland Hellenic Kingdom (Greece), and much bloodshed followed. The study of ancient sites was not an option in Crete at this moment: 'No study was so popular just now in Crete as the study of arms.'[82]

It is not entirely clear who or what was behind this insurrection, but certainly outside politics were involved, particularly with Great Britain, Italy, France and Russia ('The Powers') taking a keen interest in who would have control of the island, and 'It became manifest that the heart and the sinews of the insurrection were not in Crete, but … in the foreign agitation.'[83]

The Turks could not see that there was a problem. As far as they were concerned the Cretans had all they needed. In an article in *Lippincott's Magazine*, written in 1878 by an unnamed English naval officer, simply cited as E.S., it was reported:

> They [the Cretans] had lentils, oil, flour and firewood, a shelter for their heads, and their rugs and rags to sleep under. The Turkish officers asked, What more could people want? What they wanted was the Turks out of the island for ever, but it was of no use to say that. Such a remark on our part might have been thought personal.[84]

The Turks left chaos in their wake, with little regard for the small nation of Christians. The 19th century traveller Edward Postlethwaite, commented of some of the villages:

> Many were the blackened walls I here beheld of roofless cottages, mementos of the Ottoman torch (which seems ever to have accompanied their march) but imperfectly masked by the veil of foliage dawn round then by compunctious nature. They told not only of burnt abodes, but of burnt subsistence, and extinguished hope.[85]

The final resolution came in 1896, when a Greek mainland force landed in Crete causing war to break out between Greece and Turkey. The Powers imposed a settlement: the French took responsibility for Sitia; the Italians, Hierapetra; the British, Heraklion; and the Russians, Rethymnon; all four looking after Khania with a joint fleet in Suda Bay.

---

[81] Dapper, 1688: 454-55.

[82] Skinner, 1868: 17.
[83] Miller, 1925-26: 108.
[84] E.S., 1878: 74.
[85] Postlethwaite, 1868: 65.

The involvement of The Powers (aka 'Europa') was not necessarily for the benefit of Greece (Fig. 3.1) or for the good of the Cretans as it was considered a good idea to leave the Turks in control (Fig. 3.2)[86] but rather for its (The Powers) own interests. However, the Turks continued to be troublesome and were eventually removed from the island by The Powers by 1898, whereafter Prince George, heir to the Greek throne, was appointed ruler of the island. By 1913 a union between Crete and Greece had been created.[87]

During the mid 19th century, the American Bayard Taylor recalled, 'Travellers are yet so scarce in Crete as to be personages of some importance.'[88] Even towards the end of that century, the English traveller Charles Edwardes was told, 'As for apartments, there is no such accommodation heard of in Crete. No one comes here, and therefore preparations are never made for travellers like you.'[89] The reason was that it was not safe.

When Crete was returned to the Greeks and at peace, Arthur Evans was about to show that the island had once had its very own civilization albeit a civilization which was to be later intruded upon by the mainland Mycenaean 'Greeks' themselves. However, Pococke, Pashley and Spratt had led the way for Evans to follow. Archaeology is not just a case of putting a spade into the ground; it also involves searching and discovery and that includes what is today known as 'field survey'. Pococke, Pashley and Spratt must be credited for this form of archaeological survey of Crete.

---

[86] "It appears to me, and I believe it appears to all the Powers, that it would be a rash act to at once withdraw the Turkish troops, who are really the only safeguard against disorder." - *Lord Salisbury in the House of Lords, Tuesday, March 2.* (fn. to Fig. 3.2).
[87] By 1922 all Turks had been expelled from Greece and all Greeks from Turkey.
[88] Taylor, 1859: 138.

[89] Edwardes, 1887: 23-4.

4. Richard Pococke

Biography

Pococke (Fig. 4.1) was born in Southampton in 1704. His father, also named Richard, was headmaster of All Saints Grammar School but died when Pococke was only six years old. His mother, Elizabeth, thereafter moved him for schooling to the rectory of her father, the Rev. Isaac Milles, at Highclere in Hampshire. His grandfather was an accomplished scholar and clergyman, and it was through him that Pococke received his Classical and Christian education. With this background it was not surprising that Pococke would be ordained in the Church of England. He matriculated from Corpus Christi in Oxford on 13th July 1720 aged 15, was appointed the College Chapel Clerk on 3rd February 1721, took his Bachelor of Arts in 1725, his Bachelor of Common Law in 1731 and his Doctorate of Common Law in 1733. He was a prelate and a member of a number of societies, including the Royal Society and the Spalding Society. He died of apoplexy in September 1765, having been Bishop of Ossory (in 1756), of Elphin, and of Meath (the latter two in the last year of his life).

In his will he left some of his travel journals to the British Museum but with very few references to Crete. He also left a manuscript of papers to his cousin Jeremiah Milles, his travelling companion in Europe, who bequeathed them to the British Museum, but they relate mainly to Pococke's travels to Ireland.

Traveller

Pococke's main recorded travels are of England, Ireland, Scotland, Egypt and the Middle East, the latter of which gained him a 'distinguished reputation',[1] and his book on Egypt and the Middle East was translated in the 18th century into German, French and Dutch. It must be true to say that he was one of Great Britain's first true scholarly travellers.

Although 'archaeology' may not have been a recognized term in the 18th century, the study/collection of 'old things' was prevalent. For example, numismatists were hard at work and the past was coming alive to the more practical researchers and travellers (see references to the antiquarians in the chapter 3). Pococke was one such traveller who had an eye for antiquities – including the ancient ruins of Crete. He reported his findings in his book, *A Description of The East, and Some Other Countries*. The first volume was printed by Bowyer in 1743, and the second volume was in two parts, the first part containing his experiences in Crete, published in 1745.[2]

There have been certain interesting views of Pococke. He was believed to be a man of 'mild manners and primitive simplicity ... In his carriage and deportment he seemed to have contracted something of the Arab character [see Fig. 4.1], yet there was no austerity in his silence, and though his air was solemn, his temper was serene.'[3]

In 1761 Mrs Delaney described Pococke as 'the dullest man that ever travelled ...'.[4] Whatever her view, Pococke was certainly not dull with regard to his travels. Kemp, the 19th century biographer of Pococke's tour of Scotland, reported that 'His [Pococke's] contemporary, Bishop Forbes, has preserved a pen-picture of Dr Pococke ... and represents him rather as a pleasant, genial, jocular man, able to adapt himself to every circumstance and society – qualities essential to travel.'[5]

Pococke said he travelled to Europe to give an account of antiquities and natural history.[6] In fact, many of the countries he did visit and commented on, including Crete, were not part of the Grand Tour in the 18th century (see chapter 3). However, his tour did include a search for Troy. What he found were some ruins described as 'hewn stones, columns and pieces of entablature' which he presumed to have been Ilium (his 'old Troy')[7] but not of the Bronze Age or Hissarlick, now believed to be 'Homeric' Troy. Pococke had a belief in the Homeric heroes as he referred to the 'grave of Hector'; the sepulcher, statute and possible tomb of Ajax; the destruction of ancient Sigeum by the Trojans; and 'in this plain of Troy most the battles mentioned by Homer were fought'.[8] Unfortunately he made no comment as to when he considered the last of this list took place. Did he really believe it was part of the then known Classical period, or some other distant past? This is not something that can be answered, only speculated upon. Could the same be said of his findings in ancient Crete?

Travels in Crete (Map 2)

The 19th century historian James Augustus St John commented of Pococke, 'His researches, although conducted with haste, throw much light on the ancient

[1] Mavor, 1803: 1 (on Pococke in Egypt).
[2] Pococke, 1745, Vol. II, Part I, Fourth Book: 'Of the island of Candia' (hereafter 'Pck').
[3] Cumberland, from Kemp, 1887: xxxix.
[4] Quane, 1950: 41 (from a letter of 2nd January 1761), but this was because he had no time for small talk or tittle-tattle at her tea parties (Hegarty, 1989: 32).
[5] Kemp, 1887: i-ii.
[6] Pococke, 1745, Vol. II, Part II, Preface: iv, having already said that Crete was 'famous in history' (at iii).
[7] Pococke, 1745, Vol. II, Part II, Second Book: 106; see also his description and plan of the ruins of Troas (108-10).
[8] *Ibid.* 104-6.

geography of the land of Minos …'[9] Geography perhaps, but what about ancient prehistory? John Pendlebury was rather critical of Pococke's work on Crete as giving 'a wealth of inaccurate information'.[10] Trevor-Battye observed, 'By about the middle of the last century [19th] various investigators had made researches into both physical and archaic questions in Crete. We need not go back as far as Strabo, but in 1745 Pococke, in his *Descriptions of the East*, gave many interesting facts.'[11] But were these interesting facts about ancient pre-history? In order to answer this question it is necessary to try and identify what Pococke saw during his travels on the island.

He was there in 1739, but it is not entirely clear exactly when in the year this may have been. He mentioned approaching Candia on the 4th September and anchoring off Sfachia on the 9th, setting out for Canea on the 12th.[12] Did he mean September? Then on the 3rd September he set off for Chisamo.[13] He later referred to setting out from Canea on the 17th August.[14] His first letter to his mother, which mentioned his arrival at Canea, is dated 16th-27th August 1739. The two dates must refer to the Julian and Gregorian calendars (being 11 days difference)[15] and he told his mother that he set off for Canea during the 12th–23rd August.[16] He would be writing his book from his journal and may have been misreading these dates. More likely a confusion with the usage of the two calendars, as August rather than September would appear to be the month of arrival, assuming the date on the letter to his mother is correct.

On arriving in Canea (Khania) on the northwest coast he called upon the only English house on the island, that of the English Consul General.[17] With the Consul and the Bishop of Kisamo he set off to see the sites on the western part of the island. His first encounter with the ancients was on Cape Spada at Dictynnaeon, and he related to the cities by way of mythology and connections with Minos,[18] but to no ruins. The first ancient remains seen by Pococke, at Magnia, were small and of marble, possibly of the Dictynnaeon Temple mentioned by Strabo.[19] At the port of Cysamos (Kisamos) he saw foundations of some 'considerable buildings, which might be warehouses … a city of no small extent, as one may judge by several heaps of ruins about the fields; but there are no signs of the walls of the city …'.[20] He gave no indication of the age of the

city, but Kisamos was most likely Minoan in origin[21] and the port to Aptera. Today the ancient city lies beneath the modern town.

Pococke found a ruined city at Aptera and, although concurring with Robert Pashley's later observation about the size of wall (chapter 6), he did not concur with Pashley's positioning of the site, placing it 'about five miles from the port of Chisamo'.[22] It is 30 miles east of Kisamos and, surprisingly, the ever-critical Pashley, who located it where it is today, did not comment on this error.

Pococke wrote to his mother about Palicastro:

> Came near to the sea west of Cape Spada …
> and went south west about 4 miles to Palaio
> Castro, the old ruined city of Aptera on a high
> hill, at the foot of which, the muses and the
> sirens had a trial of musick & the sirens being
> vanquished lost their wings. We viewed the
> Antiquities.[23]

This reference to the 'trial by musick' relates to the mythological tale of the victory of the Muses (an Homeric term) over the Sirens following a musical contest which took place at the city and after which the Sirens plucked off their feathers in sorrow and threw themselves into the sea. Aptera is Greek for 'featherless'. The antiquities he viewed included a very antique bas relief, a sepulchral monument, which he purchased.

At Artacina, or Rocca, he saw the remains of some rooms which, he said, 'the people say belong to the ancient Greeks, and they have some fables relating to it of a giant whom they call Ienes',[24] but his lack of description does not help identify these rooms in any manner.

His next observation led to some contention later by Pashley. Pococke observed that:

> About five miles to the south south west of
> Canea there is a hill among the mountains,
> on which there are some ruins; I conjecture
> that this hill is Tityrus, on which, according to
> Strabo the city of Cydonia seems to have been
> situated.[25]

Pashley (chapter 6) totally disagreed with this, quoting Strabo as saying that Cydonia was not on a hill 5 miles inland but situated by the sea.[26] Pashley was correct in his understanding of Strabo. Also, Pashley, referring to Olivier and his *Voyage dans l'Empire Othoman*, identified the ruins on Tityrus hill as a Medieval fortress,[27] although Strabo did refer to a mountain called Tityrus in Cydonia

---

[9] St John, 1835: 118.

[10] Pendlebury, 1939: 16. Pendlebury was the Knossos curator and a renowned archaeologist of Crete; he was a larger than life character and devoted supporter of the island, but was murdered by the Nazi's at the beginning of their occupation of the island (see Grundon, 2007).

[11] Trevor-Battye, 1919: 137.

[12] Pck: 240, 241, 241 respectively.

[13] Pck: 243.

[14] Pck: 248.

[15] Great Britain did not adopt the Gregorian calendar until 1752, but the difference had extended from 10 days to 11 by then.

[16] Pococke to his mother, letter 16th – 27th August 1739, British Museum, 22998, Vol. XXI (letter XXXI).

[17] Pck: 243.

[18] Pck: 244.

[19] 10.12 (Jones, 2000).

[20] Pck: 245.

[21] Davaras, 1976: 167.

[22] Pck: 246.

[23] Pococke to his mother, letter, 29th September 1739, British Museum, 22998, Vol. XXI (letter XXXII); also Pck: 246.

[24] Pck: 247.

[25] Pck: 247.

[26] See Strabo, 10.4.13.

[27] Pashley, 1837, Vol. I: 16.

on which there is the Dictynnaeon temple.[28] So it is an ancient site even if not recognized yet as Bronze Age. In any event, Pococke found no ruins, 'it is not very much to be wondered at that no other ruins should be seen here, as they would, without doubt, carry the stones from this place to build the city of Canea, which is but five miles distant, whereas the quarries are ten miles from that city'.[29] Ancient stones were re-used for building later cities, but it is not entirely clear what Pococke was looking at.

A word of caution may be raised at this point regarding Strabo, as he will be mentioned on several occasions in the next chapters because both Pashley and Spratt relied upon his observations and measurements. With regard to mainland Greece, it has been suggested that Strabo may not have visited all the sites to which he referred. The British traveller Colonel Leake wrote, 'As his account of the sea-coast is generally more accurate and detailed than that of the inland districts, we are tempted to believe that few parts of the interior were visited by him, but that his travels were principally performed by sea.'[30] William Clark, a traveling contemporary of Leake, also doubted Strabo's calculations of the distances between Mycenae to Argos and Mycenae to the Heraeum – 'Strabo was wrong in both.'[31] Weller commented, 'Quite as important as the quotations and errors that have been discussed is the fact that Strabo's entire description of Greece lacks the touch of the first hand observer.'[32] Jones suggested, 'it cannot be maintained with positiveness that in Greece he saw any place other than Corinth – not even Athens, strange as this may seem'.[33] Could the same apply to some of the sites of Crete? Jones made no mention of Strabo being in Crete, but commented 'we may infer that it was in the Alexandrian library that he made from the works of his predecessors those numerous excerpts with which his book is filled'.[34] Strabo said he was not alien to Knossos,[35] but the reference was probably to his connection with his ancestor, Dorylaus, who had lived in the city, rather than Strabo himself having lived there.

Pococke left Canea and headed eastward to Retimo (Rethymnon) in order to make a tour round the island,[36] although he was not to achieve this intention. He then headed southeast to Matala, one of the ports of Gortyns, where he came across some ruins of Castro Matala and cut into the rocks semicircular niches 'hollowed in like graves, and a stone laid over them,'[37] but gave no indication of date. He then said that, 'In searching for Lebena further to the west, I found a place which I thought to be of greater consequence … that is the fair havens, near unto the city of Lasea; for there is a small bay about two leagues east

of Matala, which is now called … Fair Havens.'[38] This is confusing as Lasea (Lisia) is about two leagues (around 6 miles) south east of where Matala is today and Lebena is the same distance east of Lasea. He was misplacing these sites, putting Lasea ('Fair Havens') where Lebena is today and Matala where Lasea is today. He made no further mention of finding Lebena but, on his map (Map 3), he positioned Lebena where Matala is situated today. He remarked that 'the Tables [Tabula Peutingeriana] place Lisia, which must be Lasea, sixteen miles from Gortynia'[39] whereas it is no more than about twelve (as is Matala). He made lengthy references to the possible whereabouts of some of the sites in a footnote, not all of which have proven accurate (see Appendix D for this footnote).

Pococke was aware of the early origins of Gortyns, referring to Homer's mention of it as a walled city,[40] and that the walls had since been destroyed.[41] There are no Bronze Age walls remaining at the city, although it does date back to this period. He described several ruins which would have been most likely Roman, including a theatre (possibly one of the two Belli drew in the 16th century - see chapter 10). He did mention the 'labyrinth' but believed it to be 'nothing more than a quarry, out of which Gortynia was built … and they might choose to hollow out such a large grotto, rather than work this quarry in the common way, that their families might retire to it on any invasion, and secure their riches'.[42] It is difficult to believe that this 'labyrinth' could have just been for use as a quarry considering its immense and complex passages (see chapter 11).

He then recalled that it had been said that Agamemnon (Homer's Bronze Age King of Mycenae) had landed on Crete due to a storm and named three cities after his victory at Troy. The cities were Mycenae, Tegea and Pegamus, but he could learn nothing of these places other than a Pergamo to the south east of the labyrinth at Gortyns.[43] Pergamos and Tegea are both in Cydonia, south west of Khania, but have left no visible evidence of any ruins. It is not clear where Mycenae was supposed to have been located as there is no such town of that name on the island today nor in Pashley's or Spratt's time.

Knossos
The city of Knossos was referred to by Homer in his catalogue of ships.[44] As mentioned in chapter 2, Homer was supposedly referring to cities many years before his own time, and so was Knossos the city of King Minos? This is obviously something that will never be proven but between c.1900 BC and c.1450 BC Knossos was an important and wealthy 'palace'. Much has been written on it during the 20th and 21st centuries, most of it based around Sir Arthur Evans' excavations at the beginning of

---

[28] 10.4.12.
[29] Pck: 248.
[30] Leake, 1841: 32.
[31] Clark, 1858: 81.
[32] Weller, 1906: 355.
[33] Jones, 1997: xxiv.
[34] *Ibid.* xxiii.
[35] Strabo, 10.4.10.
[36] Pck: 248.
[37] Pck: 250.

[38] Pck: 250.
[39] Pck: 250.
[40] Homer's *Iliad*, 2.646.
[41] Pck: 252.
[42] Pck 254.
[43] Pck 254.
[44] Homer's *Iliad*, 10.263-4.

the 1900s,[45] and it is from this latter work that Crete came to the fore as a 'prehistoric' civilization as far as modern 20th/21st century historians were/are concerned.

Pococke came upon what he thought was the ancient city, adding:

> … it is famous for having been the residence of king Minos, where he had his palace: The labyrinth also was here … but even in the time of Pliny, there were no remains of it … In the time of Minos, Amniso was used as its harbour … which possibly might be at the mouth of Cartero nearer Candia …[46]

Certainly his reference to Amniso (Amnissos), a Minoan port, 'In the time of Minos' supports the idea that he believed in and recognized an earlier civilization. He then went on to describe some ruins that he saw including several large arches which he described as platforms for seats of a theatre. Perhaps this was theatre referred to by Belli (see chapter 9), although not of the Bronze Age.

Not far from Knossos, to the south, is Mount Iouktas (Joukta),[47] the supposed burial place of Zeus. It appears that Pococke did not visited the top of the mountain as he talked of what the modern Greeks said was up there (a temple and tomb) rather than what he saw for himself, '*They relate* that there was a temple dedicated to him [Zeus] on this hill …' (added italics).[48]

Turning north, he headed for Candia (Herakleion), but other than assuming it may have been the port to Knossos, he found no ancient remains. He made a brief footnote reference to Eleuthernia and the old tower he saw that

Spratt identified (see chapter 10). Stampolidis suggested Pococke visited Eleutherna[49] but this did not appear to be the case. Pococke said, 'I saw a tower *at a distance* called Teleuterna, which I conjectured to be some remains of the old Eleuterna' (added italics).[50] Mount Ida he did ascend and it is the site where Zeus was said to have grown up, hiding from his father, Cronos, but Pococke was not impressed. He made a mere reference to a small rough grotto on the north side of the mountain[51] which was possibly the cave that was later to reveal many Minoan artifacts (Figs. 4.2a and b).

On his return to Canea via Retimo (Rethymnon), he passed through several villages but commented very little upon them. They included Apokorano, Armiro, Corunna, ancient Minoa (Paliocastro, or possibly Aptera), Suda Bay, Cape Melecca (Cape Trypiti or Akrotiri) and Sternes. Finally he commented, 'Having seen everything that was curious, I returned to Canea.'[52]

Well, not everything that was curious, as his ancient site reports are somewhat disappointing on an historical point of view and do not give very much away with regard to dating. Even so, the travel historian Damiani commented that 'he [Pococke] was to make substantial contributions in the fields of *archaeology*, natural history, geography and science …' (added italics).[53] Although this was very much more a reference towards his activities in Egypt rather than Crete, it is interesting the word 'archaeology' is used. Certainly Pococke trod upon ground beneath which lay evidence of a Bronze Age civilization, and while his geographical observations of Crete were of interest, they lacked the antiquarian detail later supplied by both Pashley and Spratt.

---

[45] See his 4 volumes (in 7) *The Palace of Minos*, 1921-35.
[46] Pck: 256.
[47] Pococke said four leagues (p.256), which is rather excessive if one league is equivalent to three miles, as it is only about five miles from Knossos.
[48] Pck: 256.

[49] Stampolidis, 2004: 22.
[50] Pck: 259 (also his footnote on p.258, wherein he was wrongly informed that the tower was the work of the ancient Greeks); see Spratt, Fig 10.8 for the tower.
[51] Pck: 260.
[52] Pck: 264.
[53] Damiani, 1979: 71.

5. Robert Pashley
The Traveller

Biography

Robert Pashley was born in York on the 4th September 1805. He was a Fellow of Trinity College, Cambridge, having been admitted on 3rd May 1825, and matriculated at Michaelmas the same year. He became a Scholar in 1828, gaining his Bachelor of Arts in the following year and his Master of Arts in 1832. As a barrister he was admitted to Lincoln's Inn in April 1825 and the Inner Temple in June 1837, where he was called to the Bar in November 1837. Thereafter he achieved the status of Queen's Counsel, Bencher of Inner Temple in 1851 and from 1856 an assistant judge of the Middlesex sessions until his death. He failed in his attempt to gain a parliamentary seat at King's Lynn but was deeply concerned with the poor, publishing works on pauperism.

He died on the 29th May 1859, leaving his personal estate to his trustees to hold for his eldest surviving son. In fact he only had one child, Robert Edmund Pashley, who died on 18th August 1878 at the age of 21, leaving no heirs. It is not clear where Pashley's journals/papers may have ended up although a number of his finds and documents, particularly relating to Crete, were destroyed in a fire at Inner Temple shortly after his return from the island, 'Every scrap of my unpublished materials respecting Crete and Asia Minor were destroyed by the fire in the [Inner] Temple in March 1838.'[1]

Preparation for Crete

It is worth looking to see how Pashley became involved in travelling to Crete. The historian Sir Moses Finley said of Pashley and the fact that, as far as most people were concerned in the 19th century, Crete had no ancient historical ancestry:

> The first important breakthrough [in Crete] was made in 1834 by a young man from Trinity College, Cambridge, named Robert Pashley … he joined that remarkable constellation of nineteenth-century British explorers and archaeologists … who were opening up vast new and exotic fields of inquiry … a modern expert could say of his seven-odd months work that Pashley 'identified most of the important sites with accuracy which had never before been attained and has in few cases since been challenged.'[2]

During the 19th century it was becoming common practice for experts in various fields, particularly geology and natural history, to join Royal Naval survey expeditions. The Royal Naval hydrographer, Captain (later Admiral) Francis Beaufort (of the 'Beaufort Scale') was keen to investigate the ancient antiquities of the Aegean and was fully supportive of any persons wishing to join a ship for the purpose of such research. He was to become a prime motivator toward the archaeological survey of Crete.

Beaufort wrote to Captain Richard Copeland of HMS *Beacon*, prior to the latter's departure for a hydrographic survey of the eastern Mediterranean, enquiring:

> Would you like to have a classical traveller in the Beacon to hunt for antiquities while engaged on the coast of Asia Minor? I have no one in my eye nor do I know whether their Lordships [at the Admiralty] would permit it but before I ask them or enquire at the universities I wished to ascertain your candid opinion of the utility of the scheme, and still more your personal feeling about it.[3]

Copeland obviously agreed, as Beaufort wrote to him again, 'I am much pleased that you approve of the idea of having a savant to accompany to you.'[4] In fact Pashley was not Beaufort's first choice as he added in his letter to Copeland:

> … and I will take care that none but a 1st rate man, and gentleman, [be] sent out. There is somewhere in Italy the son of the Master of Trinity College Camb who I understand would likely to jump at such an offer.[5]

The man he had in mind was the son of Christopher Wordsworth (brother of the poet), the Master of Trinity College, Cambridge. Both Wordsworth's sons, Christopher Jnr and John, were on the Grand Tour at the time, and whichever son Beaufort was considering did not 'jump at such an offer' as neither wished to interrupt their travels.

Sir John Barrow, Second Secretary of the Admiralty, wrote to Pashley in December 1832 informing him that their Lordships of the Admiralty had approved him to investigate 'the antiquities, the Geology and the botany at the parts of

---

[1] Pashley to Beaufort, letter, 20th May 1852, Hydrographic Office (HO), Letter Book (LB) 18: 133.
[2] Finley, 1991: 19. This was somewhat unfair on Spratt as Finley went onto Evans with no reference to Spratt, who, to some extent, made a better identification of ancient ruins than did Pashley (see chapters 9 and 10).
[3] Beaufort to Copeland, letter, 18th July 1832, HO, LB4: 90.
[4] Beaufort to Copeland, letter, 26th July 1832, HO, LB4: 98-99.
[5] *Ibid.*

the Coast of Asia Minor and Greece on which he [Copeland] may be employed surveying'.[6] The Admiralty obviously got the idea that Pashley was a geologist or naturalist from Beaufort who was covering his options. Beaufort informed Copeland of Pashley's appointment:

> I have at last the great pleasure of introducing Mr Pashley to you – he is a Fellow of Trinity College Cambridge - not only a distinguished scholar, but imbued with a proper zeal for *antiquity hunting*. That zeal will I am quite sure meet with every possible encouragement and assistance at your hands … and the *important aid* you will derive from the company of such a person on the *interesting service* in which you are engaged ...'[7] (added italics)

The 'antiquity hunting' is a clear reference to the intention of seeking antiquities. The 'important aid', as Beaufort told Pashley, would be the 'determining of the ancient names and places as may be included in his Survey'.[8] This was Beaufort's excuse for the usefulness of Pashley's attendance. The 'interesting service' is possibly a reference to Beaufort's own frustration at failing to secure antiquities on his own visit to the Mediterranean, as he commented to Pashley, '… as I well recollect the provoking opportunities I lost on the coast of Asia Minor, and the feebleness of my last efforts to rescue a few vestiges of ancient geography from oblivion'.[9]

At the same time Beaufort wrote to another naval officer, Lieutenant Thomas Graves, to introduce him to Pashley.[10] The reason was that Graves was also surveying in the Mediterranean and one of his junior officers was Midshipman Thomas Abel Brimage Spratt.

Accordingly, Copeland 'welcomed a classical scholar Robert Pashley of Cambridge to help him identify ancient sites [in the Aegean]'.[11] Pashley was very enthusiastic about the early undiscovered history of Crete and wrote to Beaufort:

> I believe we know but little indeed in England of the value and capabilities of this island. I must say a word of its history, which is so very interesting from the earliest dawn of Grecian civilization down to the present hour. You know how it is connected with many of the ancient theogonies & myths with the origin of laws, of the fine & useful arts, in fact with everything of any importance in the progress of society before the wars of Troy.[12]

'Before the Wars of Troy' is before the Classical era and was the Bronze Age, a period Pashley had clearly identified with, and he would have been aware of a rough date for it at around 1250 BC as he surely had read Herodotus who referred to Homer's Trojan War as being 'eight hundred years or thereabouts' before his own time of *c*.450 BC.[13] Admittedly Pashley made no inroads to date some of his early architectural discoveries although he gave some indications.

Pashley reported back to Beaufort on his finds of ancient sites with mixed feelings. He did not always find the sites where he had anticipated them to be from reference to his maps but was pleased with what he had seen:

> I have visited the sites of nearly twenty ancient cities, most of which I am sorry to say are either not placed at all or are placed entirely out of their proper places in all the maps I have seen. Many of the remains are extensive, most of them interesting, & some are very singular… I consider the two months I have spent here as more profitability employed as worth more in every point of view than all the rest of my eastern travels.[14]

Then, with more optimism of discovery he wrote, 'The sites of which I believe I have been the first European visitor are Chersonesus, Miletus, perhaps Lycastus, and Axos. The number however will be increased by the time when I have next the pleasure of writing to you.'[15] Beaufort replied, 'It delights me and will delight all your friends to find that you anticipate such a rich harvest in Crete.'[16] From Nauplion, on the mainland of Greece near Mycenae, Pashley wrote again to Beaufort of his discoveries in Crete:

> Since I last wrote to you I have found remains of Elyrus, Suria, & Tarrha as well as four other *very ancient* cities in the same neighbourhood (between Colanni [?] & Loutro of Lapie). I have also visited Eleutherna, which [has kept?] its ancient name; Sybritus, the excavation called the labyrinth, and the remains of Lyttus.[17] (added italics)

When he had completed his travels he was convinced that he had seen nearly all the cities of ancient and 'very ancient' Crete and informed Beaufort accordingly, '… as for Crete, you will find … that I have visited most of the ancient sites'.[18] That was to prove somewhat of an over-estimation.

His visit and discoveries on the island are logged in his book, *Travels in Crete*.[19] One of his purposes was to consider the present state of Crete; the other was to

[6] Barrow to Pashley, letter, 17th December 1832, LB 4: 186.
[7] Beaufort to Copeland, letter, 17th December 1832, HO, LB4: 190, although he did mention in another letter to Copeland of the same day that Pashley's studies must not interfere with the progress of the survey (Beaufort to Copeland, letter, 17th December 1832, HO, LB4: 186).
[8] Beaufort to Pashley, letter, 17th December 1832, HO, LB4: 189.
[9] *Ibid.*
[10] Beaufort to Graves, letter, 17th December 1832, HO, LB4: 191 and again 6th February 1833, HO, LB4: 234.
[11] Fisher, 1989: 3.
[12] Pashley to Beaufort, letter, 15th February 1834, HO, Incoming letters prior to 1857 (IL): P115.

[13] Herodotus, 2.145.
[14] Pashley to Beaufort, letter, 3rd April 1834, HO, IL: P112.
[15] Pashley to Beaufort, letter, 18th April 1834, HO, IL: P113.
[16] Beaufort to Pashley, letter, 1st May 1834, HO, LB5: 190.
[17] Pashley to Beaufort, letter, 16th June 1834, HO, IL: P111.
[18] Pashley to Beaufort, letter, 9th October, 1834, HO, IL: P110.
[19] Pashley, 1837, Vols. I and II (hereafter 'Psh I' and 'Psh II').

establish the position of various ancient sites, but only the Classical, Hellenistic and Roman periods were known to him at the time. This does not mean he did not discover earlier Bronze Age sites (his 'very ancient'?). He utilized ancient sources such as Strabo, Pliny, Polybius, Pausanias, Herodotus, Ptolemy, Juvenal, Meletius and the Stadiasmus to assist him in his identifications. He also made several references to the 19th century geographer and historian Dr J.A. Cramer. His search for ancient cities was not an easy task and he remarked, 'Crete has been so little explored that it was necessary to enquire everywhere for ancient ruins.'[20]

Of Pashley's venture, the historian Llewellyn Smith rather short-sightedly wrote, 'A large part of his book is wasted in speculation about topography of the ancient Cretan cities: a fashionable game at the time, but exceedingly boring for the reader today. Skip the topography, for the rest is pure gold.'[21] Obviously this was only a matter of opinion and it depends upon the purpose for which the book was being read, but it cannot be classed as 'boring' if the reader has any interest in the archaeology of the island. Nor could it be said that it was written as it was fashionable to do so at the time, as it was written as a serious observation of the island which had not been achieved before, not even with Pococke since Pashley's was a much more detailed account of the island.

The historian and traveller of the early 20th century Aubyn Trevor-Battye commented on Pashley's two volumes:

> It is impossible to over-estimate the value of the work done in Crete by Pashley in the year 1834. It must be borne in mind that at that time most of the ancient sites were undetermined. The clue to many of them rested upon illusions, often very obscure, made by virtue of the Roman period long after the golden age – the age of "the hundred cities of Crete" [from Homer] - had passed away; and even the references of Strabo's writings, though the author lived much in Crete, and though more reliable than others, were based in part on guesswork. Pashley determined or confirmed the sites of Aptera, Lappa, Eleutherna, Axos, Biennos, Praesos, Phalasarna and other ancient settlements, and was the first to visit the cave of Zeus on Iuoktas.[22]

All those sites mentioned by Trevor-Battye have since been established to be of the Bronze Age.

Pashley then set out on his extensive exploration of antiquities on the island of Crete with the aid of Captain Manias (a guide from Sfakia in the southwest Crete), Antonio Schranz (an illustrator) and a mule.

---

[20] Psh I: 125.
[21] Smith, 1973: 21.

[22] Trevor-Battye, 1913: XVI.

6. Robert Pashley
Travels In Crete, Vol. I

To Crete (see Map 4)

Pashley (Fig. 6.1[1]) left England in January 1833, but, according to his letter to Beaufort, he did not reach Copeland on the *Beacon* until August,[2] and it was not until February 1834 that he arrived on Crete. He reported to Beaufort with much optimism:

> I had the pleasure of receiving your letter before I left Malta and am happy to be able now to write to you from this island [Crete] which I was so anxious to visit, & which I find interesting beyond my most sanguine expectations. As to its antiquities I believe there will be no great difficulty in making out most of its ancient sites[3]

Pashley began his investigation of Crete at the northwestern end at Khania (Canea) and sought out ancient Cydonia/Kydonia. He made no attempt to date the city's origins other than to say it had 'existed in very ancient times … long before the age of Polycrates'.[4] Polycrates was a 6th century BC tyrant of Samos, and Cydonia is referred to in Linear B as *ku-do-ni-ja*,[5] which is possible evidence of its existence in the Bronze Age (as with all other city references to Linear B[6]).

Pashley was satisfied that ancient Cydonia was around Khania based on the account of the 6th century BC Carian sailor Scylax that it was a harbour that could be closed (by a chain).[7] Strabo said it was 'situated on [by?] the sea, facing Laconia, and is equidistant, about eight hundred stadia [approx. 130 km], from the two cities Cnossus and Gortyna, and eighty stadia [approx. 13 km] distant from Aptera …'.[8] Laconia is in the southern Peloponnese of mainland Greece which would put Cydonia on the northwest coast of Crete. A stadia is an ancient Greek measurement equivalent to about 160–180 metres, or just under 1/8th of a mile (similar to a furlong). However, working on this premise the distances from Knossos and Gortyns do not fit as they would put Cydonia in the sea.

This means either Strabo was inaccurate or our modern day conversion does not relate to his stadia. The former is more likely as Strabo himself was relying, to some extent, on ancient writers whom he observed were inconsistent with distances.[9] Today ancient Cydonia is considered to be Khania and any ancient ruins have long since been built upon although remains of Minoan tombs are still evident of the outskirts of the town.[10]

Travelling east past Sudha Bay, at Palaikastro Pashley found considerable remains of walls of the ancient city of Aptera (Fig. 6.2a), some of which were made up of varying sizes of blocks which is indicative of Bronze Age architecture (see chapter 1). He supposed their construction was before the Romans but did not suppose how long before other than to say that some of the walls were very large, 'Their massiveness gives them almost as good a claim to admiration as those of Tiryns itself.'[11] Tiryns, although not then excavated but visible,[12] was a Bronze Age fortress of the Mycenaean period (Fig. 6.2b). Polygonal walls remain today at Aptera (Figs. 6.2c and d) and they bear a fair resemblance to those of the Bronze Age. Pashley further observed that 'the ruins of Palaeokastron [Aptera] shew that its establishment belongs to the very earliest period of civilisation …'.[13] In fact the walls of Aptera are considered to be of a later Hellenistic period and this is certainly true of Pashley's second sketch of its walls (Fig. 6.3a) which can be compared with other walls that also remain today at the site and are Hellenistic (Fig. 6.3b). Regardless, his comparison of the walls with Tiryns is further evidence that he believed in an earlier civilization of the same era as Tiryns, and his second comment regarding an 'earliest period of civilisation' begs a pre-Classical one. Aptera is believed to be *a-pa-ta-wa* in Linear B[14] and so of the Bronze Age.

Pashley then mentioned the finding of a small headless winged statue standing on a sculptured pedestal. It is not of the Bronze Age, but its method of discovery is interesting as Pashley 'pointed out for *excavation*, a spot to the south of the monastery; and owing to the zeal with which the work [excavation] was executed, an elegant little winged statue … was found' (added italics).[15] This confirmed

---

[1] This *may* be an image of Pashley, otherwise no other image appears available.

[2] Pashley to Beaufort, letter, 4th December 1833, HO, IL: P116.

[3] Pashley to Beaufort, letter, 15th February 1834, HO, IL: P107.

[4] Psh I: 12.

[5] McArthur, 1993: 153. However, some of the similarities of Linear B names with known names today could be coincidence (see Rackham & Moody, 1996: 103).

[6] See McArthur, 1993: 120, Fig. 8.1, for map of Crete showing places with possible Linear B evidence.

[7] Psh I: 13 – Scylax of Caryanda from Hudson's *Minor Greek Geographers*, Vol. 1, pp.18 and 265, Gail's edition.

[8] Strabo, 10.4.13.

[9] Strabo, 10.4.3.

[10] Macdonald, 2005: 199

[11] Psh I: 38.

[12] Excavated by Schliemann in 1876.

[13] Psh I: 47.

[14] McArthur, 1993: 126-7.

[15] Psh I: 42.

that his work did include some limited excavations.[16] He also referred to this instance in a letter to John Murray, his publisher, '… a small statue standing on a sculptured pedestal, and found by me (by excavating) at an ancient site in Crete'.[17] This does show that he was not adverse to excavation if the need required it and that this method of discovery was not restricted to a later breed of archaeologist. He wrote to Beaufort in April of 1834:

> I have found an ancient site for instance where a few hours excavation would in all probability find at least a few medals, & thus afford evidence of the same. It's true such slight excavations would not be expensive if performed by Greeks but then I would first find the men then remain on the spot & then my examination of the island would go on but slowly.[18]

Pashley journeyed eastward to Rethymnon which revealed nothing to indicate any Bronze Age activity other than a reference to Lappa (just southwest of Amphimalla) which he reported, 'Stephanus of Byzantium tells us … was found by Agamemnon'.[19] As previously mentioned (chapter 4), Agamemnon was Homer's King of Mycenae who according to Homer led the Greeks, including King Idomeneus of Crete, against Troy sometime (perhaps) around the 13th century BC. At Rethymnon Pashley remarked that 'The ancient Rhithymna … does not seem to have been a place of much importance.'[20] The 16th century Venetian physician, traveller and artist Onorio Belli (1550-1604) remarked that most of its antiquity has been obscured by the modern city and by Turkish destruction in 1571.[21] But there were Minoan and Mycenaean settlements situated there.[22]

The Melidoni (Melidhoni) cave was of great interest to Pashley with regard to both its 'modern' day history and mythology of the Classical period. The cave dates back to the Minoan period where it was utilized as a cult site evidenced by finds of earthenware pottery and a double-bladed axe.[23] It is a typical 'grotto' for Minoan cult practice (Figs. 6.4a-d). It is quite a spectacular site and is mentioned in some detail in Murray's 19th century *Handbook for Travellers to Greece* as an excursion.[24] Also, the room Pashley actually discovered bears his name (Fig. 6.4b).

South east of the Melidoni Cave is Axos (referred to by Virgil as Oaxen: of the river Oaxes[25]) and nearby Eleutherna, 'where there are many ancient remains', or so Pashley was told by the locals.[26] After a false start he did find ruins of interest at Axos 'carefully fitted together without cement … they belonged to the earliest style of the so-called cyclopean or pelasgic walls'.[27] This suggests the Bronze Age but the general opinion is that the walls are Archaic/Hellenistic, although late Minoan potsherds have been discovered there.[28] Also Axos is possibly *e-ko-so* in Linear B.[29]

Another site of known Minoan origin is Panormos[30] on the coast due north of Melidoni. Unfortunately, although Pashley was aware it was an ancient city, on his own admission he did not visit it.[31]

One major Minoan site he did visit was Tylissos, just southwest of Herakleion. Although he found no traces of ancient ruins, he said, '… yet I felt little or no doubt that I was standing on the site of the ancient Tylissos'.[32] Tylissos was of Minoan origin as it is referred to in Linear B as *tu-ri-so*.[33] The Minoan site was excavated by Joseph Chatzidakis between 1902 and 1913, and restored, initially under the control of Nicolas Platon, between 1952 and 1962 and again between 1990 and 1994.[34]

Around Knossos

Pashley made little comment on the ancient possibilities of Knossos, although he obviously believed it to have been a city of some antiquity and was aware of the time scale of what we now know as the Bronze Age: '… the dance of these Cretan youths and women [of Rhogdhina] … which still preserves some of the chief features of the Cnossian chorus of *three thousand years ago*' (added italics).[35] His reference to 'three thousand years ago', *c.*1200 BC, was to Homer's *Iliad*,[36] but whether it had ever occurred to Pashley that Homer may have existed at a different time to his Trojan War is not clear. This does give some indication that Pashley had a timescale in mind for his 'ante-Homeric' sites and other sites he linked with the Homeric heroes (see next chapter).

Pashley was quite convinced that Makroteikho (Makryteichos) was 'undoubtedly the site of Cnossos'.[37] Of Knossos' ancient remains he reported only some rude

---

[16] Excavation was a fairly innovative technique in the early 19th century but not unknown (Gell had certainly done some digging): 'but to explore a tomb still seemed akin to desecration. The reverent tourist must admire the flesh, but it was not done to lay bare the privacy of the skeleton which time had slowly shrouded' (Stoneman 1987: 155).
[17] Pashley to Murray, letter, 26th May 1836, National Library of Scotland, *Robert Pashley Correspondence* (NLS), Acc. 12604.
[18] Pashley to Beaufort, letter, 3rd April 1834, HO, IL: P112.
[19] Psh I: 85.
[20] Psh I: 102.
[21] Belli, 1586 (from Falkener, 1854: 25); see also chapters 9 and 10.
[22] Vasilakis, 2000: 150.
[23] Davaras, 1976: 356-7/83 & 358-9/92.
[24] Murray, 1854: 358. This travel book, first published in 1840 by John Murray's publishing company, makes various references to Pashley (one to Pococke). In fact, the travel guide follows Pashley's route (including omitting the eastern side of the island) and says as much (p.363).

[25] *Bucolics,* Eclogue I.66. Oaxos, according to mythology, was the grandson of Minos.
[26] Psh I: 145.
[27] Psh I: 152. 'Pelasgic' means pre-Hellenic people.
[28] Davaras, 1976: 356-7/102 and 358-9/166.
[29] McArthur, 1993: 134-153.
[30] Vasilakis, 2000: 138.
[31] Psh I: 157, fn 40.
[32] Psh I: 161.
[33] McArthur, 1993: 153.
[34] Vasilakis, 2000: 15; Davaras, 1976: 356-7/12 and 358-9/16.
[35] Psh I: 246.
[36] See Homer's *Iliad*, 18.590-605, wherein Homer refers to youths dancing on a floor at Knossos.
[37] Psh I: 204. The village of Makroteikho is just northeast of the palace of Knossos.

masses of Roman brickwork.[38] He commented, 'The natural caverns and excavated sepulchres seen in the immediate neighbourhood of Cnossos, call to mind the well-known ancient legend respecting the labyrinth',[39] but he did not identify them. He may have been referring to the tombs across the rivulet from Makroteikho possibly seen by Spratt (see chapter 9). But then Pashley was quick to clarify that he found no traces of any such 'monument' as a labyrinth in the neighbourhood of the village.[40]

Interestingly the Cretan guide authors, John Fisher and Geoff Garvey commented:

> It was probably as well for those who were to come after him that it never occurred to Pashley to take up the spade. That he came near to doing so is borne out by his prophetic comments on Knossós: "The mythological celebrity and historical importance of Cnossos, demand a more careful and minute attention than can be bestowed on them in a mere book of travels."[41]

Mount of Iouktas, 6 km south of Knossos, was supposedly the burial place of Cretan Zeus.[42] Many Cretans were unaware of this mythology and Pashley commented, 'I was of course anxious to hear something of the sepulchre of Zeus; but it was in vain that I inquired of my host, Dhemetrio's brother, for any cave on the mountain. He knew of nothing of the kind.'[43] The 19th century British traveller Charles Edwardes had similar trouble in searching out a cave (see chapter 12). In fact there is no cave 'of Zeus', only 'knowledge' of his tomb on the summit of the mount, a fact that Pashley soon established.[44] However, the mount has two peaks: the southern has on it the chapel Aphendis Khristos and the northern has foundations of an ancient ruin.

On the northern peak Pashley observed:

> … foundations of the massive walls of a building the length of which was about eighty feet. Within this space is an aperture in the ground, which may perhaps once have led into a moderate-sized cave; but, whatever may have been its former size, it is now so filled up, that a man cannot stand in it, and its diameter is not above eight or ten feet … I now stand on the spot, in which Zeus was supposed to be at rest from all celestial and terrestrial cares, and which was so celebrated during many ages![45]

But did he stand on the spot where Zeus rested? Interesting, Pashley made no reference to the southern peak which Spratt thought was more likely to have been the site of the tomb (see chapter 9). Pashley then added:

> On the eastern side of the mountain, and about a hundred paces from its summit, I found considerable remains of ancient walls. The construction is chiefly of very large stones, among which a good many small ones were intermixed … These fragments seem to offer a good specimen of the so-called *first cyclopean style*. They are four or five in number, and the whole length of the ground, which they partially cover, is between four and five hundred paces, of which not more than fifty paces are occupied by the actually existing remains. It is, however, evident that the old walls extended all round the summit … Above the wall I observed, scattered over the ground, many pieces of ancient pottery, which, as well as the wall, would rather serve to indicate an abode of the living than a resting place of the dead.[46] (added italics)

He did not clarify what he meant by 'first cyclopean style' (but see next chapter for 'second style'). Where does this put his initial 'foundations of massive walls'? Certainly there existed and still do 'cyclopean style walls' on the summit (see Fig. 6.5),[47] and Pashley had a sketch done of what he saw (Fig. 6.6). There is no doubt that this was a temple of some description and represented a peak sanctuary of Knossos[48] in the Minoan period.[49] It contains an altar 'to Zeus' and a number of deep fissures, one just below the altar (Fig. 6.7)[50] which may account for Pashley's reference to an aperture and cave. There are also five rooms a few metres to the east (Fig. 6.8) which may account for Pashley's belief that it was used for 'an abode of the living' if that is what he saw. Trevor-Battye commented that Pashley '…was the first of the moderns to visit the cave of Zeus on Iuktas'.[51]

---

[38] Psh I: 204.

[39] Psh I: 208.

[40] *Ibid.*

[41] Fisher and Garvey, 2004: 428 although they do not reference Pashley's quote, but it is Psh I: 209.

[42] As an 'immortal', his death, then rebirth, is explained by the fact he was a god of vegetation which died but recovered annually; this 'mortal Cretan Zeus' lead to the ancient Cretans being called 'liars' by the mainland Greeks. See the 4th/3rd century BC poet Callimachus' hymn to Zeus (8): 'The Cretans are always liars; They even built your tomb, O king; But you died not, you are for ever.' In fact Epimenides first called Cretans liars in the 6th century BC.

[43] Psh I: 211.

[44] Jameson's footnote commented that it 'has a peak, not a cave, sanctuary' (1969: 212, fn. 2, reporting Scully, 1965: 15), although Somerville referred to the 'Cave of Winds' not far below the Minoan sanctuary on the northern peak of the mountain and excavated in 1979 revealing three humans found in three chambers (2007: 139), and so more of a tomb than a sanctuary.

[45] Psh I: 212-3.

[46] Psh I: 220.

[47] The wall was 735 metre in length and over 3 metres wide.

[48] The Central Court at Knossos is aligned to the mount.

[49] The wall has been dated to MMIA (around 2000 BC) but was in use prior to this in EMII through to LMIIIB as evidenced with finds including hoards of bronze double axes, terracotta figurines, vessels, seals and jewellery (Cameron 2003: 129-30, Pat Cameron worked at the BSA, Knossos, cataloguing material for the Stratigraphical Museum); also Evans, 1921: 154-163; and Karetsou, 1981: 151.

[50] Murray only mentioned one summit, but it must be this one as he referred to 'massive foundations' and an aperture 'which may have once led to a moderate size cave' (1854: 361) but it appears that Murray is merely repeating Pashley rather than recollecting a personal visit (see fn. 24 above).

[51] Trevor-Battye, 1919: 137.

Even Evans, albeit briefly in a footnote, referred to Pashley's visit to the site and his observations.[52] Evans had identified the site as Minoan[53] and so it must be correct to say that Pashley did, here at least, come across some remnants of the 'Minoan' Bronze Age.

Pashley moved southwest to Khani (Kanli) Kastelli (also known as Prophitis Ilias) which is a village beneath the twin peaks of Rhocca (fortress) where, in the 'saddle' of the peaks lies the Venetian fortress of Temenos. However, he dismissed Rhocca as nothing more than Venetian,[54] although he did consider that the ancient site of Thenae was nearby. As will be seen in chapter 9, Spratt was more convinced. Pashley thought he had located ancient Rhaucos at the village of Haghio Myro, just west of Khani Kastelli, but there is no real evidence to support his supposition. It was based on a link with the name of the 3rd century AD bishop Myro whose native village and episcopal seat was Rhaucos, 'situated near Cnossos'.[55] It becomes more confusing when Pashley expressed the view that there might be two sites called Rhaucos in Crete and suggested the more ancient may be close to Mount Ida,[56] yet he made no further attempt to find this latter Rhaucos when he visited Ida.

Pashley had some trouble in locating Arcadia as he was confused by the 19th century village called Arkhadi which he decided was not the ancient city. This confusion came from his reading of Cramer who put Arcadioti 'north-east of the ruins of Gortys … which from the similarity of name … corresponds, doubtless, with the site of Arcadia'.[57] Pashley relied on the *Peutinger Table* to put Arcadia some 40 miles east of Knossos, east of the Lassithi plain which he refrained from commenting on. This Table/map cannot be classed as entirely accurate and reliance upon it must be treated with some caution.

He travelled northwards back to the coast to Palaeokastron which he believed to be the ancient city of Cytaeum, referred to by Pliny.[58] Cytaeum is possibly *ku-ta-to* in Linear B.[59] But he saw no more than a Venetian fortress which he presumed accounted for the disappearance of the ancient remains. He based his theory on the name he found, Palaeo-kastron, which is not the designation of Middle Age remains which would be Kastelia but of an earlier ancient site that has been purposely built over by the Venetians, indicating respect for the earlier city[60] (hence 'palaeo': ancient or old). However, he was correct in believing it to be ancient as it is Ayia Pelagia, a pre-proto and neo-palatial Minoan site.

At Herakleion he searched in vain for remains of antiquity but commented, 'From Strabo *we know* that Heracleion was the port of Cnossos in the age of Minos' (added italics).[61] By saying 'we know', he appeared to be accepting a 'bygone' age of Minos. However, it is not surprising that he found nothing as the Venetian town and port would have covered the ancient city.

At Amnissos, which he thought was Armyro, he talked of the temple of Ilithyia but was unable to find it, unlike Spratt (see chapter 9). To the east of Amnissos, Pashley came upon Kheronesos and the ruins of nearby Episkopiano, but gave no indication as to what they may have been. But he did assume that he was near the port of ancient Lyttos, some eight to ten miles south,[62] recognizing the coastal town to be of ancient origin.

He did make a brief footnote reference to a visit to Homeric Miletos/Milatos[63] (on the 14th March) where, he said, 'considerable remains of walls of polygonal masonry both, of the acropolis and city, are seen.'[64] Again he gave no further description and nothing remains there today (but see chapter 9). In the same footnote he went on to say:

> I am compelled to leave my travels in these parts of the island undecided, at all events at present: and shall resume my personal narrative, in the next chapter, at Hierapetra.[65]

He completely cut out reference to his travels further eastwards, giving no reason. John Pendlebury merely commented, '… private affairs having prevented him from arranging his material from the East end of the island'.[66] This is most unfortunate, particularly as the majority of his personal papers and diaries, which may have shed some light on his findings over this part of the island, were destroyed in the fire (see previous chapter).

Towards the west

Pashley picked up again at Hierapetra on 26th March[67] on the south coast, travelling west. At Arvi he was aware that it had ancient connections but could find no traces of such a city other than fragments of a sarcophagus which were located near the shore. He was assured by the inhabitants of the nearby village of Hagio Vasili that there once existed remains of an ancient city.[68] Arthur Evans established that Arvi was Minoan[69] as was its surrounding area.[70]

Likewise, at Viannos/Biennos, Pashley was convinced of its ancient origins but found nothing in evidence. Hood reported of 'two worn fragments of tripod feet … [so]

---

[52] Evans, 1921: 154, fn. 3.
[53] Evans 1921: 155.
[54] Psh I: 224.
[55] Psh I: 234-5, Spratt had other ideas (see chapter 9).
[56] Psh I: 235.
[57] Cramer, 1828, Vol. III: 385 (Psh I: 230).
[58] Pliny, 4.20.
[59] McArthur, 1993: 138.
[60] Psh I: 260.

[61] Psh I: 264, and it was Minoan (Davaras, 1976: 358-9/10).
[62] Psh I: 268-9.
[63] Homer's *Iliad*, 2.647.
[64] Psh I: 269-70, fn. 48. 'Polygonal' is sometimes used as another name for 'cyclopean'.
[65] Psh I: 269-70, fn. 48.
[66] Pendlebury, 1939: 17.
[67] Psh I: 271.
[68] Psh I: 275-6.
[69] Evans, 1896b: 464-5; Davaras, 1976: 358-9/83.
[70] Hood *et al.*, 1964: 89-93.

should be Minoan',[71] and nearby, at Galan Charakia, Platon excavated two tombs containing Early Minoan and Middle Minoan vessels and a Middle Minoan four roomed building has also been found.[72] Also near modern Vianno Minoan sites have been found at Ligarus and Ayios Nikolaos.[73] Pashley linked Inatos and Priansos and identified them just west of Biennos. Inatos is possibly *wi-na-to* in Linear B.[74]

Pashley' reference to Gortyns is very brief and he only 'made a rapid survey' of its ruins and referred only to previous descriptions by Belon, Tournefort, Pococke and Savary of the ruins and Cockerell regarding the 'cavern/ labyrinth'.[75] He obviously decided that it was of little value to add anything further which is unfortunate as his views of the 'cavern' may have been of interest as to its existence as merely a quarry. It can only be assumed that he considered it of little consequence.

Pashley continued westwards, passing Mount Ida to his right, beforehand 'ascertaining' at the monastery of Arkadhi the existence of ancient remains at Eleutherna[76] but said very little about what they were. It is not clear whether he had seen the site. He did not say he had in his book, and just under a month previously, on February 25th, he had been told that it was inaccessible due to snow.[77] However, he did inform Beaufort that he had visited it (see reference to letter in previous chapter[78]).

He then sought ancient Sybrita which he believed to be near Eleutherna. Looking at his positioning of Sybrita on his map, he puts it just off to the east of where the site is today and where Spratt found it, which may account for Spratt's comment that Pashley had missed the site altogether (see chapter 10).

He considered there had been some confusion with Priansos and Praesos as he believed scholars supposed Praeos to be in this area.[79] He was able to clarify the whereabouts of Praesos near Sitia with reference to an inscription he copied at the Plu-Monasteri,[80] now Toplou Monastery, east of Sitia, south of Itanos, below Cape Sideros on the northeast side of the island. He put Stelae and Homeric Rhytion near Priansos but found nothing of ancient interest.

Pashley made an interesting comment in the conclusion of his first volume when referring to spring water and comparing 'modern day' (19th century) Greece/Crete with Homeric Greece, 'Thus the characteristic credulity of the Greek is as strongly developed at the present day as it was *three thousand years ago*, when Homer described the warmth of one of the two springs … in the neighbourhood of Troy'(added italics).[81] Regardless of the spring water reference, Pashley was again indicating a timescale of Homer and therefore the possibility of a civilization during that period, 'three thousand years ago', *c.*1200 BC, which is the Bronze Age.

[71] Hood *et al.*, 1964: 83; also Davaras, 1976: 358-9/135.
[72] Vasilakis, 2000: 76; see also Nowicki, 2000: 138-9.
[73] Hood *et al.*, 1964: 76.
[74] McArthur, 1993: 152.
[75] Psh I: 297, but see chapter 11 on the labyrinth.
[76] Psh I: 309.
[77] Psh I: 146.
[78] Pashley to Beaufort, letter, 16th June 1834, HO, IL: P111.
[79] Psh I: 288.
[80] Psh I: 290.
[81] Psh I: 320.

7. Robert Pashley
Travels In Crete, Vol. II

To the west coast (see Map 4)
Returning to Khania, Pashley came upon the River Platania and Platanias, otherwise possibly ancient Pergamos. He was certain that the river Platania was the same river Iardanos as mentioned by Homer in the *Odyssey*,[1] 'There he [Menelaus] cut the fleet into two parts, and drove some on Crete where the Kydonians lived around the streams of Iardanos.'[2] Pashley's identification of ancient Pergamos[3] was based on Pliny placing it between Cydonia and Kisamos.[4]

He became somewhat lost whilst searching for ancient Ierami (Gerani), just west of Platanias. He had followed an extract from the book of the 19th century historian Dr Cramer who had said the ruins of Ierami were to be seen at Cydonia[5]. Pashley commented, 'Neither ancient authors, nor modern travellers, as far as I am aware, afford any ground or colour for Dr Cramer's assertion.'[6]

Around where Pashley did locate Ierami, northwest of Pyrgos, are the ancient ruins of Modea. However, the coinage found at the site would indicate that the ruins are not as early as the Bronze Age, although there is evidence of a Minoan peak sanctuary.

Pashley referred to Pococke's reference to the ruins at Dictynnaeon on the cape of Spadha (see chapter 4), but chose not to visit the area himself, not thinking it worthwhile spending a whole day in going to see few remains which existed of a city already found.[7]

He was not able to find Kisamos as most of the ancient city lies beneath the modern town. However, just south of Kisamos he found the ruins of Polyrrhenia:

> I should think there can be no doubt that these are remains of the walls built by the Achaeans and the Laconians, when they came and settled with the Polyrrhenians and fortified this strong place.[8]

It was Homer in his *Iliad* who referred to the Bronze Age Mycenaeans as the Achaeans, a point of which Pashley would have been well aware. The remaining walls are Hellenistic, even though Pashley went as far as commenting, 'It was here that Agamemnon, when driven into Crete, came and offered sacrifice.'[9] The point, again, is his belief in an earlier period even if he was confusing its structures. Even so, Final Neolithic and Late Minoan IIIC, Protogeometric and Geometric sherds have all been seen at the site, although very little wall remains today.

At Phalasarna (ancient Korykos), the far western port of Polyrrhenia, Pashley found ancient ruins including a 'great chair' or 'throne' (Figs. 7.1a and b). He referred to Herodotus reporting that Midas, King of Phrygia, dedicated his throne to Delphi,[10] but he did not say it was made of stone. Pashley also mentioned Pausanias' references to thrones being donated to Classical Grecian temples for the god 'whose statutes were generally in a sitting posture on them'.[11] No such statutes were found at Phalasarna. Eight smaller but similar shapes were discovered around the 7th century BC Temple B at Kommos, just south of Phaistos (Fig. 7.2). They were described as 'a series of curious small U-shaped, open compartments ... one wonders if they were covered over by a cooking lid – or were actually small hearths, open on one side, used for boiling limpets'.[12] This is not an identification that could be given to Pashley's 'great chair'. Hadjidaki, in 1988, was still referring to it as a throne,[13] but Bowman had considered it an 'up-turned sarcophagus'.[14] Neither appears very likely, and more probably it was a cult area for 'offerings' before entering the city. Minoan sherds have been found scattered some 500 yards from Phalasarna,[15] proving that the site was of the Bronze Age and Pashley had visited it.

Pashley became rather disillusioned with the western coastline south of Phalasarna and, hearing of no remains of antiquity in that vicinity, he headed around to the south coast. He did find ancient ruins, mainly temples, at Lissos (Lyssos, west of Sougia Bay), but they were predominantly Hellenistic and Roman rather than Minoan. Lissos would have been the harbour to Elyros and Hyrtakina. At Lissos

---

[1] Psh II: 23.
[2] Homer's *Odyssey*, III. 291-2.
[3] Or Pergamea as founded by Aeneas in Virgil's *Aeneid*, 'Until at last we glide to the ancient shores of Crete. Eagerly setting to work on the walls of my chosen city, I name it Pergamea' (III.131-3).
[4] Pliny, *Natural History*, IV.20.
[5] Cramer, 1828, Vol. III: 366.
[6] Psh II: 25.
[7] Psh II: 29.
[8] Psh II: 47.

[9] Psh II: 49, but reflecting Hoeck, 1823-29, Vol. I: 48, and Zenobius, v. 50.
[10] Herodotus, 1.14.
[11] Psh II: 64.
[12] Shaw, 2006: 130-1. Thousands of limpet shells were found around these 'curious compartments'.
[13] Hadjidaki, 1988: 464, identifying a similar structure behind it but facing the other direction.
[14] Bowman, 1974: 266.
[15] Hadjidaki, 1988: 466-7 and fn. 11; see also Frost & Hadjidaki, 1990.

he turned inland believing he should find some antiquities at Elyros.[16] Nearby at Syia he observed Roman remains and appeared disappointed that they were not of a much earlier date.[17] He found Elyros and favoured it as the birthplace of the poet Thaletas, who lived 'before the time of Homer'.[18] This is further belief in a pre-Homeric period in Crete. There is very little at the site today other than a few stones and a view of the harbour at Sougia, or ancient Syia/Suia, the port of Elyros.

Just west of Elyros, Pashley came across the ancient site of Hyrtakina:

> ... on top of which [summit of hill] I yesterday learnt that there are *Hellenic* remains: I find all my hopes fully realized ... Along the south-western and western sides, however, considerable remains of ancient walls still exist: their height above ground varies from two to five or six feet. After following their course on the south-western side for about two hundred paces, we arrive at an entrance ... Soon after passing this entrance, we find a considerable piece of outer wall, which is five to twelve or thirteen feet high. The piece sketched is perhaps more regular, in size and forms of stones, the greater part of the walls which remain; but the whole may be considered as a near approach to what has been termed *second style of cyclopean masonry* ... I observe on the ground numerous pieces of pottery, and also notice that the stones are, in some places, more massive than those sketched.[19] (added italics)

Pashley's usage of 'Hellenic' is a generalization of ancient Greece rather than a specific period. As with his 'first cyclopean style'[20] (see previous chapter), he does not make it clear what he means by 'second style of cyclopean masonry', perhaps smaller but still heavy weight, or may be to distinguish between his idea of 'earliest style of so-called cyclopean or pelasgic walls'[21] (the first style?). The wall he sketched (Fig. 7.3) certainly gives that impression, and Vasilakis reported that 'Tthethox believes that Yrtakos [Hyrtakina] was the capital city of the Achaians [Homer's 'Greeks'], and was destroyed by the Dorians [end of Bronze Age] ... There were two cyclopic walls [Pashley's?], parts of which can be seen today.'[22] However, the walls of the actual 'city' on the summit today bear little relation to 'cyclopean'. Pashley's external walls seem very extensive and have disappeared over the last one hundred and seventy years or so, perhaps for building usage elsewhere over the centuries.

Nothing Minoan has been found at the site of Hyrtakina yet, but it bears a remarkable resemblance to the typical late 'Minoan retreat' positioned high up on the summit of the hill (such as Karphi) with a commanding view into the valley below.

Pashley said of the ruins of Hyrtakina and Khadros (Kantanos) that they were 'as yet unvisited ante-Homeric cities'.[23] His reference to 'ante-Homeric' implies a date before Homer but he did confuse the issue by discussing coins from Hyrtakina[24] which could not be pre-Homeric as coins did not exist then (see chapter 9). This could be a confusion by him of dating generally or simply a reference to, in his mind, a later period of ancient Hyrtakina. The same may apply to other sites he links with coins, such as Knossos, Axos and Tylissos. He sketched the walls of Kantanos,[25] and there remain some remnants of walls on the eastern side of the hill today, but these are not exactly cyclopean. However, Kantanos is possibly *ka-ta-no* in Linear B[26] and hence of Bronze Age origin.

Similar remains of large ancient walls were seen by him at Vlithia and on his return to Kalymides.[27] Such walls are indicative of the Bronze Age era, but this causes difficulties as they appear to be Archaic/Hellenistic. Again the emphasis is on Pashley's belief in an earlier period to which they might belong.

Pashley then found ancient Anopolis overlooking the harbour of Lutro, the ancient port of Phoenix. Of the walls of Anopolis he said, 'The chief remains are on the west; where a considerable piece of ancient walling, of the *very earliest style* still exists ... The chisel has been nowhere used on any stones' (added italics).[28] This is similar to a description of Bronze Age walling.

Despite the confusion with the style of walls at theses sites (Hyrtakina, Khadros/Katannos, Kalymides, Polyrhennia, Anopolis/Aradhena), it is probable that they were inhabited during the Bronze Age and Pashley had discovered them. However, the point is that at least Pashley had an earlier society in mind by making reference to this cyclopean style of walling, and this cannot and will not be under-emphasized.

Finally in his travels, Pashley was the first to detect the location of the ancient Hellenistic city of Tarrha on the south coast. There has been some debate about the city's origin[29] prior to the 4th century Hellenistic period, but it could be *ta-ra* in Linear B[30] and so of the Bronze Age.

Certainly, as far as the western part of the island was

---

[16] Psh II: 101, having read it in Pausanias, X.16.3.
[17] Psh II: 102.
[18] Psh II: 108.
[19] Psh II: 111-112.
[20] Psh I: 220.
[21] Psh I: 152.
[22] Vasilakis, 2000: 158.

[23] Psh II: 116.
[24] Psh II: 113.
[25] Psh II: 115
[26] McArthur, 1993: 173.
[27] See Psh II: 129 and 123 for his drawings of walls from these two sites.
[28] Psh II: 242.
[29] See Weinberg, 1969: 90-108.
[30] McArthur, 1993: 149.

concerned, Pashley's discoveries of anything clearly of the Bronze Age were limited. Sites of this period are by today's standards relatively scarce and so this is hardly surprising. This is not to say that earlier cities did not exist at these sites during the Bronze Age, as they are located in the places which were attractive for settlers, but the Archaic/Classical/Hellenistic/Roman activity usually covered and/or destroyed earlier evidence.

It appears from his book that Pashley completed his travels around Crete at the beginning of May,[31] but in a letter to Beaufort he said that he finished all his researches in Crete in July and August.[32] It is not clear why there is this discrepancy other than he may have lingered on in Crete or it took him that length of time to return home by ship or he continued his researches after he had returned home. Regardless, at the end of his travels he was a little pessimistic about his achievements and wrote to Beaufort:

> I have been now employed for more than a
> fortnight with my papers on Crete and may
> perhaps succeed by Christmas in putting
> them in order. I confess however that I feel
> some little disappointment at discovery … so
> many discussions on dry questions of ancient
> topography will they contain.[33]

On the contrary, what he had discovered was an earlier civilization than the known Hellenistic/Classical, hence his confusion with the topography. He just did not realize its actual date.

Publication

When Pashley was arranging the publication of his book with his publisher, John Murray, he had reservations of its impact.[34] He said in a letter from Trinity College, Cambridge, to the publisher:

> A learned friend who has read over my first
> chapter … thinks it "amusing." I fear the
> feeling cannot be general of all events since
> parts of my book - for instance chapters II &
> III & others, will be lighter reading, & I should
> think much more generally palatable.[35]

He was also concerned about the number of illustrations to be included, but considered the cyclopean walls to be of importance and indicated as much when writing again to his publisher:

> Do you think they [the lithographs] will help
> the book? Some of them I should give at all
> events – for instance the cyclopean walls – but
> unless they would be of some use to the book,
> for its general reader I mean, I might perhaps

content myself with a head piece for each chapter …[36]

He was worried about the cost of the lithographs/woodcuts and made comment of this in the same letter. The following month he again took issue with this factor, hoping to 'do a deal':

> I enclose the list of wood cuts. It would
> probably be of little use for me to comment on
> the prices mentioned. I will only observe that
> the £1.15.0 illustrations seem to me to be dearer
> than those at £3.10.0. [presumably relatively].
> Perhaps the consideration that I wish to have,
> in all probability, at least 40 similar illustrations
> for the work, may also have influence on the
> price.[37]

As previously discussed, his drawings to some extent confuse the issue as to his sightings of possible Bronze Age ruins as, at a first glance, they are indicative of such structures but on further investigation this may not to be the case. In saying this it is not entirely clear whether all the walls drawn by Pashley have been excavated and identified. However, his resulting belief in the existence of some earlier architecture is evidence of a belief in an earlier civilization, that of the then unknown Bronze Age.

Beaufort was unable to replace Pashley but instructed Copeland's successor, Thomas Graves, to continue archaeological study of antiquities in the Mediterranean. These intentions were made clear in a minute book relating to HMS *Beacon*:

> The situation and event of all ruined Temples,
> Theatres, Aqueducts, paved roads, excavations
> and other vestiges of antiquity which are at
> no great distance from the shore should be
> considered a prominent part of your operations
> … for in a national survey like this it would be
> a great reflection on us if such an opportunity
> were lost of assisting the literary world their
> researches in ancient geography …
> When time does not press, and the remains
> appear interesting, more may be done, and
> even the inscriptions copied, in doing which
> the exact form of letters should be imitated,
> and those of which there are any doubts should
> be noted; even fragments should not be hastily
> rejected as they often contain a syllable or a
> few letters from which the name of the place
> may be inferred.…
> In the same spirit other remnants of antiquity
> might be obtained, sarcophagi examined when
> not in opposition to the prejudices of the
> inhabitants, and remarkable pieces of sculpture
> described or drawn; but the Commander and
> the officers who are employed on the shore are
> strictly enjoined to permit no mischief to be

---

[31] Psh II: 266.
[32] Pashley to Beaufort, letter, 9th October 1834, HO, IL: P110.
[33] Pashley to Beaufort, letter, 28th February 1835, HO, IL: P107.
[34] It would appear he was seeking a run of between 500 and 750 copies (Pashley to Murray, letter, 7th June 1836, NLS, Acc. 12604) and 500 was agreed with a possible 250 cheaper editions for the German market (Pashley to Murray, letter, 8th July 1836, NLS, Acc. 12604).
[35] Pashley to Murray, letter, 26th May 1836, NLS, Acc. 12604.

[36] Pashley to Murray, letter, 18th April 1836, NLS, Acc. 12604.
[37] Pashley to Murray, letter, 5th May 1836, NLS, Acc. 12604.

done to those remains, and leave them as much protected as possible for examination of future travellers, or benefit of the natives themselves when they revive such pursuits.[38]

Beaufort's reference to 'if such an opportunity were lost' is reflective of his comment in his letter to Pashley (see chapter 5) wherein he lost the opportunity to travel to and research the island for antiquities himself.[39] It should be noted that he was not insisting on monuments being brought back to England, merely that they should be recorded in as much detail as possible so as to be useful for future research. As far as Crete was concerned these orders were shortly to be taken up by Thomas Spratt.

As a final word on Pashley, in his work on Edward Lear, Levi commented, 'Crete was more or less unexcavated until Sir Arthur Evans dug at Knossos in 1900, though its innumerable ancient sites were charted by Pashley.'[40] Some of these 'innumerable ancient sites' may well have been of the Bronze Age.

---

[38] Beaufort, Minute Book, 2: 306, 1st September 1836.
[39] Beaufort to Pashley, letter, 17th December 1832, HO, LB4: 189.

[40] Levi, 1995: 197.

8. Thomas Spratt
The Traveller

Biography

Vice-Admiral Thomas Abel Brimage Spratt (Fig. 8.1) was born in Teignmouth, Devon in 1811. His father was Commander James Spratt (who distinguished himself at Trafalgar[1]) and his mother was Jane (*nee* Brimage), and of their thirteen children, Thomas was the eldest of nine that survived. He began his naval career at the age of sixteen in 1827 and joined the *Mastiff*, an HM Surveying Vessel, on 22nd June 1832 with the junior officer rank of Midshipman.[2] He spent most of his seafaring time surveying in the Mediterranean Sea, including the waters around Malta and Crete, to produce Admiralty charts for shipping. He also served during the Crimean War which interrupted his activities in Crete. He was made Lieutenant on 15th October 1841, Commander on 3rd March 1849, Captain on 3rd January 1855, Rear-Admiral on 20th October 1872 on the retired list, having retired in April 1870, and Vice-Admiral on 9th March 1878.[3] He received a good service pension in 1867.[4] During the Crimean War he was 'gazetted with especial praise for his services at the fall of Kimbourn'[5] for planning the attack to capture the Turkish city and placing buoys which led the fleet to its position.[6] He received the Baltic, Crimean and Turkish medals and the Azof clasp and was awarded Companion of the Commander of the Bath after the Crimea War in 1855.[7]

He was clearly a respected individual who contributed a great deal to science. His many publications included work on Troy, Rhodes, Smyrna, Tunis, Samos, Boeotia, Danube, Serpent Island, Varna (Bulgaria), Dobrutcha (Romania), the Sea of Marmara (Dardanelles), Skiros, Constantinople, the Nile, Santorini and the Suez Canal.[8] He also reported on his time in Chalcis, capital of prefecture of Euboea, northeastern Greece.[9] He was made a Fellow of the Geological Society (FGS) in 1843; Fellow of the Royal Society of London (FRS) in 1856; Fellow of the Royal Geographical Society of London (FRGS) in 1859; Fellow of the Society of Antiquaries of London (FSA) in 1873; and Fellow of the Zoological Society of London (FZS) in 1883.

He died in Tunbridge Wells on the 10th March 1888, leaving a widow, Sophie Dean Spratt (*nee* Price)[10] and three sons, Edward James, Frederick Thomas Nelson and Arthur Graves Spratt. He left his journals to his second son, Frederick. Frederick died on the 4th February 1934, leaving his property to his son, Frederick Graham Spratt Bowring[11] and his daughters, Margaret and Isabella. Frederick Graham died on the 14th June 1977, but without heirs and his will made no mention of his grandfather's journals. He did leave some of his great grandfather's items to the Maritime Museum at Greenwich, so it was likely he would have inherited his grandfather's journals if his father had kept them, but they are not at the Maritime Museum.

Traveller

In 1838 Spratt visited Bunarbashi in Turkey, believing it to be Homer's Troy, 'These and other fragments I saw on the heights above Bunarbashi convinced me that a great city once stood there. That city could be no other than Troy itself.'[12] Spratt was wrong as the ancient city of Troy was further west at Hissarlick.[13] However, if he believed in the early site of Homeric Bronze Age Troy, there is no reason not to assume he could also believe in similar early sites elsewhere such as at Crete, particularly as Homer made references to Crete. The problem at that time was that he had no Bronze Age timescale label for such sites other than 'early/crude/rude' or 'cyclopean' (see next two chapters).[14]

Whilst on the *Mastiff*, Spratt's commander was Lieutenant Thomas Graves (as mentioned in chapters 5 and 7). Spratt was appointed to HMS *Beacon* on 21st June 1836, serving as mate, and therefore would have only missed

---

[1] J. Spratt to Beaufort, letter, 22nd January 1839, HO, IL: S420, setting out the details of his involvement in the battle.

[2] ADM 37/9336, The National Archives.

[3] ADM 196/37, Officer's Service Records 1756-1966, National Archives; also The Navy Lists: 359. A senior captain promoted to admiral on retirement was known as a 'yellow admiral' (or admiral of the yellow) and, although not on the active list, presumably Spratt's continued work as a hydrographer lead to further promotion to vice-admiral.

[4] PMG 23/76, The National Archives.

[5] ZJI/290 1855 Oct-Dec, *The London Gazette*, The National Archives.

[6] *The Times*, 15th March, 1888 ('Obituary').

[7] *Ibid.* Dawson commented that '…had his seniority been a little greater rumour asserted he would then have received the KCB for his excellent war and scientific services combined' (1885: 43).

[8] See Maempel, 1986: 296-300 for a full list of Spratt's publications.

[9] Spratt to fellow naval officer, Leycester, letter, 4th December 1880 (D. Moore collection).

[10] PMG 19/54, The National Archives.

[11] His father had adopted the surname of Bowring. What property was passed down is not known, but Frederick 'senior' had sold his father's Cretan marble statute of Aphrodite at Sotheby's in 1929.

[12] Spratt to Leake, letter, 4th February 1855[56], National Maritime Museum (NMM), SPR/3/9.

[13] Discovered by Schliemann in 1870 (see Schliemann, 1875); see also Allen, 1999.

[14] As with Pashley, Spratt's references to 'cyclopean' may not have been the identification of Bronze Age structures, but it is an assumption of an earlier civilization than the Hellenic.

Pashley by two years. Graves was given command shortly afterwards on 2nd August 1836.[15] The task was to survey the Mediterranean and produce a navigational chart of the waters for the Admiralty. Earlier in the century, the German traveller F.W. Sieber had commented:

Among the charts of Candia [Crete] all are very faulty … and no nation has ever been permitted to make a chart of the Archipelago. We shall scarcely obtain an accurate topographical knowledge of it, till Greece falls into the hands of a civilized nation.[16]

However, Spratt's relationship with Francis Beaufort (see chapter 5) did not run smoothly as Spratt obviously failed to attend Beaufort with a report of Graves' activities in the Mediterranean. Beaufort wrote to Graves:

Sir, I hoped that 'ere this Spratt would have made an appearance in this room, and have furnished me with matter about which I should have to write to you – that not being the case I have only to express a hope that he will bring me a large harvest of your usually excellent work.[17]

Francis Beaufort had suggested to Graves a survey of Crete in 1847,[18] and Graves was to commence this in 1849, but it was postponed as he was redirected to a more urgent survey of Cyprus.[19] In 1849 the *Beacon* had been pronounced unseaworthy and Graves took over as captain of HMS *Volage*[20] for the survey of Cyprus. He was then to go on to Crete in 1850 but shortly afterwards the ship was recalled to England. In May 1851 Spratt was sent to Malta and given command of his own ship, the paddle steamer HMS *Spitfire* (Fig. 8.2), with instructions to continue the survey of Crete.[21] Beaufort wrote to him confirming his daily (diem) pay:

Cmmdr TAB Spratt –	20s per diem	[£365 a year]
Lieut AL Mansell -	8/ - do -	[£146 a year]
Mr John Stokes – Master -	5/ - do -	[£91.25 a year]
" GB Wilkinson - Mids -	5/ - do -	[£91.25 a year][22]

From Malta Graves reported (lacking punctuation) Spratt's arrival to Beaufort, adding his disapproval of the *Spitfire* and general conditions:

Spratt has arrived with his staff but as he has I know reported progress I will say nothing more about his establishment to whom I will give every assistance and information in my power than that his "Spitfire" is the worst miserable [time] out I ever beheld and that with all my love for Hydrographical pursuits I am only too glad to be clear of and unconnected with the petty economy and annoyances surveyors are now subject to.[23]

He wrote again to Beaufort in February 1852 with reference to Spratt's ship:

… and how can I better commence [my letter] than by reporting the great improvement that has taken place in Spratt's health since his return to Malta – he is now almost himself again – despite of his "Spiteful" [as he called the *Spitfire*] and her miserable accommodation he has done good work during the Summer.[24]

Beaufort instructed Spratt to proceed to Crete and, as he had instructed Pashley, collect antiquities. He also reminded him to read Pashley's books:

… I have no doubt you will rapidly go on – but not too rapidly to do full justice to your work. I am a great admirer of zealous & eager workman, but still more [admiration] of those who leave nothing for subsequent workman to glean … Do not forget all I said to you about variations on shore & on board – Pick up inscriptions and antiquities – Read Mr Pashley as you go along the coast …[25]

On the 4th December 1851 Beaufort wrote to Pashley, sending him a copy of a letter from Spratt reporting on Crete and asked what Spratt should look out for on the island.[26] Beaufort then wrote to Spratt on the 19th December, not really giving Pashley much time to respond, saying, 'I sent your letter of Oct 15 to Mr Pashley who is I suppose out of town as he has not replied nor returned it [Spratt's letter].'[27] In the end Pashley did not reply until June the following year which clearly upset Beaufort, as he wrote to Spratt, 'I have just retrieved from Mr Pashley's hand your letter of Oct but without any remarks wh[ich] could be of use to you or wh[ich] cd[could] alone to me for the wanton rudeness of not answering my note for 6 months …'[28] What Beaufort failed to mention to Spratt was that

[15] ADM 196/1, The National Archives.
[16] Sieber, 1823: 18.
[17] Beaufort to Graves, letter, 19th January 1848, HO, LB15: 108.
[18] Beaufort to Graves, letter, 18th September 1847, HO, LB15: 13.
[19] Beaufort to Graves, two letters, both 9th March 1849, HO, LB16: 46 and 47.
[20] Deacon commented that the *Volage* was active in the Archipelago in the seasons of 1847 and 1848 but Graves did 'not appear as her captain in the navy list till 1849' (1978: 62, fn. 1). Dawson's memoirs of Spratt reported that he, Spratt, commanded *Volage* between March 1847 and April 1848 (1885: 42), but at some stage during that period he returned to England due to ill health because on the 18th April 1848 the Hydrographic Office wrote and asked Spratt if he was fit to rejoin *Volage* (HO, LB15: 184); Beaufort told Graves that Stokes had been offered the *Volage*, but he could not take it up immediately. This offer may have happened with Beaufort having Spratt's ill health in mind (letter, Beaufort to Graves, 2nd December 1847, HO, LB15: 62).
[21] Dundas and Stewart (of the Admiralty) to Spratt, letter, 12th May 1851, (Admiralty Order) NMM, SP/2/1.
[22] Beaufort to Spratt, letter, 12th May 1851, HO, LB18: 150.
[23] Graves to Beaufort, letter, 30th May 1851, HO, LB, IL: G160. Dawson reported that Graves had command of the *Spitfire* prior to Spratt, it having succeeded the *Volage* as the principal surveying ship in the Mediterranean (1885: 42).
[24] Graves to Beaufort, letter, 7th February 1852, HO, IL: G161.
[25] Beaufort to Spratt, letter, 7th July 1851, HO, LB17: 410-11.
[26] Beaufort to Pashley, letter, 4th December 1851, HO, LB4: 133.
[27] Beaufort to Spratt, letter, 19th December 1851, HO, LB17: 340.
[28] Beaufort to Spratt, letter, 8th June 1852, HO, LB18: 352. This is very much a 'change of tune' to Beaufort's comments to Copeland when

Pashley did say in his reply (to Beaufort), albeit somewhat late, that his papers had been destroyed by fire in Inner Temple (see chapter 5).[29]

It was Graves who encouraged Spratt, when surveying the sea, to look beyond the coasts they visited and consider the topology, geology, people and settlements of the country, including the visible remains of its history.[30] Taking Graves' advice Spratt travelled around the island of Crete and observed its topography and ruins which led him into the new science of archaeology. He was aware that the island held secrets to an ancient past and believed it must have been involved as a link or port of call of the ancients. He observed:

> Having but late of returned to England from a short tour of the Island of Crete and being aware of the many imperfect knowledge … in the remote part was the calling place between great and [?] civilized powers those of Egypt & Greece or Rome.[31]

He was assisted in his tasks by very able personnel, including Lieutenant Mansell and the surveyors George Wilkinson and Edward Wolfe Brooker, which enabled him to successfully research the island and write up his findings in his two-volume book, *Travels and Researches in Crete*.[32] One of the interesting discoveries which resulted from his combination of surveying, archaeology and topography was the way in which relative levels of land and sea had changed over the island in historic times. He wrote to the geologist, Sir Charles Lyell:

> Dear Sir Charles,
> Fearing you may be impressed with the idea that the eastern end of Crete had gone down as much as the west. I am induced to write a line to rectify it, if so; and to state that movements in the eastern half of the island have neither been as great nor apparently as uniform as the western movement. Both are subsequent to the historic period and the evidences are in both instances indicated by the elevation or partial submergences of some ancient Greek building or city.[33]

The letter was written on the on the 28th of February 1856, which was a Thursday. The two must have met the previous evening because the following day Spratt wrote again to Lyell confirming the situation:

> My dear Sir Charles,
> You understood me quite right on Wednesday evening in respect to the fact that the western half of Crete having been elevated, and the eastern half depressed or gone down a few feet.[34]

The submergence of the east coast can be seen today at the Minoan palace site of Kato Zakros, as part of it is underwater even in mid summer (Fig. 8.3). In 1977, Hopkins wrote, 'He [Spratt] noted quite correctly, that much of western Crete had risen by a whole eight metres. It was also believed, wrongly, that eastern Crete had sunk by a comparative extent.'[35] Hopkins did not make it clear as to whom he meant by 'it was believed' but the above letter of the 28th February to Lyell showed that Spratt did not believe this.

However, the movements were not restricted just to the east and west. Spratt observed that there was a maximum elevation of nearly 26 feet occurring on the south coast at the base of the White Mountains to the west of Sphakia, 17 feet to the extreme west of the island and declining to 6 or 7 feet along the north coast to Suda Bay.[36] He added that 'all the ancient cities included in this line of coast have been affected by the elevation by the conversion of their ancient ports into dry land'.[37] At first he found this puzzling and not thinking until a little later that the elevation must have 'occurred subsequent to the existence of these cites'.[38]

Spratt had discovered this occurrence at Phalasarna, a port on the western end of Crete, and had written to his friend and traveller Colonel William Leake with the information. The letter is of much geological interest as well as lending weight to the suspicion of an earlier inhabitation of the area. Leake sent an extract of the letter to the Royal Geographical Society (RGS) to be read out at a meeting (see Appendix E). Of particular note was Spratt's reference to possible ancient activity some distance from the sea:

> On going to Phalasarna I looked for its ancient port, mentioned by Scylax … but I could find no artificial work in the sea. There is however, a long ledge of rocks, or rather an islet which lies off it, helping to form a natural but not an artificial harbour. This satisfied me in part, till, on examining the ruins, I saw in the plain a square place enclosed by walls and towers, more massive and solid than those of the city … I was instantly impressed, for several, reasons, that here was the ancient port or artificial port, although full 200 yards from the sea and nearly 20 feet above it. My first idea was, that the ancients had a means of hauling

---

Pashley left Crete: 'My endeavours to get a proper person to succeed Mr Pashley have not yet succeeded – but I trust that before Spring you will be joined with some one with equal zeal and learning - I do not believe it would be easy to find anyone who could exceed Mr P in these qualities.' Beaufort to Copeland, letter, 1st October 1834, HO, LB4: 282-3.

[29] Pashley to Beaufort, letter, 20th May 1852, HO, IL: P595.

[30] Deacon, 1978: 3.

[31] SPR/2/17, Report, 'Crete and the Cretans', NMM. Unfortunately the report is undated and so gives no clue as to when this 'short' visit was.

[32] Publication had been delayed until 1865 because of the Crimean War and his work thereafter.

[33] Spratt to Lyell, letter, 28th February 1856, Edinburgh University Special Collections Department, 5420.

[34] Spratt to Lyell, letter, 29th February 1856, Edinburgh University Special Collections Department, 5422.

[35] Hopkins, 1977: 78.

[36] Spratt to Lyell, letter, 29th February 1856, Edinburgh University Special Collections Department, 5422.

[37] *Ibid*.

[38] *Ibid*.

their vessels into it as a dry dock; but at last the coast elevation was [uncumbered] and on measuring the sea mark at its upper level here I found that the bed of this anc[ient] port is now 3 or 4 ft below that level …[39] (Figs. 8.4a and b)

In his letter to Leake he originally dated this 'movement' of the island to a date prior to history (presumably pre-776 BC - date of first Greek writing) but was unsure, suspecting a more recent date due to a possible change in the markings on the landscape, concluding with a period 'subsequent therefore to the decline of the Roman Empire'. In his journal he dated it to the late Roman period.[40] The tectonic displacement has been dated to the 5th century AD[41] (see chapter 10 regarding Spratt on Phalasarna).

In 1859 (after serving in the Crimean War) Spratt returned to the Mediterranean in command of HMS *Medina* and was involved in the submarine cables for deep-sea soundings, including soundings from Malta to Crete. On completion of his work in Crete in 1859 he received a letter of appreciation from Captain Washington acknowledging the contributions from Spratt's subordinate officers:

> Sirs,
> Having submitted for the inspection of the Board of Admiralty the chart of the Island of Candia [Crete] recently completed by the surveyors of HMS Medina under your command. I have the justification to acquaint you that I have received direction to express to you that their Lordships highly approve of that work, and I have to request that you will convey this expression of the Board's approval to Commander Mansell, Lieutenants Wilkinson and Brooker, to Mr Stoker and the other assistants who have been employed on this survey.
> I am, Sir, your obedient servant,
> John Washington
> Hydrographer[42]

The Cretan gems

Gems or sealstones appear to be the instigator of research for archaeologists seeking the prehistory of Greece and Crete. Arthur Evans found his sealstones in a flea market in Athens which led him to Crete (see chapter 3), and Heinrich Schliemann found them at Mycenae. Spratt also discovered similar stones. The following is an extract from a report read by Spratt to the Society of Antiquaries, in 1879, on the archaic gems from Crete:

> Considerable interest having been awakened in regard to certain engraved stones of rude cut but undoubted early work, since researches and excavations of Dr. Schliemann, who had procured a few of them at Mycenae, I am induced in consequence to exhibit to the society several of these archaic or lentoid gems, as they are sometimes called by Dr Schliemann, from the generality of them having of that form, with a double convex surface.
> There is now a very interesting and important collection of these gems in the jewel room of the British Museum, which have been recently obtained from Crete, as well as the neighbouring Greek coasts and islands.
> The seven engraved gems which I now exhibit … were procured by me in Crete in various localities, but chiefly in the eastern part of it. As I have always regarded them as deserving more recognition as specimens of early art, both from their rarity and from their archaic and rude style; differing so strikingly from the well known types and forms, I had them set as now seen, the better to preserve them.
> But no previous collection had existed for comparison with them until that now in possession of the Trustees of the British Museum. The interest felt in them always by myself has consequently been considerably enhanced by their now fully-recognised importance as relics of archaic work of a special and highly interesting character, viz. that of personal or family seals or crests. And as the small group in my possession fortunately contains good typical specimens of these signet gems, if such they may be called, both from the subjects engraved upon them and their rude style, and also from the different character of the stones - for these archaic gems exist in steatite, hermatite, and also in carnelian or agate in its several varieties of colour and translucency – they therefore seemed to me to be deserving of exhibition to the members of the Society, and of venturing to accompany them with a few observations by way of description, etc.[43]

What is particularly interesting about this part of the report is his reference to the similarity of his gems to those found by Schliemann in Bronze Age Mycenae.[44] This implies similar dating which means that Spratt had in his hands evidence of the Bronze Age of Crete.

He then went on to describe the gems (see Fig. 8.5) and then continued with an observation of their probable origin as being from Caria, previous inhabitants of the Greek coast and Aegean islands[45] and possibly linking them with Crete. So who were the Carians and what was their connection with Crete?

---

[39] Spratt to Leake, letter, 18th September 1853, Royal Geographical Society (RGS), JMS 15/33. It was read out on the 13th March 1854 and published in the *Journal of the Royal Geographical Society*, 1854, vol 24: 238-9 (Appendix E).
[40] Spratt, 1865, Vol. II: 123 and 246.
[41] Cameron, 2003: 431; see also Flemming (1978) and Dermitzakis (1973) on coastal movement; and more recently Rackham & Moody, 1996: 194-201.
[42] Washington to Spratt, letter, 26th May 1860, NMM, SPR/3/3.

[43] Spratt, 1879: 119 (also SPR/2/28, May 1879, NMM).
[44] See Schliemann, 1878.
[45] Spratt, 1879: 121-2.

Caria

Caria is on the southwest coast of Anatolia (Asia Minor/ Turkey) and was first mentioned in the cuneiform texts of old Assyrian and Hittites Empires (*c*.1800-1200), and Pausanias was of the opinion that the Carians had occupied Crete.[46] Homer referred to the Carians in his catalogue of ships and said that they lived in Miletos.[47] Miletos itself was situated on the south-western coast of Anatolia (not to be confused with the Miletos in Crete – see below) and Strabo mentioned it in his *Geography*, linking it with the Carians who originated in Crete.[48] Herodotus, who came from Halicarnassus on the coast of Caria, said that the Caunians were aborigines of Caria although 'by their own account they came from Crete'.[49]

According to Herodotus, Anatolian Miletos was a stronghold of Caria.[50] It had supposedly gained its name as its settlers were from Miletos (Melatos) on the northern coast of Crete.[51] There are both Minoan imports in the early period of settlement at Anatolian Miletos and imitations of Cretan shapes. There are some fragments of Late Minoan IA and IB marine style sherds, but this in itself is not evidence for actual Minoan presence, just for imports. However, there is a great deal of locally produced domestic ware of Minoan types: 95% of pottery is Minoan in character and only 5% of local southwestern Anatolian. Also found were numerous flat discoid loomweights of the Minoan kind as well as many fragments of wall paintings in the Minoan technique. As for religion, there are fragments of an offering table of Minoan type and stone vessels of ritual, rhyton and an alabaster chalice, again in Minoan style.[52]

Travels in Lycia

Lycia is the southern neighbour of Caria and Herodotus referred to the Lycians as being 'from Crete and their customs were partly Cretan, partly Carian'.[53] According to Homer, Sarpendon, son of Zeus and ally to the Trojans, was ruler of Lycia.[54]

In April 1839 the antiquarian Sir Charles Fellows travelled to Lycia in search of antiquities and ancient sites.[55] Perhaps the most spectacular of his discoveries were the ruins of the city of Xanthos. The date of these remains he considered to be 'a very early one' and the walls 'Cyclopean'.[56] He did not clarify how early but three temples at the site have since been dated to the Classical 5th century BC.

Spratt and his two colleagues, the naturalist Edward Forbes and the historian the Rev. E.T. Daniell, joined Fellows in January 1842 just before the completion of the latter's work. Spratt's ship, the *Beacon*, then under the charge of Captain Graves, had been 'commanded to bring from Syria [actually Anatolia] the remains of antiquity discovered at Xanthus by Sir Charles Fellows'.[57] This may not have been considered an entirely popular venture by some in England, as Forbes, although not clarifying, commented:

> There had not been a little discussion too, in
> London circles, with regard to the doings of the
> 'Beacon' when procuring the Xanthus marbles,
> and the part Captain Graves took in that
> expedition had been much misinterpreted.[58]

It would appear that the monuments of Xanthos were causing as much controversy as the Elgin Marbles had done forty years earlier. Along with Graves, both Spratt and Forbes appeared uneasy about this mass clearance of a site and its removal to England. Spratt himself was to send items back to the British Museum and the Fitzwilliam Museum in Cambridge, but not on this scale. In fact Graves had given orders that two of the large tombs (Harpy and Payava) should not be dismantled until further instructions had come from Malta to construct suitable boats for their transportation down river, orders that were ignored.[59]

Spratt, Forbes and Daniell intended to travel to Lycia for surveying, naturalist and antiquarian purposes respectively. They came upon some eighteen ancient major cities and several other minor sites, and managed to trace the marches of Alexander the Great through Lycia. Unfortunately Daniell was taken ill with malignant malaria and died before the completion of the expedition.

They began their tour at Makri harbour (ancient Telmessus), the nearest safe anchorage to Xanthos, and travelled to Caria. It was not long before they came across the Cyclopean conglomerate stone architecture of Pinara. More Cyclopean walls were discovered at Arneae, but unlike many other ancient walls of Lycia they bore no inscriptions, possibly indicating an earlier phase of architecture. Likewise at Cyaneae, where they reported, 'within the walls was a confused row of buildings of early and late date; but we saw no sculptured fragments, columns or inscriptions'.[60]

The earliest finds appear to have been 6th century BC[61] and a great deal were mainly Classical/Hellenistic, Roman or Byzantine. However, Lycia did have Mycenaean

---

[46] Pausanias, *Guide to Greece*, 7.3.1.
[47] Homer's *Iliad*, 2.867, hence Spratt's reference to them being 'referred to by tradition'.
[48] Strabo, 14.2.1, 3.
[49] Herodotus, *Histories*, 1.172.
[50] And when the Persians captured it, they recovered Caria, *Histories*, 6.25.
[51] Homer referred to this Miletos as one of Crete's 'hundred cities', *Iliad*, 2.647.
[52] Niemeier & Niemeier, 1999: 547-8.
[53] Herodotus, *Histories*, 1.173.
[54] Homer's *Iliad*, 2.876-7; and Herodotus also referred to Sarpendon as reigning in Lykia in his *Histories*, 1.273.
[55] Fellows, 1839; Pococke had also travelled to Lycia in 1739-40.
[56] Fellows, 1839: 225.
[57] Bennett, 1855: 9.
[58] From Wilson & Geikie, 1861: 408. Graves had refused to transport the marbles (Friendly, 1977: 259) (see fn. 59 below).
[59] Cook, 1998: 141-2. Fellows had his finds ready for transportation in January but Graves said he would have to make the request for the boats to Beaufort who was in Malta and did not expect a reply until March – Fellows was furious; Stoneman commented that Graves was a constant frustration to Fellows, 'It was the bureaucrat pitted against the explorer, a battle of will against obstinacy' (1987: 213).
[60] Spratt & Forbes, 1847: 111.
[61] See Akurgal, 1983.

connections, as Miletos, just further north, was a Minoan/Mycenaean colony (as mentioned above), and so there is some reason to speculate that some of the cyclopean architecture may have belonged to that age.

Spratt's and Forbes' findings were published in their book *Travels in Lycia*,[62] and so Spratt had possibly found Cretan links in Asia Minor before he visited the island of Crete itself. This is another indication of his interest in the search for ancient civilizations. Spratt was obviously unimpressed with the lack of credit he had received for his work in Lycia, as his colleague William Leake wrote to Sir Roderick Murchison, the President of the Royal Geographical Society (RGS):

> Capt Spratt complains that his discoveries geographical and archaeological in Lycia and the adjoining parts of Asia Minor have never [been] noticed by any President [of the RGS] in his annual address, and I think he complains not without reason, those discoveries having been some of the most important that have been made in that country and of a nature particularly fitted to the objects of our Society.[63]

The same may have applied to his discoveries on Crete.

Crete

Spratt had more than one purpose for visiting Crete, which he mentioned in the introduction of his book, *Travels and Researches in Crete*.[64] He commented that he was there to survey but also to collect reliable information regarding ancient cities, many of which were yet undiscovered and this would be of importance to the island's geography and topography.[65]

As seeking out ancient cities was part of his business, so too was the search for an ancient Cretan civilization. He was not the scholar Pashley was, and as Pendlebury remarked, 'Neither his scholarship nor his knowledge of the language can compete with Pashley's, but his common sense, enthusiasm and simple directness have produced a valuable book.'[66] He may not have had the scholastic skills or academic background of Pashley,[67] but he had a keen eye and his observations of ancient sites and cyclopean ruins were second to none. The Cretan archaeologist Stampolidis was of the opinion that Spratt's work was the transition from travel journal to academic study, 'The dynamic set in motion in these years [second half of 19th century], after the publication of Spratt's two-volume *magnum opus* on Crete, is obvious also in the publications that follow, which are less travel orientated and more antiquarian in nature.'[68]

Sir Roderick Murchison in an address to the Royal Geographical Society, perhaps reflecting on Leake's letter (above), said of Spratt's book:

> 'The Travels and Researches in the Island of Crete' by Captain T.A.B. Spratt, RN., is a work which will rivet the attention and enrich the minds of various readers, whether they be antiquaries and scholars, or geographers and men of the sciences ... for here we see produced by one of them [Royal Naval surveyors] a masterly illustration of the physical geography, geology, archaeology, natural history, and scenery of the diversified Island of Crete.[69]

The book was written in two volumes and (amongst other matters) recorded Spratt's antiquarian finds on Crete.

[62] Spratt & Forbes, 1847.
[63] Leake to Murchison, letter, 15th January 1854, RGS, CB 1851-60.
[64] Spratt, 1865, Vols. I and II (hereafter 'Sp I' and 'Sp II').
[65] Sp I: 2.

[66] Pendlebury, 1939: 17.
[67] Although he was knowledgeable of the classics as he relied very much on ancient authors such as Herodotus (c484-425 BC), Thucydides (c.460/55-400 BC), Strabo (c.64 BC-AD 25), Pliny (AD 23-79) and Plutarch (c.AD 45-125) as sources of identification of ancient sites.
[68] Stampolidis, 2004: 23.
[69] From Dawson, 1885: 44.

9. Thomas Spratt
Travels And Researches In Crete, Vol. I

To Crete (see Map 5)

Although Spratt was not specific about dating sites or finds, he did observe, as early on as page 24 of the first volume of his 1865 Cretan travels' book (Sp I) , 'Sometimes, too, we shall be amidst the relics which tell of the power, wealth, and civilization of the past – of the cultivated race of Cretans twenty or thirty centuries ago …'. *Thirty centuries ago* was the time of the Bronze Age 'Minoans' and hence a clear recognition by Spratt of an such a society. On his first visit to Crete Spratt ascended Mount Ida in the centre of the island. In mythology Mount Ida was the birthplace of the Olympian god Zeus (Jupiter), but Spratt dismissed this ancient tale and felt no enthusiasm for the Mount other than for its views and flora as he had 'no learned interest in the mythological features and faith of the men of the time of Minos'.[1] His purpose was purely scientific and he was to make observations for the purpose of his survey and not, he said, for the pursuit of classical study.[2]

However, his observations were to include sites of antiquity, and although his interest was mainly scientific this did lead him on to archaeological pursuits. He was prepared to base some of his assumptions concerning the whereabouts of ancient cites on the words of ancient classical authors and so did consider classical study. But he found nothing to indicate Mount Ida's 'sacred character' other than a fragment of identifiable earthenware and a few pieces of charcoal and incense.[3]

His indifference to the Mount because of its connection with the mythological Zeus is interesting as he did not feel the same about King Minos. He referred to Knossos as 'the capital of Crete under Minos'[4] and considered the 'laws of Crete, by Minos' to be the model of the laws of Lycurgus and Crete as a school of art at the time of Minos.[5] The same seemed to apply to his belief in Daedalus, King Minos' mythological architect of his labyrinth, as he referred to him as 'the father of Cretan art under Minos'.[6] He did make reference to the fact that Daedalus may have been a fiction, '… and whether Daedalus was a man or a myth, as some assume, it was at Gnossos, according to the writings of all, that the school of art, under the mythical name, was planted and flourished.'[7] Here he appeared to be leaving

his options open on the subject.[8] There would be those in the 19th century who may also have assumed King Minos to be a myth, but it would appear not Spratt. This is possibly an indication of his belief in a bygone age of Crete prior to the Classical period.

The visit to Mount Ida was on the 31st of May but he said it was 'a few years ago'.[9] This was a previous visit to 1851 and almost certainly in 1843. On this particular occasion he was accompanied by Colonel Henry Drummond Hay who was visiting the island for his interest in vegetation and was a guest of Graves. In a letter to Sir Francis Beaufort in June 1843, Graves commented on his own invitation to Hay to join his ship the HMS Beacon sailing from Malta to Crete.[10] Not only that, but both Spratt and Drummond Hay visited the Gortyns' labyrinth in 1843 as they marked their names on a wall, accompanied by the date '1843', and Spratt added 'HMS Beacon' (see end of chapter 11 and Figs 11.6a & b).

Hay was something of an ornithologist and could contribute with observations in the stead of the ship's previous naturalist, Edward Forbes, who Graves had been missing, '… as I have to regret the loss of my worthy friend Mr now Professor Forbes as a companion'.[11] Forbes had taken the chair of botany at King's College, London. In October 1843 he wrote to James Balfour, the Professor of Botany at Edinburgh University, referring to his 'pupils' from *Beacon*, sending him a 'beautiful parcel from Mount Ida'. This may have been a reference to Spratt's visit to Mount Ida, Spratt being one of Forbes' natural history 'pupils'.[12]

With Forbes, Spratt had collected various plant and flower species but had learnt nothing of the ancient civilization. On his return to Crete in 1851 in command of the steamship *HMS Spitfire*, Spratt was convinced that he would be 'amidst the relics which tell of the power, wealth, and civilization of the past – of the cultivated race of Cretans *twenty and thirty centuries ago* …' (added italics).[13] He

---

[1] Sp I: 6.
[2] *Ibid.*
[3] Sp I: 11.
[4] Sp I: 58.
[5] Sp I: 68-69.
[6] Sp I: 69.
[7] Sp I: 70.

[8] He put obvious mythology, such as the escape of Daedalus and his son, Icarus, from the island on wings, down to a 'poetic indication of the need of undue ambition and weakness … fiction in which there is some fragment of fact …' (Sp I: 70).
[9] See Spratt's comment 'Thus, as my first introduction to the island of Crete was by an early visit to the summit of Ida' (Sp I: 23).
[10] Graves to Beaufort, letter, 29th June 1843, HO, Miscellaneous Papers, 27c.
[11] *Ibid.*
[12] See Forbes to Balfour, letter, October 1843 (from Wilson & Geikie, 1861: 346).
[13] Sp I: 24.

intended to seek out evidence of this civilization as well as localities 'left undescribed by Pashley'.[14]

Candia (Herakleion), Amnissos and Knossos
Candia, or modern Herakleion, in north central Crete was where Spratt began his travels. It was, and still is, a port and an obvious starting point for Spratt, as it was possible to anchor his ship within the protection of the bay. However, the only ancient Cretan relics Spratt was able to report from the town were a Roman statue and a sarcophagus, both he believed to be from Knossos. When Spratt was there the sarcophagus was being used as a drinking-trough for cattle.[15] This does give an indication of Spratt's interest in the island's past early on in his visit and his interest in archaeology.

Herakleion was of Bronze Age origin[16] and it is a likely position for a port of Knossos during the Minoan period, but it is not surprising that Spratt found nothing of pre-historical interest in or around the town because the Venetians would have built over any such ancient remains. Herakleion was later to prove an important area for evidence for Minoan activity. A boar's tusk helmet was found at a chamber tomb at Katsambas (Poros),[17] the Minoan harbour at the mouth of the Kairatos River at Herakleion which compares with Homer's description of such a helmet as being worn by Odysseus.[18] Therefore the helmet found at Katasambas subsequently linked Crete to the Mycenaeans, although such a civilization was not then known to Spratt.

Spratt believed that Herakleion was a port for ancient Knossos and that Amnissos, being about a 6 km to the east of Herakleion, was its secondary.[19] Amnissos is situated in a protected bay with a coastline of some 2.5 km suitable for beaching ships. It is also referred to in Linear B as *a-mi-ni-so*.[20] Obviously Spratt would not have been aware of Linear B, but he did suggest that Amnissos was also the site of Matium,[21] which Pliny mentioned as being opposite the island of Dia. Amnissos was once the name of the river now called Kairatos. This is contrary to Pashley's belief that Matium was Candia/Herakleion. It really depends on how accurate Pliny intended the phrase 'being opposite'. Amnissos is right opposite Dia, and working on this assumption, Spratt is possibly correct with his identification of Matium.

In the *Odyssey*, Homer referred to Odysseus being forced by the wind to pull into Amnissos on his way to Troy, 'He stopped at Amnissos, where there is a cave of Eileithya, in difficult harbors, and barely had he escaped from the stormwind.'[22] Strabo referred to Amnissos as a seaport used by Minos, 'where there is the temple of Eileithuia'.[23] The cave at Eileithyia[24] contained artefacts from the Neolithic, Middle Minoan and Roman periods[25] but was missed by Spratt.

Amnissos was excavated by Spyridon Marinatos in 1929-1938, and he found the 'House of the Lilies', a Minoan Villa with paved corridors which was part of a Minoan settlement but destroyed by fire in the fifteenth century BC.[26] Spratt was therefore correct to link Amnissos with ancient Knossos.

Spratt believed Knossos was one of the earlier seats for the development and cultivation of art, using its coins as an example.[27] Although he was correct, he had the wrong reason. The oldest currency coins of Crete, so far as they have been identified, cannot be assigned to an earlier period than *c*.500 BC,[28] but Spratt did date some of the sculptures as far back as 777 BC.[29]

Clearly Spratt was aware of Knossos as an important site and speculated as to its position in a low undulating plain and terminating at the village of Fortezza (Fortetsa).[30] Certainly Knossos is situated in a low plain descending east into a ravine ('river' Kairatos) and dropping down below Fortezza. He saw nothing much to impress him but commented:

> But in the time of the Venetians, Belli shows
> that there was still existing the remains of a
> curiously constructed theatre or circus; the plan
> of it however, was not sufficiently distinct,
> to Belli, to be given in the manuscript, the
> relics of which have been recently published
> by Mr Falkener in the 'Museum of Classical
> Antiquities'.[31]

In 1586 Onorio Belli (see chapter 6) described the area of Knossos:

> The hills upon which the city was built are
> of low elevation, and the walls may be four
> miles in circumference … It is now almost
> completely destroyed, and none of its buildings
> remaining entire. Several large masses of
> walling exist in different places, built of stone,
> but much decayed. The foundations of a theatre
> or other building, of great size, are visible, but
> it is not easy to determine its plan.[32]

It is unfortunate that Belli was not able to record the plan of

---

[14] He considered Pashley's account incomplete (Sp I: 23), but then so too was his own.
[15] Sp I: 44-5.
[16] Davaras, 1976: 358/10 and 1976: 5; also Evans, 1928: 229ff
[17] Vasilakis, 1999: 235; Evans, 1928: 229.
[18] Homer's *Iliad*, 10.263-4.
[19] Sp I: 66.
[20] McArthur, 1993: 106.
[21] Sp I: 67.
[22] Homer's *Odyssey*, XIX: 188.

[23] Strabo, 10.4.8.
[24] The cave where Hera gave birth to Eileithyia, the Goddess of childbirth (Pausanias, I.18.5).
[25] Vasilakis, 2000: 89.
[26] Davaras, 1976, 5-6; Schafer, 1991: 112.
[27] Sp I: 71.
[28] Although gold 'coins' (for decoration) were found in the 16th century BC Grave Circle A at Mycenae (Schliemann, 1878).
[29] Sp I: 71 – but mainly 'Roman or inferior art' (Sp I: 80).
[30] Sp I: 58-60.
[31] Sp I: 60.
[32] From Falkener, 1854: 24 (a supplement to his 'Museum of Classical Antiquities').

the theatre in his manuscript 'History of Candia'[33] and so it is not clear to what he is referring. However, as Belli considered the site of Knossos to be four miles in circumference it may be somewhere as yet undisturbed. He did record a large monument, but it was not a theatre, more of a basilica (Fig. 9.1),[34] and it is not clear where it was situated.

So it appears that foundations of Roman buildings were visible to Spratt, unlike when Evans visited the area nearly fifty years later. What were not evident to Spratt were the ruins of an impressive city that lay beneath the surface. Evans' palace excavations were only a small portion of the whole urban area if both Belli and Spratt are referring to its circumference in mileage terms. Strabo suggested its original circuit was 'thirty stadia'.[35] 30 stadia is about three and three-quarter miles but this cannot be relied upon (see chapter 6 on stadia).

Spratt searched for the 'mythical' labyrinth which he thought may originally have existed as a subterranean quarry in the heart of the hills that surrounded Knossos. He looked to the ridge on the east side of the Makryteichos (Makriteikron/Makroteikho) village (over the rivulet of the Kairatos river) and compared what he saw with that at the 'labyrinth' at Gortyns (see below and chapter 11):

> … that [Makryteichos hills] is said by the natives to be the entrance to extensive catacombs, which, however, have become choked up by falling in of its sides, and cannot be explored … This entrance to the supposed Labyrinth or Catacombs of Gnossos has the same character as that of the entrance to the Labyrinth of Gortyna, excepting that the Gnossian excavations have been used as sepulchres, but whether originally or subsequently to Minos cannot be determined so as to identify it as the true Labyrinth, of which the tradition only existed for twenty-five centuries.[36]

It is not entirely clear what he was looking at, but it is most likely either the MM III Black Cave (Makro Spilio) or one of the many tombs of the adjacent cemetery on the hill overlooking the village of Makryteichos and possibly referred to by Pashley (chapter 6). There is a Bronze Age 'labyrinthian' tomb in the Mavro Spilio cemetery, Tomb IX (Fig. 9.2),[37] which could have been what Spratt saw.

Mount Iouktas

As mentioned in the chapter 6 (see also Pashley Figs. 6.5-8), Mount Iouktas has two peaks and Spratt referred to the ancient foundations on the northern peak as 'Cyclopean',[38] as had Pashley. Spratt was not convinced that these Cyclopean walls were part of the sacred Tomb of Zeus, as Pashley had presumed. Spratt thought it would have been where the modern chapel stood on the southern summit, being the site of an older chapel.[39] His theory was based on the fact that new chapels were usually built on the same spot as old ones and therefore this was the sanctified or sacred place. The problem is that it is not known what is beneath this chapel, and if another chapel, what lies beneath that one. The later Greeks may not have considered the Minoan site on the northern summit sacred and may have simply utilized this southern summit to create a new sacred position. The 15th century traveller Buondelmonti first considered the tomb of Zeus to have been on the southern summit, but by the 19th century the northern peak had become the favourite site for the tomb as a result of Pashley's observations,[40] despite Spratt's later theory.

Evans was to identify the northern summit as a Middle Minoan refuge site,[41] and he received the credit for 'first' investigating this peak sanctuary in 1909,[42] but both Pashley and Spratt had been there before him. Admittedly the latter two were not involved in excavation, but they had searched it out and recorded their views on its possible ancient usage.

From Iouktas Spratt visited Archanes and, similar to Pashley, reported nothing of archaeological interest, again being unaware of the Bronze Age architecture that lay beneath its earth.[43]

Rhaucos and Lycastos

From the summit of Mount Iouktas Spratt looked down on 'two remarkable craggy peaks … two miles to the southwest of Iuktas',[44] which, unlike Pashley dismissing it as no earlier than Venetian (see chapter 6), he believed to have been ancient Rhaucos, which may be *da-ra-ko* (Draukos) in Linear B.[45] Between the twin peaks today are the ruins of the Byzantine fortress of Temenos, built in AD 961. Spratt's belief was supported by 'local tradition' and the fact that Khani Kastelli is an abbreviation of Roucani Kastelli (the Castle of Roucani),[46] and the hill of the peaks is still referred to as Rocca, but that was its Venetian name. It is not clear whether Spratt actually went up onto the summits of either peak as he made no mention of such a visit. This is unlike his graphic descriptions of most of the areas he ventured into. Nor did he mention the chapel of Panayia or the adjacent Roman cistern half way up the western peak, nor any of the other four ruined Venetian

---

[33] Abstracts written by Apostolo Zeno (1608-1750) are preserved in St Mark's Library in Venice.

[34] Although Belli's drawings are not of the Bronze Age, it is worth reproducing them (as done here and below) as they are rare, and they do show that Spratt was not adverse to his own research.

[35] Strabo, 1.4.7.

[36] Sp I: 66, another reference to the possible belief in the existence of Minos.

[37] See Forsdyke, 1927; also Hogarth, 1899-1900: 81 on possible settlement.

[38] Sp I: 79 and 84.

[39] Sp I: 84; supported by Bickford-Smith, 1898: 28.

[40] Rutkowski, 1986: 2, 3.

[41] Evans, 1928: 156.

[42] Cameron, 2003: 129.

[43] See Sakellarakis & Sakellarakis, 1997.

[44] Sp I: 84.

[45] McArthur, 1993: 130.

[46] Sp I: 85. Another view is that it means 'Bloody Castle' in memory of a battle in 1647 when the Venetians defeated the Turks (Spanakis, undated: 181; Evans, 1928: 74; Cameron, 2003: 132).

chapels situated within the two hills, all of which must have been visible at the time, as they still are now.

Spratt's opinion differed from the then general view that the site was that of ancient Lycastos (as it is accepted as so today). Homer did not mention Rhaucos in his catalogue of ships but he did refer to 'silver-shining Lycastos',[47] and it is possibly *ru-ki-to* in Linear B.[48] Neither did Strabo mention Rhaucos but Polybius did, 'the Gortynians, who sought in every way to depress the Gnossians, deprived them of a portion of their territory called Lycastrium, and assigned it to the Rhaucii ...'.[49] This implies Rhaucos and Lycastos were separate but near to each other.

The plain below Rocca was inhabited in the Bronze Age and Evans reported that he found Minoan sherds scattered around Visala, near to Khani Kasteli.[50] Also Marinatos found a Late Minoan III sarcophagus in its entirety.[51] So Spratt was close to a Bronze Age site.

Some confusion arose with Lycastos. Spratt queried Pashley's positioning of it in the district of Mirabello, just south of Milatos, and he suggested that Pashley relied upon natives' tales rather than his own observations.[52] Pashley did not actually mention the whereabouts of the city but Spratt was referring to his map reference. Spratt believed Lycastos was (K)Astritzi where he saw a mixture of Cyclopean and later Hellenic walls and square towers from 12 to 15 feet high.[53] There is certainly no evidence of either walls or towers there today. Strabo said that Lycastos no longer existed in his time and its territory had been shared between the Lyctians and Knossians.[54] So if Khanli Kastelli was Lycastos and no longer existed in Strabo's time, it is unlikely that Spratt would have seen any evidence for it if he was not excavating. However, Spratt thought Strabo was mistaken. As these cities must all be in the same vicinity based on Homer's description and as Astritzi was the only nearby ruins Spratt found, he assumed that site to be Lycastos. It is more likely that Spratt himself had made the mistake rather than Strabo, which means it is unlikely that Lycastos was at Astritzi.

As well as Archaic and Classical, there was a large Late Minoan site at Astritzi, but nothing is visible today as it has been cleared of its stonework.[55] More recently another possible Minoan palace has been found at Astritzi's neighbouring village of Galatas, so clearly Spratt was on the right track.

Lyttos
According to Spratt Lyttos (Lyktos) was one of King

Minos' cities of central Crete: 'This central part of Crete, which comprised several other cities of Minos, viz. Lyttus, Lycastus, Gortyna, and Phaestus ...'.[56] All four cities are of the Bronze Age and again a reference to Minos and a possible belief in an early era. To get to Lyttos Spratt passed over the plain of Pediada and through the ancient walls of Saba, or Sapa, which he thought to be Thenae.[57] Today there is nothing of archaeological interest to see above the ground at Saba.

At Smari (Smarvi), near Saba, Spratt referred to one of the thirty seven inscriptions he found on the island.[58] He also reported that the walls of the Smari 'are purely Hellenic, and not Cyclopean, and are in better preservation than those at Kastrtizi'.[59] The inscription would support this Hellenic observation but it is interesting that Spratt is differentiating between the two styles of walls, Hellenic and Cyclopean which would suggest a recognition of different periods. The site of Smari is on top of a hill above the village and there are Hellenic (Hellenistic) ruins as Spratt reported. There are also Minoan ruins which cannot have been visible to him at the time, which include very small rooms and a typical lustral basin which may be a place for ceremonial purification. So again Spratt was within the precincts of the Bronze Age civilization even if he was unaware of it.

Ancient Lyttos/Lyktos (called Xidhia when Spratt visited) is about 30 km due east of Khani Kastelli or, as Strabo calculated, 120 stadia from Knossos,[60] which is approximately 22 km (although it is further than that at about 38 km). Lyktos may be *Ru-ki-to* as inscribed in Linear B tablets from Knossos,[61] rather than Lycastos (above), and Spratt referred to it as 'of very great antiquity',[62] possibly meaning long before the known Classical period.

Spratt observed that the site at Lyttos occupied a very commanding position on the western summit of the Lasithi Mountains, made up of terraces on the hill to support it,[63] and there is no doubt of its commanding position. Due to terracing, Spratt reported that most of the remains of the buildings of the old city had fallen into the valleys.[64] He gave no indication of the age of these 'old buildings', although he found several sculptured Roman marbles and on the summit of the ruins two headless marble statues[65] near the small chapel. He added that there where no

---

[47] Homer's *Iliad*, 2.647.
[48] McArthur, 1993: 146. Although it has also been suggested that the script reference may be Lyctos/Lyttos (see below) (McArthur, 1993: 143).
[49] Polybius, *Histories*, 22.19.4.
[50] Evans, 1928: 73.
[51] Cook, 1951: 252.
[52] Sp I: 115.
[53] Sp I: 91.
[54] Strabo, 10.4.14.
[55] See also Nowicki, 2000: 179; Pendlebury, 1939: 342, 351, 361.
[56] Sp I: 77.
[57] Sp I: 92.
[58] Sp I: 93 and 414 - all of them in ancient Greek and therefore either Classical Greek or Roman. Accordingly, it is not proposed to refer to them (they can be found in the appendix to Sp II: 411-35, reproduced by Rev. Churchill Babington; see also Babington, 1855: 97-109).
[59] Sp I: 93.
[60] Strabo, 10.4.7.
[61] McArthur, 1993: 145-6; Vasilakis, 2000: 126.
[62] Sp I: 89.
[63] Sp I: 96.
[64] *Ibid.*
[65] One a draped female and the other the lower half of a colossal statute of Jupiter. It is not clear where these are now, but there are several headless Roman statues at the museum at Hierypetra, although they do not appear to have come from Lyttos.

remains of building, not even the Venetian theatre drawn by Belli in the 16th century (Fig. 9.3).[66]

Homer mentioned Lyktos, albeit by name only,[67] and Nowicki reported vestiges of Late Minoan IIB/C pottery, leaving no doubt that a Minoan settlement existed during that period.[68] There is very little else in evidence of the Bronze Age today as time and nature have removed most the evidence of ancient activity.

Khersonesos, Malia and Milatos
Moving on from Lyttos, Spratt headed north to the coast at Khersonesos ([C]Hersonesos), keeping in touch with his ship which anchored close under the cape forming the bay. He then went in search of an early Christian church which he was convinced must exist due to the town being the see of a bishop. He found the foundations of a large 5th century AD Basilica (112 feet long and 52 feet broad) with several columns supporting its roof and 'just under it … there is a small cave that is still used as a chapel, and dedicated to Hagia Paraskevi, or Holy Friday'.[69] This chapel is still used today (Fig. 9.4). The foundations of the Basilica (of Kastri) still remain, with its mosaic floor, which Spratt did not mention and so presumably was not visible to him at the time (Fig. 9.5). Underwater, around the west side of the basilica peninsula, are three ancient rectangular fish tanks which would have been part of the Roman harbour[70] and must have been visible in Spratt's time but he made no mention of them.

Spratt also came across a large cistern and aqueduct near the western entrance, neither of which is now evident. However, he did observe, adjacent to the harbour, the tessellated fountain with four triangular sides, each side representing aquatic figures and fishermen[71] which does still exist today (Fig. 9.6). His only other find was the ruin of a small Roman theatre which had been in a much more complete state in the Venetian period as it had been drawn by Belli (Fig. 9.7). Spratt reported that 'the foundation of the proscenium and a part of the wings and back alone remain'.[72] Today only a wall-buttress survives. All these are of historical and archaeological interest but not in relation to the Bronze Age.

What is relevant to the Bronze Age is that Spratt also found evidence of a 'broad road having once connected Lyttos with its emporium Khersonesos … indicative of a period of great populousness, prosperity, and advanced civilization'.[73] It is likely, from its position, that Khersonesos would have been the port for Lyttos. Unfortunately modern Khersonesos is very much urbanized and practically nothing of ancient interest remains other than the ruins of a recently excavated Minoan building and road amongst the cafes on route to

the seafront. It could well be the old road from Lyttos as it heads towards the bay and harbour of today, which almost certainly would have been the ancient port of the city, as confirmed by Spratt, 'we have a fine view of the Bay of Khersonesos, and of the ancient port of the city that stood upon the west shore of the bay'.[74]

On the other side of Khersonesos Bay to the east is Malia Bay and the Minoan 'palace' of Malia.[75] The Cretan archaeologist Adonis Vasilakis credited Spratt as the first to detect ruins in the area of Malia in the 19th century.[76] Spratt found evidence of the site a few hundred yards from the coast, 'The remains consist chiefly of some few foundations of ancient inhabitants, portions of cyclopean terraces or walls, and a massive platform ninety-five feet square, formed of slabs of limestone, which must have supported or been the approach to a temple.'[77] He added that a shepherd had found scales of gold and the natives had found only a few ounces of precious metal.[78] It is not entirely clear where he was referring to, but there are several burial grounds around this area, the cemetery of Chrysolakos being the most prominent.[79] Here gold burial goods, including the famous 16th century BC gold bee pendant, were found. There is also the large site of the 'palace' of Malia, *c.*1900-1450 BC, which is about 600 yards or so from the coast. If either this palace or the cemetery were in the region that Spratt referred to, then the natives should have persevered.

Spratt was unable to locate Homer's Milatos but was not surprised and referred to Strabo's understanding that it had been destroyed.[80] He queried Pashley's map reference of the ruins west of the modern city, although the map is not that exact. When questioning the local natives, 'they pointed to a conical peak jutting off from the higher hills on the east side of the bay, and not far from the sea-shore as the only true Hellenic site in the neighbourhood … on the sloping ground extending nearly to the sea from its base'.[81] He was only to perceive heaps of stones which seem to have been the 'remains of ancient and rude inhabitants of an early city like that of Miletus'.[82] Minoan and post-palatial finds at a nearby tholos tomb would indicate a Bronze Age settlement,[83] perhaps Spratt's 'rude inhabitants', as would two chamber tombs containing clay larnakes and vases.[84] Also, Late Minoan III pottery has been found at Kastellos within the Milatos area.[85] As mentioned in the previous

[66] Sp I: 97.
[67] Homer's *Iliad*, 2.647.
[68] Nowicki, 2000: 177 (referring to Taramelli, 1899 and 1901).
[69] Sp I: 105-6.
[70] Leatham & Hood, 1958-9: 266-73.
[71] Sp I: 106.
[72] Sp I: 107.
[73] Sp I: 104.

[74] Sp I: 105.
[75] Vasilakis suggested it could be *se-to-i-ja*, as inscribed in Linear B from Knossos (2000: 129), but McArthur thought this to be Siteia (1993: 147) which would seem more likely (see next chapter).
[76] Vasilakis, 2000: 128.
[77] Sp I: 112.
[78] *Ibid.*
[79] See Soles, 1992:160-176.
[80] Strabo, 10.4.14.
[81] Sp I: 114; Fisher & Garvey commented, 'Although you'd never guess from what remains today, ancient Milatos has a distinguished past' (2004: 170).
[82] *Ibid.*
[83] Cameron, 2003:230.
[84] Davaras, 1976:197.
[85] Nowicki, 2000: 170-1. 'The ancient city was probably on Kastello hill'

chapter, according to Cretan tradition, the Anatolian city of Miletos was founded by inhabitants of this Cretan Milatos, '… the Cretans, who founded, among other places, Miletus [in Anatolia], having taken Sarpedon from Cretan Miletus as founder'.[86]

Mirabello Gulf (Lasithi)

Spinalonga, on the inner west coast of the Mirabello gulf, is connected to the mainland by the isthmus of Porus. Within this isthmus is the ancient city of Olous, but it is submerged due to the rise in seawater over the centuries (see chapter 8). Under the water, but close to the shore, there is a small area of wall and some squared and shaped stones. Further out in slightly deeper water there are cracked flagstones and the remains of a pavement and more walls, possibly shipsheds.[87] Spanakis suggested that this submerged city was due to 'a local subsidence' and not, as Spratt thought, a general subsidence.[88] The modern town of Olous is Elounda and as far as its history is concerned several inscriptions have been discovered, the earliest dating back to the 4th century BC.[89] However, Olous does date back to the Early Minoan Bronze Age.[90]

Spratt considered this submerged site to be Olontion and not Olous. He had other ideas about the whereabouts of Olus/Olous, or Olerus.[91] He believed it to be about 12 km further south at a town his guide called Goolas, near Kritsa. He was basing his thought simply and very thinly on the name similarity: 'The name [Goolas] is so near to Olus that it cannot be doubted that these ruins are really those of that city – called also Olerus…'.[92] This is not a tenable conclusion and he was clearly wrong. Olous must be the same place as Olontion, people from Olous being Olontians and being an independent and autonomous city of ancient Crete it minted its own coins marked with the word ΟΛΟΝΤΙΩΝ.

On route to his Olous (Goolas) Spratt observed 'massive Cyclopean ruins on the hillside'[93] and at the site discovered ruins of terraces, '…upon every one of which were the ruins of habitations of the earliest and rudest Cyclopean style …'.[94] He added that 'no Roman or middle-age remains are to be seen, to break the harmony of this unique Cretan city of *heroic* times (added italics)'.[95] 'Heroic' implies the Homeric era. What he found could have been the ancient city of Lato which is very large in ruins as he described, although he went on to record that he had travelled half-an-

hour southeast to Kritsa.[96] Lato is about half-an-hour from Kritsa on a mule, but to the southwest, and it would be unlike Spratt to mistake such directions unless, which may be assumed, part of the 'road' headed in a southeasterly direction before turning east (the road today heads south before turning southwest).[97]

Lato has been described as being founded in the 7th century BC and flourished until Hellenistic times with hardly any evidence of Roman occupation.[98] Judging by the ruins there would appear to be a particular Mycenaean influence in architectural design. Spratt described some of the walls as Cyclopean (Figs. 9.8a and b), and the narrow and high entrances are reminiscent of the Late Mycenaean world (Figs. 9.9a and b), as are some of its house entrances. Picard simply referred to 'LM III traces'.[99] LM (Late Minoan) III is the Mycenaean period in Crete and this Mycenaean style architecture would seem more than just 'traces' of the era. There are Late Minoan finds from a cemetery at Kritsa in the museum at Aghios Nicholias, and so, with a Minoan cemetery so close to Lato, it is likely it has Minoan origins.

Both Federico Halbherr and Arthur Evans were convinced that the site was 'prehistory',[100] despite the later views that it was not.[101] Basing it on Spratt's record perhaps, Evans also referred to the site as Goulas (Goolas), 'with heaps of Cyclopean ruins', adding '… more than one building of the Sixth or Mycenaean City of Troy – the true Homeric Pergamos'.[102] As with any of these Archaic/Classical/Hellenistic sites, there is no reason to suppose that they were not once flourishing in the Bronze Age. Also, Lato is possibly *ra-to* in Linear B.[103]

On the coast to the northwest of Lato is Aghios Nicholias, or ancient Kamara, which Davaras referred to as of the Bronze Age.[104] Spratt found a few remains of Cyclopean walls, believing the site to have been the port of his Olus [Lato] and Kritsa.[105] It may have been the port for Kritsa and Lato (Spratt's 'Olus'), but Olus/Olontia was probably its own port. There is no reason not to believe that there were several ports around this coast and particularly within the protection of the gulfs. Such ports would not be the modern-day interpretation of large harbours but simply safe areas for beaching ships.

Further south Spratt came upon Istrona, or ancient Minoa,

(Vasilakis, 2000: 133).

[86] Strabo, 12.8.5. Although a Homeric character, in mythology Sarpendon was also the brother of Minos.

[87] Burch, 1989: 177.

[88] Spanakis, undated: 98 (referring to Sp II: 232).

[89] Vasilakis, 2000: 136; although Bickford-Smith suggested Olous to be 'full of ruins of great age … Most of the houses have massive walls …The spot seems to have been undisturbed for thousands of years …' (1898: 11).

[90] Stillwell, 1976: 646.

[91] Sp I: 122-3.

[92] Sp I: 134.

[93] Sp I: 131.

[94] Sp I: 132.

[95] Sp I: 133.

[96] Sp I: 137.

[97] Otherwise this would put his 'Olus' around Agios Ioannis and there is nothing evident there today.

[98] Cameron, 2003: 225-6.

[99] In Myers, Myers & Cadogan, 1992: 154.

[100] Brown, 1993: 51. Evans began excavations there before handing over to the French.

[101] Although Hutchinson said it 'certainly straddles the period from the Sub-Minoan to archaic Greek times, but the individual buildings are very hard to date.' (1968: 330).

[102] Evans, *The Times*, 29th August 1894.

[103] McArthur, 1993: 144.

[104] Davaras, 1976: 356/66, 357/116, 359/161.

[105] Sp I: 143 - there is nothing to see of these walls today and the town was urbanized in the late 19th century.

near Minoan Kato Khorio.[106] Although it is marked as an ancient site, there is nothing there of any consequence to be seen today. Strabo positioned it at the narrowest point of the island, '... the shores again converge to an isthmus narrower than the former [Gulf of Georgioupolis, just west of Rethymno], about sixty stadia [about 7miles/11 km] in width, which extends from Minoa, city of the Lyctians, to Hierapytna and the Libyan sea; the city is situated on the gulf [of Mirabello]'.[107] Spratt accounted for the lack of ruins by assuming they had submerged as Olus (his Olontion), but there is no evidence for this.

East coast
Peninsula of Sitia
From Minoa in the southern dip of the gulf of Mirabello Spratt travelled along the northern coast of the peninsular of Sitia, the territory of the Eteo-Cretans, the 'Cretans of the old stock' (see chapter 2), in search of Mount Dicte and the Dictaean Cave, the birthplace of Zeus. Strabo said of the site:

> Prasus [in Sitia] belonged to the Eteo-Cretans;
> and the temple of Dictaean Zeus was there;
> for Dicte is near it, not "close to the Idaean
> Mountain," as Aratus says, for Dicte is a
> thousand stadia distant from Ida ...[108]

Based on Strabo's distancing, Spratt considered that Mount Dicte was what is now the Ornon Mountain range in the middle of the Sitia peninsula and the temple of Dicte was at Kopra Kephalo (now Limnes).[109] However, the Idaean Mountain is in central Crete and 1000 stadia is about 160–180 km which would take it some 60 km into the sea. 100 stadia is about 16 km which would place it about 10 km southeast of the town of Sitia, whereas Spratt positioned it about 15 km southwest of Sitia on the northeastern part of the Ornon Mountain range. Again it depends upon Strabo's idea of the stadia compared with the modern-day view (or his source). He distanced Knossos to the northern sea at 25 stadia (approximately 4 km), Knossos to Gortyns at 200 stadia (approximately 30 km), Knossos to Lyttos at 120 stadia (approximately 20 km) and Gortyns to the Libyan Sea at 90 stadia (approximately 14 km),[110] all of which are about right. Perhaps he was just more accurate with shorter distances.

The 'Dictaean' Cave is above the Lasithi plain, south of Malia (55 km east of Mount Ida). The cave is a spectacular cavern on two levels and gained its prominence from the wealth of deposits suggesting it was a cult centre of the ancients from the Late Neolithic period or Early Minoan I, but more prominent from the Middle Minoan period.[111] It was excavated by Hadzidakis and Halbherr in the 1880s

and Evans visited it in 1894.[112] Dicte is *Di-ka-ta* in Linear B.[113] The arguments as to its exact position in Crete are somewhat immaterial considering Zeus was mythology and, as far as the 'Minoans' were concerned, possibly an unknown deity.[114]
Spratt then considered the issue of the Eteo-Cretans and referred to Strabo's findings. Strabo believed the Eteo-Cretans occupied the southern part of Crete and centred at Prasos.[115] This belief was based on Staphylus of Naucratis in Egypt (date unknown), but it is not known where his information came from.[116] This creates a problem as to the actual whereabouts of Prasos. Strabo initially said it bordered on Lebena, 70 stadia (approximately 11 km) from the sea, 180 stadia (approximately 28 km) from Gortyns.[117] Taking these approximate measurements, this would place it at Priansos (see below), not Prasos as Spratt observed,[118] and give Lebena a very large territory. It may well have been called Prasos when Strabo was there. But was this the Prasos of the Eteo-Cretans?

As previously mentioned (chapter 2), Homer said of the people of Crete: 'Language with language mix together. There are Achaians, there are great-hearted Eteokretans, there are Kydonians, and Dorians in three divisions, and noble Pelasgians...'[119] Strabo had obviously made a note of this passage, putting the Dorians towards the east and the Cydonians in the west and the Eteo-Cretans in the south.[120]

Based on Strabo's distancing of Dicte from Ida (above), Prasos (Praesus) would also be in the sea. But he then added that it was 'a hundred stadia [about 16 km] from Samonium ... situated between Samonium and the Cherronesus, sixty stadia above [from] the sea'.[121] This does not relate at all with the 'Prasos' that Strabo said was 180 stadia from Gortyns (above). So where was Samonium? Strabo referred to it as a sharp promontory sloping in the direction of Egypt and Rhodes[122] which would put it on the southeastern coast although there is no 'sharp promontory' on that coast and that would be about 15 stadia from today's Prasos. Spratt seemed to think Samonium was on the northeastern part of the island,[123] assuming Cape Sidaro (the 'sharp promontory'), although he added later that it may represent the entire eastern promontory.[124] Working on Strabo's Dicte being 100 stadia from Samonium and Prasos being 60 stadia from the sea between Samonium and the

[106]Myers, *et al.,* 1992: 286-9, for Minoan reference.
[107]Strabo, 10.4.3.
[108] Strabo, 10.4.12; see also 10.4.6 on Prasus belonging to the Eteo-Cretans.
[109] Sp I: 169; the Dicte Temple is not to be confused with the Dictynnaeon Temple in Cydonia, western Crete.
[110] Strabo, 10.4.7.
[111] Cameron, 2003: 240; Boardman, 1961.
[112] See Evans, 1921-35 (various references).
[113] McArthur, 1993: 130.
[114] He is mentioned in Mycenaean Linear B, but it is not known who or what the earlier Minoans worshipped, possibly the mother goddess. We only have Homer's 'word' that such a god 'existed' prior to the Classical period, and he was composing late in the 8th century BC, over 600 years after the Minoan palace period.
[115] Strabo, 10.4.6.
[116] Strabo, 10.4.6 and fn. 1.
[117] Strabo, 10.4.12.
[118] Sp I: 156.
[119] Homer's *Odyssey*, XIX: 175-177.
[120] Strabo, 10.4.6.
[121] Strabo, 10.4.12.
[122] Strabo, 10.4.3.
[123] Sp I: 166 and 201; as did Spanakis (undated: 173).
[124] Sp I: 191.

Chersonesus,[125] he concluded that Dicte was 40 stadia further from Samonium than Prasos was. This conclusion does not make any sense because Strabo did not actually say how far Prasos was from Samonium. Spratt assumed that Strabo was saying Prasos is 60 stadia from the sea at Samonium and actually said this later in his text.[126] On today's positioning Prasos is about 60 stadia from the sea at Sitia on the northern coast.

The present remains of Prasos are mainly post 12th century BC but there are some Late Minoan wall remnants still evident.[127] Spratt found ancient terraces that had supported buildings and scattered heaps of stones but nothing of the early building, concluding that it could only be identified as an ancient site due to it retaining a close proximity to its ancient name of 'Prasoos'.[128] As the city was built over three hills it is not clear which one Spratt was investigating. Obviously reliance upon 'modern' names, even in the 19th century, is a dangerous way of locating sites without archaeological evidence. Prasos was excavated by Bosanquet who began work in 1901.[129]

As mentioned above, to the east of Prasos is Kopra Kephalo/Kefali (Limnes) where Spratt was convinced that he encountered the ruins of the Temple of Dicte.[130] Today there are the remnants of a Mycenaean/Minoan (Late Minoan IIIA) settlement.

Spratt identified Sitia with ancient Etea but could find no indication of an ancient site at the Venetian city of Etea.[131] Although Sitia has now been urbanized, some Minoan material has been found around the modern town, but the remains of an ancient city of Sitia are possibly at Petras. Spratt 'found some detached remains of massive Cyclopean walls and terraces of a very early city of Crete … probably it was the capital of Eteo-Cretans under the name of Eteo or Etea …'.[132] It is not exactly clear what Spratt may have seen as the walls are not that 'massive', but Petras has proven to be a small Minoan 'palace' with its typical 'Central Court', storerooms and lower terraced town. During the 1950s a series of neopalatial (17th–15th century BC) finds were discovered following the opening up of a new road and it is believed that the site administered the entire Sitia basin.[133]

The British archaeologist Robert Carr Bosanquet came across Petras in 1901 but only briefly investigated it over two days as he decided it was of little interest.[134] After his visit he heard stories about two Moslems demolishing

ancient masonry in order to make cultivation terraces in the hillsides. He believed this story since he saw many 'roughly-dressed megalithic blocks of limestone and a certain amount of ashlar making it evident that there was extensive building here'.[135] This removal had happened 15 years before Bosanquet's visit, around 1886, which meant that the Cyclopean walls mentioned by Spratt may have already been demolished long before Bosanquet's arrival which may explain why he did not mention any in situ. Bosanquet then proceeded to excavate Palaikastro, presumably assuming there was nothing left to investigate at Petras, and so it was not only Spratt who visited the site and failed to realize its true value.

From Sitia Spratt went on to the far northeastern end of the island towards Cape Sidaro, and came across Eremopoli, or ancient Etera (now Itanos).[136] This is on the coast and was possibly a port. Vasilakis referred to it as 'prehellenic',[137] and Spratt reported that there were remains of Cyclopean walls on the southern bay and ascending into the hills and drew a map (Map 6).[138] It is certainly a protected bay and may well have been used as a safe haven for anchorage (or beaching) to protect against the northerly gales and for trade links within the Aegean with Anatolia and the Cycladic islands. Spratt found some inscriptions at the site, including a broken Graeco-Roman sepulchral slab, the letters of which are very unclear, and a rock inscription of a dolphin,[139] possibly of the 6th century BC.[140] Although these inscriptions are not Minoan, evidence of Spratt's 'Cyclopean walls' still remains (Fig. 9.10), and the ruins of an equally early town have been uncovered indicating a Bronze Age settlement, possibly u-ta-no in the Linear B tablets.[141]

Just south of Eremopoli is the Minoan site of Palaikastro.[142] Here Spratt first noticed remains of a period 'between the rude and early and middle age, being formed of square stones as in the better Greek period. The foundations of these walls …on the west side of a low, flat-topped hill …'[143] (Fig. 9.11). This 'dating' is very unclear, but 'better Greek period' may imply Classical. Then in the bay he found remains of what he believed to be 'one of Homer's hundred cities that composed the Cretan community under Minos ….'.[144] Spratt's very belief of a Homeric city implied that he considered the existence of an early civilization in Crete. As had Pashley, Spratt suggested that the site could have been 'Samoniun or Grammoniunm [Grammion]' but again based only on names as mentioned by ancient authors.[145] The site has been identified as Minoan and must have been used as a port even though so close to Itanos,

[125] This is not very helpful as [K]**Chersonesus is over 100 km from Samonium.**
[126] Sp I: 167.
[127] Spanakis, undated: 312, 313; see also Bosanquet, 1901; Whitely, 1992 &1998; Whitely et al., 1995.
[128] Sp I: 165.
[129] Bosanquet, 1901/02: 231-81; see also Nowicki, 2000: 59; and excavations continue today under Whitely and the British School at Athens.
[130] Sp I: 169.
[131] Sp I: 161.
[132] Sp I: 161-2; see Homer's reference to Eteocretans in chapter 2.
[133] Tsipopoulou, 2003 : 44-51
[134] Bosanquet, 1901/02: 282-5.

[135] Ibid.
[136] Although Spratt had some doubts as he thought it may have been Arinsoe (Sp I: 195), and he placed Itanos near Kato Zakros.
[137] Vasilakis, 2000: 106.
[138] Sp I: 194.
[139] Sp I: 197 (the dolphin now in the Fitzwilliam Museum, Cambridge.
[140] See Budde & Nicholls, 1964: 9-10.
[141] McArthur, 1993: 151; Davaras, 1976: 153; Cameron, 2003: 275.
[142] Davaras, 1976: 241.
[143] Sp I: 210.
[144] Ibid.
[145] Sp I: 211.

also a port, and both with suitable beaching terrain.[146]

What Spratt also saw were fragments of a tomb:
> I was shown some ancient tombs that had been
> dug out of the side of Palaio Kastron hill ... I
> saw the fragments of one that had recently been
> opened, which was formed of large and thick
> slabs of terra cotta, rudely ornamented; and
> some other fragments visible seem to indicate
> that, in this city, entire coffins or sarcophagi
> were formed of this material. A very curious
> terra-cotta figure was obtained from one by
> a lay priest on a neighbouring farm; it seems
> to be of Phoenician origin, and to indicate
> Phoenician settlement or a place of call in
> their trading-voyages between the eastern and
> western worlds.[147]

It has been observed that 'This was one of the first references to pre-Hellenic antiquities discovered in Crete.'[148] The 'high point' of the Phoenicians dated from around 1200 BC and so this may indicate a Bronze Age discovery by Spratt.

The main maritime site on this eastern coast would have been further south at the Minoan palace of Kato (lower) Zakros. Here Spratt found 'Cyclopean remains of a very ancient and very considerable city ... consisting entirely of Cyclopean walls and the foundations of rude and massively constructed buildings and terraces ...'.[149] He thought this to be Itanos because Ptolemy placed the site in the most eastern part of Crete.[150] However, he added, 'but the name of Zakro, which the place now bears, has evidently no connexion with the ancient city'.[151] There is some confusion here on Spratt's part as the site is a Minoan 'palace'. He must have simply been referring to Zakros as not being an ancient name. The site was first excavated in 1901 by David Hogarth on behalf of the British School at Athens[152] and then again in the 1960s by Platon.[153] The latter credited Spratt with identifying the valley of Kato Zakros as an archaeological site but added that it was Arthur Evans 'who obtained and made known the first archaeological information about it'.[154] We return again to the clarification of the meaning of 'archaeological information'. Spratt supplied 'archaeological information' by finding the site, although he may not have supplied 'archaeological detail'. As Spratt observed, it clearly was 'very ancient' and 'very considerable', and similar in style, although smaller, to the three other main Minoan palaces of Knossos, Malia and Phaistos. Its sheltered bay and

beach made it a prime candidate for the site of a port for the eastern coast.

Southern coast
Spratt reported that the route to Hierapetra (Ierapetra/ Gierapetra) by the southern coast road was long and tedious and had nothing to attract attention.[155] He was not far wrong, as even judging by today's discoveries very little has yet materialized on the Bronze Age archaeological front along this part of the coast. Spratt did refer to ancient ruins at Hierapetra and drew another map (see Map 7) including two theatres referred to as smaller and larger, both having been drawn by Belli (Figs. 9.12 and 13), and an amphitheatre.[156] Spratt did discover the ruins of these buildings but in nothing like the condition they were in when Belli was there in 1590 although the larger was more conspicuous than the smaller.[157]

Spratt did come across two sculptured sarcophagi at Hierapetra which were found in a tomb, and he reported, 'During some *excavations* by one Kluveraki ... between the theatre and the amphitheatre at the east end of the city, a sunken chamber was struck upon ... from 6 to 8 feet below the soil (added italics)'.[158] The sarcophagi in the chamber were not of the Bronze Age[159] (although they depicted Homeric heroes, Achilles and Hector), but the point is Spratt's references to excavations, and so the term, and method of discovery, was not unknown to him. Also, Spratt was of the opinion that the sarcophagi may originally have been from elsewhere on the island, as he said:
> Heroes and monarchs alone were worthy of
> such a tomb and monument, wherever it stood
> originally, whether Hierapetra or elsewhere.
> But Hierapetra was never a city of such
> celebrity as to possess either, so far as we know
> of Cretan history. To whom, of all Cretans, was
> such a monument so appropriate as to the hero
> king Idomeneus himself, one of the suitors of
> Helen, and companion of Achilles in the great
> war ...[160]

Idomeneus, King of Crete, was a Homeric character, and this comment of Spratt's suggests that he believed that Idomeneus did exist in 'Cretan history' and that would have been in the Bronze Age. Hierapetra is considered to have been inhabited in the Minoan period[161] and from its position it is difficult to believe that it was not used as a Minoan port. It is now urbanized and so further excavations are not currently possible. Other evidence of Hierapetra's connection with the Bronze Age era is 7km northwards at Episkopi where an impressive Late Minoan II larnax was found.[162]

[146] See Bosanquet 1901/02: 286-316; Dawkins, 1903-4: 192-231; Sackett *et al.*, 1965: 269-314; MacGillivray *et al.*, 1986: 135-54; Nowicki, 2000: 50-3.
[147] Sp I: 210.
[148] Farnoux, 1996: 26.
[149] Sp I: 234-5.
[150] As did Pashley.
[151] Sp I: 235; see also Spratt's report of 1860.
[152] Referred to by Cadogan, 2000: 24 (Report *BSA* 7, 1000-1).
[153] See Platon, 1971.
[154] 1971: 24.

[155] Sp I: 253.
[156] Sp I: 256.
[157] Sp I: 260-2.
[158] Sp I: 281-2.
[159] 2nd century AD (Robinson, 1969: 196-5, fn 18D; also Walker, 1984: 207). Both sarcophagi are in the British Museum.
[160] Sp I: 283-4.
[161] Davaras, 1976: 358-9/157; see also Papadakis, 1986.
[162] Now in the Hierapetra Museum (see Davaras, 1976: 177, fig. 105).

Lieutenant Mansell, Spratt's junior officer, ventured further west and inland to Anatolia hoping for vestiges of ancient ruins. Spratt recalled, 'he [Mansell] was not more fortunate than Mr. Pashley in the discovery of any ancient city of importance between Girapetra [Hierapetra] and Arvi'.[163] What both travellers were unaware of were the Minoan sites of Myrtos Pyrgos and Fournou Korifi[164] that lay beneath the earth. Further along the coast at Arvi Spratt merely made reference to Pashley's identification of the site as Greco-Roman with the temple of Jupiter Arbius and his removal of the impressive sarcophagus for the Fitzwilliam Museum in Cambridge.[165]

At Keraton Spratt found nothing to confirm his belief that it was an ancient, albeit the Hellenic, city of Ceraitae, as professed by Dr Cramer[166] and mentioned by the Greek historian Polybius (c.203–120 BC).[167] However, there was an extensive Minoan site situated there.[168] Turning inland, he headed towards Biennos determined to find the ancient city that Pashley was unable to. He discovered 'foundations of walls of an early date, between Cyclopean and Hellenic'.[169] This concept of dating would mean they were of the Archaic Age (750-480 BC), but although Spratt's dating references have to be treated with some caution, it is clear here that he is distinguishing the two styles, Cyclopean being earlier than Hellenic (Hellenic being Classical/Hellenistic). As seen in chapter 6, Biennos was a Minoan settlement.

Travelling westwards, through 'Roman' Ene (Spratt's Inatos), the search for ancient (Cretan) Arcadia was perplexing and Spratt did not concur with Pashley's conclusion that it was on the east side of the Lasithi Mountains adjacent to the Gulf of Mirabella. At one point he thought the site might have been at Agio Thomas, having seen Hellenic remains.[170] This was just south of Khani Kastelli. Arthur Evans found Minoan remains of a terrace wall at Agio Thomas.[171]

After some fruitless searching brought about by unreliable native (mis)information Spratt did receive some hopeful news of an old city on a 'mountain' above Melidokhori. On climbing the mountain with his guide he was delighted to find portions of an old Hellenic wall and a fountain described by Pliny:

Arcadia … being razed to the ground, the springs and water-courses, which before were

very numerous in that locality, all at once dried up; but that, six years after, when the city was rebuilt, the water again made its appearance, just as each spot was again brought into cultivation.[172]

This convinced Spratt he had found ancient Arcadia (nothing to do with the mythical Arcadia of ancient literature), particularly as he then found a massive 'Cyclopean' tower on the west side of the crag.[173] Spratt's evidence of this being ancient Arcadia is very flimsy and mere supposition on his part. Today ancient Arcadia is mapped just north of Biennos rather than to its west, as Spratt presumed, and typical Minoan houses and tombs were excavated between 1924 and 1931 by Professor Vincenzo La Rosa.[174] Spratt's 'Arcadia' is Oxi Kefali (Axee Kefala[175]).

Spratt then turned south back towards the coast to seek out what he referred to as the Homeric cities of Rhyton, Stelae and Priansos. The reason for his 'Homeric' reference to the latter two is unclear as Homer only referred to Rhytion in his catalogue of ships.[176] Unlike Pashley, Spratt came across remains 'of the earliest time' at Rhytion (now Rotassi)[177] and some Minoan relics have since been found.[178] Of Stelae, Spratt appeared again to be speculating as to its whereabouts having no real evidence himself. His speculations also applied to Priansos which he placed on the coast by the gulf of Tsoutsouros (Sudsuro Bay). It has since been suggested that it may be 6 km further north, near Kasteliana[179] which may be Spratt's Stelae. Spratt did find ruins in the 'bold crags and hills'[180] that rise from Sudsuro Bay, possibly its harbour, but there is no evidence of anything ancient thereabouts today.

Spratt moved on twenty miles westwards to the coastal town of Lebena (Lenda, Leda) which, he commented, was celebrated for its 'salubrity' and a natural place 'that the inhabitants should raise there a temple to the god of health [Aesculapius], for it was the Brighton of the central part of Crete; and finally became the emporium of Gortyna'.[181] He came across relics of a possible temple of Aesculapius and in his handwritten Description of Crete, he reported:

… the ancients no doubt hauled their vessels ashore under the town – it was also celebrated for its temple of Aesculapius – the citizens of Gortyna no doubt found relief there from inhaling the pure sea air and hence the temple.[182]

[163] Sp I: 293. Spratt also commented that he was now treading upon Pashley's ground (Sp I: 291), meaning reported ground as Pashley had travelled to the eastern part of the island but did not report his findings (see chapter 6).
[164] Hood, et al., 1964: 94; Whitelaw et al., 1997: 265-74; Warren, 1972b.
[165] Sp I: 294.
[166] Cramer, 1828: 391 (based on what he had read in Polybius' Histories - see fn 167 below).
[167] Referred to as Cere, Polybius' Histories, 4.53.5.
[168] Evans, 1896b: 465; see also Hood, et al., 1964: 82-5.
[169] Sp I: 302.
[170] Sp I: 313; although he was unable to come to any conclusion on the identification of this site leaving it to 'the future traveller or antiquary' (Sp II: 63), in this case, Arthur Evans.
[171] Evans, 1928: 77.
[172] Pliny, 31.30.
[173] Sp I: 322.
[174] See Pendlebury, et al, 1932/33: 84.
[175] Spratt did use this name on his plan of the site (Sp I: 325).
[176] Homer's Iliad, 2.648.
[177] Sp I: 334.
[178] Vasilakis, 2000: 152; Davaras, 1976: 358-9/156.
[179] Spanakis, undated: 316.
[180] Sp I: 339.
[181] Sp I: 349, as Brighton was perhaps the 'emporium' (seaside resort?) of London in the Victorian era
[182] Spratt, 1860.

Spratt briefly mentioned Belli identifying Lebena as having 'some remains',[183] but he made no reference of Belli's drawing of what appears to be the Temple of Aesculapis (Fig. 9.14a).[184] This may be the temple which Spratt saw and is still partly visible today (Fig. 9.14b). Spratt found nothing of 'early' interest at Lebena but he was convinced that the early Greeks would have chosen this area for an upper city or fortress.[185] A Minoan site did exist in the Early Bronze Age (2500-1900 BC) as Early Minoan tombs were discovered by Alexiou in 1958-60.[186] Minoan tholos tombs can be seen today at nearby Yeragambos. This was another town that was believed to have been no earlier than the Hellenistic period until further excavations had taken place.

---

[183] Sp I: 353.
[184] Although Falkener thought it resembled a bath rather than a temple (1854: 19).

[185] Sp I: 350.
[186] See Alexiou & Warren, 2004.

10. Thomas Spratt
Travels and Researches in Crete Vol. II

Southern Crete (see Map 5)

Before heading inland Spratt called in on Kaloi Limenes/ Limionas (ancient Lasea) and compared it with Homer's Lisse Petra and quoted the *Odyssey*, 'xvii. 293',[1] but no such reference appears to exist in the Homeric text relating to this city. Evans considered it 'impossible not to believe that this harbour was not made use of in the great days of the Minoan sea dominion'.[2] Minoan chamber tombs have been found in the vicinity of Lasea.[3] Spratt then located the cove and sandy beach of Metallum (Matala), possibly the port to ancient Gortyns. Here he found the cove 'studded with ancient tombs, excavated in the rocks and cliffs'.[4] He identified a small fortress and other foundations as Roman which is not surprisinging as Gortyns was the Roman capital of Crete. Evans believed Metallum to have been a Minoan town.[5]

Moving inland and northwards Spratt came across Phaistos, 'a town of considerable antiquity and importance, and founded by Minos'.[6] He believed it to be ancient because of its coins but he was unable to find its actual location. It was more ancient than its coins, of course (see previous chapter regarding reference to coins), and Spratt must have considered this if he believed it had been 'founded by Minos'. Of the coins, Spratt accepted that none had been struck prior to Knossos losing its status as capital of Crete to Gortyns, and that, he said, had been 'after the Trojan War'.[7] This is further indication of a belief in its existence as a civilization in a bygone time of the Bronze Age. Long before Gortyns became the capital of Crete in the Roman period (see below), Phaistos was a thriving Minoan city and probably *Pa-i-to* in Linear B.[8] Spratt further observed, '… but its vestiges show even now that it was once a well-built and very extensive city, and it must have been for some time the chief republic city of this part of Crete'.[9] But he did not identify these 'vestiges' other than by reference to coins. Strabo said it no longer existed in his day but was 60 stadia from Gortyns.[10] That is about 10 km, whereas the actual distance is about 14 km.[11] What was beneath the

ground Spratt was deliberating upon was a sizeable palace second only to Knossos.

Gortyns (Gortyna/Gortys) in the Messara valley was taken over by the Romans as the island's capital and it was clearly an impressive city during the Roman rule. Spratt's plan of Gortyns (Fig. 10.1), which can be compared favourably with today's plan,[12] shows the large 2nd century BC Roman theatre, remains of which were seen and drawn by Spratt (Fig. 10.2). It was drawn in detail by Onorio Belli in the 16th century (Fig. 10.3). Spratt had missed Belli's drawing of the smaller theatre (Fig. 10.4) which was not visible to him at that time but is now under excavation (Fig. 10.5).

Although these are not Bronze Age remains, it is still of interest to note how the site has knowingly changed over seven centuries, as this gives an indication of the difficulties of finding three thousand year old sites that had not been recorded. Although Gortyns was originally a Minoan town (see chapter 4), evidence of its early civilization had been built over by the Romans. Even so, Spratt had a belief in the existence of the labyrinth of Minos. He tried to rationalize the maze of passages cut into the hill just outside Gortyns but came to no clear conclusions (see chapter 11 for Spratt's observations on the 'labyrinth' at Gortyns).

On leaving Gortyns, Spratt headed back to Herakleion to turn his attention to the western side of the island that Pashley had also visited and referred to in his book. In doing so Spratt commented, '… for his [Pashley's] volumes more particularly refer to the western half of the island; and yet he has left much interesting matter undiscovered or undescribed'.[13]

North central and western coastal area

Whilst anchored in the harbour at Herakleion, Spratt went in search of Tylissos where he was shown some ancient tombs and some ruins of large blocks close to the village of Upper Dylisso/Tylissos. He was also shown additional ruins at Lower Dylissos, thus indicating the extent of the 'old city', and he supported Pashley's view of feeling at upper Dylisso that he was at the ancient site of Tylissos even though no antiquities were evident. However, he was somewhat surprised that Pashley was not shown the ruins of the lower town.[14] As seen in chapter 6, Tylissos was Minoan.

---

[1] Sp II: 9, but again relying on name similarities.
[2] Evans, 1928: 85.
[3] Blackman & Branigan, 1975: 22-23.
[4] Sp II: 21.
[5] Evans, 1928: 87.
[6] Sp II: 23.
[7] Sp II: 44.
[8] McArthur, 1993: 153.
[9] Sp II: 25.
[10] Strabo, 10.4.14.
[11] The unreliability of Strabo's distances was commented on in chapter 4.

[12] See Cameron, 2003: 169.
[13] Sp II: 63.
[14] Sp II: 65-6.

At Anoya, Spratt was disappointed not to find any signs of an ancient city. Although just over 3 km from Anoya is Axos where he found some 'Cyclopean' walls of the acropolis of ancient Axos. Again he referred to coins of the 2nd -1st century BC[15] which obviously established the town as ancient but does not rule out Bronze Age origins. As previously mentioned (chapter 6), the ruins are most likely of the 4th century BC but Spratt's reference to the Cyclopean relics and 'Those massive piles of unwrought blocks, denoting a rude and early age … they speak of a greater force of the necessities of those early times'[16] again indicates his curiosity in an earlier civilization. His sketch of ancient Axos shows terracing which 'is an art that goes back to Minoan times'.[17]

Of Eleutherna (Eleftherna), Spratt considered it an important city at one time, although he was not particularly informative with regard to his thoughts on dating. It appeared from his comments that this may have been the fortress taken by the Roman conqueror of Crete, Metellus, as he referred to his strategy in taking possession of Eleutherna.[18] He also remarked that there had been 'no previous identification (or at least description) of this interesting city by anyone, as Pashley passed it by, merely remarking [on it] in a foot-note …'.[19] This was not entirely correct as Pashley observed ancient ruins near 'the metokhi Elevtherna' and thereafter linked it with ancient Sybrita (see chapter 6). Spratt drew a plan of the site (Fig. 10.6) which incorporates the ancient acropolis (Fig. 10.7), the large tower of early medieval origin (Fig. 10.8) and the large proto-Archaic cisterns below the acropolis (Figs. 10.9a and b), but nothing of Bronze Age interest.

However, in 1964, archaeologists Sinclair Hood, Peter Warren and Gerald Cadagon commented that there was reason to suppose that Eleutherna may have been occupied in the Bronze Age.[20] Then in 1984 the University of Crete began major excavations at the site and discovered its origins in the Early Minoan period on both the acropolis and around the Iron Age cemetery site of Orthi Petra,[21] the latter being below the acropolis, down the western terraces ('Anakourtho' on Spratt's plan – Fig. 10.6). Over the other side of the acropolis (the east), on the lower slope, Spratt observed a broken Parian marble statute and an 'Hellenic' platform on which, he thought, a temple may have stood[22] (the statue is marked on his plan, Fig. 10.6, just north-east of the acropolis).

Spratt also came across two Hellenic (Hellenistic) bridges at Eleutherna one of which he sketched (Fig. 10.10a) and which remains intact today (Figs. 10.10b and c). The bridges can be seen on Spratt's plan (Fig. 10.6 – Anct

Bridge), but only a few stones remain of the eastern bridge. The rock tombs on Spratt's sketch (Fig. 10.6) are still visible above the north side of the existing bridge (Fig. 10.11).

Spratt was keen to observe the bridges and described the one he sketched in some detail. He said it was 'very early-constructed' and referred to its 'excavated [circular] arched way over a footpath by the side of the pier of the horizontal one', adding:

> The existence of two such well-built bridges here clearly shows this city to have been both wealthy and populous in early times, although at present the site itself contains so little other evidence of the fact, except its rock tombs.[23]

His reference to 'early times' is to the Hellenistic period rather than the 'very early' Bronze Age, although (as seen above) the area was inhabited by the Minoans. The circular arch he referred to (and sketched) is no longer in existence having been filled in (Fig. 10.10b again). But he was quite correct in his observation about the bridge(s) clearly showing that they belonged to a larger site, as today they are positioned in the 'middle of nowhere' in relatively dense woodland leading nowhere. This means they must have been part of an enlarged complex in the Hellenistic period and possibly earlier.

The search for Sybrita (Syvritos) was Spratt's next task and he believed this to be Veni. On visiting Veni he was disappointed only to find the remains of a Franko fortress. He was directed to the ruins of Thronos at the base of Mount Ida on the Kephala hill. Here he encountered some massive Cyclopean remains and 'a finer site for a city I have not yet seen in Crete …'.[24] Although the site was originally thought to be Hellenistic, more recent excavations have shown that it originated in the Bronze Age.[25] This is another classic example of later excavations dispelling such earlier beliefs and the site may be that referred to as su-ki-ri-ta in Linear B.[26] The remains of a Minoan settlement are visible today but there is little evidence of 'Cyclopean' structures other than the occasional boulder. Spratt observed that Pashley missed Sybrita probably due to his guide's wish to avoid Thronos as the town was made up of a Mahommedan community.[27] In fact Pashley did make reference to finding ruins at Sybritia (see chapter 6) but he may have been looking just to the west of the actual site.

Rethymnon (Rhithymna/Retimo) is the approximate halfway point between the two large towns of Herakleion and Khania. It was probably the ancient port of Eleutherna and Lappa (or Lampe) just south of Rhethymnon, but Spratt did not consider it of any great importance or size. Its Minoan remains are most likely beneath the present town and LM III chamber tombs have been found in the

[15] Sp II: 79.
[16] Sp II: 80, and, as seen in chapter 4, Axos was of the Bronze Age.
[17] Somerville, 2007: 65. The terracing is still there but no longer the Cyclopean walls or 'massive piles of unwrought blocks'.
[18] Sp II: 91-2.
[19] Sp II: 93.
[20] Hood, Warren & Cadogan, 1964: 69.
[21] Stampolidis, 2004.
[22] Sp II: 94.
[23] Sp II: 95-6.
[24] Sp II: 104.
[25] Hood et al., 1964: 71.
[26] McArthur, 1993: 147; see also Davaras, 1976: 311.
[27] Sp II: 109.

suburb of Mastaba just to the southeast.[28] Spratt accepted that Lappa was nothing other than Roman, concurring with Pashley, but did admit some fragments found in the village may have been earlier, although not 'tens of centuries'.[29]

Spratt was not entirely clear of the whereabouts of some of the ancient sites in the Apokorona district between Rethymnon and Cape Drepano (to the west) from the information given by the ancient geographers. However, upon discovering the geological movements of the island, which included this part of the coast (see chapter 8), he realized that this could give misleading information in respect of locations of such sites and made an interesting, if rather verbose, comment about his fellow travellers and the way in which care should be taken in criticism. The gist of it suggested that travellers should be careful in criticising errors of scholars in describing ancient lands based on confusing ancient texts, particularly when such travellers are able to rectify any such errors with their own visits. In this light he was critical of Pashley, who was none to complimentary about the writings of the historian Dr Cramer (Spratt appeared very keen on Cramer's work). In any event, Spratt was identifying some of the difficulties surrounding accurate identification of ancient sites without full knowledge and the efforts made by some with limited information and resources.

Spratt was quite confident of the position of Aptera. Certainly the remains of Aptera on the southern coast of Suda Bay were nothing new and Spratt commented that they had been fully described by Pashley and that Pococke had mistaken them for Minoa. Spratt identified the city walls as 'both Cyclopean and Hellenic',[30] again confirming that he was treating these two descriptions as different. As far as Minoa was concerned, he considered this to be opposite to Aptera on the shores of the Akrotiri[31] as it is today. Strabo put Aptera about 80 stadia (around 13 km) from Cydonia[32] which is further than it is considered to be today (about 10 km).

In the vicinity of Khania (Canea) Spratt located what he thought was the ancient harbour of Cydonia, confirming Pashley's view but not Pococke's. Unfortunately most of medieval and modern Khania has covered up any remaining evidence of an ancient city.[33] Even so it is likely that a Bronze Age city once flourished there.[34] Homer did refer to Cydonia and was of the view that 'the Kydonians lived around the stream of Iardanos'.[35] Spratt speculated that 'this must be modern Platanos'.[36]

Spratt then turned southwards again through the White Mountains and plain of Omalo, emphasizing that his route was different from Pashley's and that Pashley did not visit Omalo.[37] However, Spratt came across sites that had been visited by Pashley through a highway supported by 'vestiges of Cyclopean terraces'.[38] These were Hyrtakina and Elyros, 'These two cities, although very near to each other, were evidently somewhat flourishing in the early period of Cretan history, both having struck coins.'[39] He is not explicit about what he meant by early, but with the reference to the striking of coins it must be post-500 BC.[40] As Pashley had been here before him, Spratt chose not to dwell in this area.

Returning northwards to the coast to the river Platanos, Spratt was to cover more of Pashley's trail. He recalled that Pashley had been unable to discover any ancient remains at Gerani, near Platanos (Platanias). He hoped for a better result, assuming that the ancient city was Pergamus, at the root of the Dictynnaeon promontory. This was a city which had been 'founded by Aeneas and the Trojans, or by Agamemnon ... having been a place of importance in the early history of Crete ...'.[41] This is another example of Spratt referring to the earlier age of the Trojan War. He was unsure of the exact position of Pergamus but rejected Pococke's belief that it was at Cydonia, adding, 'I leave the point open still to the consideration of the archaeologist and traveller ...'.[42] His reference to 'archaeologist and traveller' is interesting here. The implication is that he did not consider himself either. He was not an archaeologist by profession, bearing in mind that archaeology as a profession had not yet really been established at that time, but he was doing archaeological work, albeit just 'field surveying' (as we know it today). A traveller he certainly was, but limited to Crete, as was Pashley, unlike some of their contemporaries who travelled afar.

The Dictynnian promontory of Cape Spada, although fairly mountainous, did reveal ancient Dictynna (visited by Pococke) but Spratt found nothing other than of Roman interest. He moved onto ancient Rhokka (noticed by Pococke but not Pashley) and found a few remains of the city's Hellenic walls and some scattered marble blocks,[43] but nothing that may have indicated any earlier settlement.

At ancient Polyrrhenia (Palaiokastron), towards the far western coast of Crete, Spratt was more hopeful and referred again to the two different types (eras?) of architecture, 'fine specimens of both the Cyclopean and Hellenic styles occur on the west side of the acropolis ...'.[44] He referred to

[28] Hood *et al.*, 1964: 60.
[29] SP II: 117-18.
[30] Sp II: 129-30.
[31] Sp II: 130-1.
[32] Strabo, 10.4.13.
[33] 'Cydonia was the third larger [*sic*] city of Crete that was located where the city of Chania is now built ...The ruins that have been unearthed testify the existence of a great palatial centre.' (Vasilakis, 2000: 79).
[34] Davaras: 1976: 358-9/59.
[35] Homer's *Odyssey*, III.292.
[36] Sp II: 141.

[37] Sp II: 164.
[38] Sp II: 181.
[39] Sp II: 182.
[40] Although, see again reference to gold 'coins' of Bronze Age Mycenae in chapter 9, fn. 28.
[41] Sp II: 190, although he was quoting Cramer (1828, vol iii: 382).
[42] Sp II: 205-6. Gonia is on the Southeast coast of the Dictynnaeon promontory.
[43] Sp II: 210.
[44] Sp II: 212.

Polyrrehenia as 'only a small city in the *very early* Cretan times, Cydonia being the capital of the western part in the time of Minos... (added italics)'.[45] His reference to 'very early Cretan times' perhaps distinguishes it from just 'early' times to which he had referred to Hyrtakina and Elyros (above). Also, again his reference to Minos is indicative of a belief in a very early civilization, almost certainly pre-Hellenic. Pococke confused Polyrrhenia with Aptera but Pashley corrected this mistake. Even so, as mentioned in chapter 7, these sites are predominantly Hellenistic but may be Minoan in origin.

In his handwritten report *Description of Crete*, Spratt commented of Kisamos, 'This part of Crete was from very early times in trading connexion or alliance with the proximate part of the Peloponnesus ...'[46] Perhaps the Mycenaeans from the mainland Peloponnese?

Spratt's Kutri at Phalasarna (ancient Korykos) on the far western coast, already identified as Minoan in chapter 7, was 'dated' by Spratt as Hellenic in style, described as well preserved and identified as the artificial port of Polyrrhenia.[47] In chapter 8 mention was made of Spratt's discoveries at Phalasarna regarding the elevation of the island at this point. Despite his efforts, Spratt was unable to reconcile himself with Pashley's theory that the port was the mere indentation of the rocky coastline under the walls of the city. Spratt could find no beach where a ship could be landed safely:

> Consequently, as the indentation was open and exposed to all south-easterly breezes, and the whole western swell for a distance of 500 miles or more, and the low outlying islet of Petaledes off it affords but little shelter to the bay, I could nowhere recognize the trading-port, and left the place with its phenomena greatly puzzling me.[48]

Spratt then recalled a visit to the island of Cerigotto (Antikythera–northwest of Crete) where he had noticed an elevation of coastland, and it occurred to him that the same may have taken place on Crete. He then measured the sea-marks at Phalasarna which convinced him that it had elevated as the new sea marks were three feet below the old marks. This justified his theory that the inland 'quadrangular space enclosed by the unusually massive Hellenic walls upon the plain in front of the chapel of Aghios Giorgis'[49] was the port. Recent excavations have revealed Hellenistic walls around the 'lagoon' (Fig. 12). Spratt added that the principal remains at Phalasarna are 'chiefly of the Cyclopean and Hellenic terraces ... all of which were built of squared unhewn blocks, and without mortar'[50] which is more consistent with the Minoan period

of which evidence has been found nearby (see chapter 7). His plan of the site was very accurate (Fig. 10.13).[51]

Spratt saw the 'chair' or 'throne' Pashley observed, but thought it a 'bema' from which to address the Phalasarnians, not a chair or a throne.[52] Spratt drew his own picture of it (Fig. 10.14) and commented that Pashley's drawing was not a true representation of what it was like.[53] In truth, Pashley's sketch is rather good and more accurate than Spratt's (see Pashley: Figs. 7.1a and b).

Spratt referred briefly to the ancient sites of Kalamydes, Kantanos, Hyrtakina (as previously mentioned), Lissos, Elyros and Suia (the port of Elyros as referred to in the 'Stadiasmus'), but added very little to what Pashley had already described other than that they all had Cyclopean and Hellenic remains, assumingly the same ones as seen and drawn by Pashley. He was convinced that Tripiti was mentioned by both Ptolemy and the 'Stadiasmus' as the port of Poecilassu.[54] Tripiti was a Bronze Age Minoan site.[55]

At Tarrha, Spratt found the basement of an Hellenic building, possibly the Temple of Apollo, but missed by Pashley. Further along the coast at Lutro, Spratt visited the ancient port of Phoenice (Phoenix), just west of Lutro, being the only port on the south coast of Crete in which a ship could find security for the whole season.[56] If this was the case, then, although Spratt reported that the ruins of Phoenice were chiefly Roman, it was most probably a port during the Minoan period for contact with Egypt.

It was at this point, in the summer of 1853, that Spratt was called from Crete prior to the outbreak of the Crimea War. He returned again to Lutro in July 1859 on HMS *Medina* to continue his investigations.[57]

Just east of Phoenice, at Safkia, Spratt found no ruins but considered that it was the only town, besides Ierapera, situated upon the south coast of Crete.[58] This is distinguishing towns from villages but it is interesting to note that very few Minoan cities have yet been found on the south coast as opposed to the north and eastern regions. This may have something to do with the fact that the Minoan 'thassalocracy' (naval power) was concentrated within the Aegean around the mainland of Greece, the Cycladic islands and the mainland of Anatolia: to the northwest, north and northeast respectively. But it may also have something to do with the fact that they are yet to be discovered.

Spratt ended his journey around the island at Franko Kastelli,

---

[45] Sp II: 213.

[46] Sp II: 219.

[47] Sp II: 227-8. Hadjidaki traced Spratt's port (emphasizing the difficulties of finding these sites 'today') and excavated the southwest tower and dated the latter to the Hellenistic period (1988: 472 and 474).

[48] Sp II: 231.

[49] Sp II: 231-2.

[50] Sp II: 233. The reference to 'Cyclopean' may have been referring to the town (no longer visible) rather than the Hellenistic harbour which would

have been the Hellenic reference.

[51] Compare it with Cameron's plan, 2003: 431.

[52] Sp II: 234-5.

[53] Sp II: 236.

[54] Sp II: 245.

[55] Davaras, 1976: 358-9/85.

[56] Sp II: 249.

[57] Sp II: 251.

[58] Sp II: 255.

east of Sfakia, and again reported no ruins of ancient interest. He concluded his ancient historical quest with:

> ... and so I leave the reader ... to awaken in his mind scholastic reminiscences connected with one of the most classic and most important islands in the East, and with its inhabitants in the archaic times, from their having been the stage in progress of civilization and art between the schools of Egypt and those of enlightened Greece ... and in regard to social liberty and civilization, a progress from Pharaonic slavery and degradation of Egypt and the East, through an improved condition under the wise legislation of Minos, to the liberal laws and philosophy finally developed by Solon and Socrates.[59]

In effect this acknowledged the existence of a civilization in Crete in between the Egyptian 'Pharaonic slavery' of the 3rd millennium BC and the Classical ('enlightened') period of Socrates of the 5th century BC. This 'in between' period was the Bronze Age of the 2nd millennium BC, part of which included the Minoan civilization.

Spratt discussed the possibly 'great catastrophes' of ancient tradition and referred to:

> ... the great Deucalionic deluge, fixed about 1500 B.C., as also the subsidence of a great land tract called Atlantis ... were so strong that the remembrance of them, vividly retained amongst the thinly scattered and rude cave-inhabiting people who proceeded the Greeks, induced both the early and the later historians of the latter to record them ... there is undoubtedly, to my mind, evidence of great catastrophes having occurred within a few thousand years prior to history, that must have swept away some of the settlements of those early men ...[60]

His Bronze Age 1500 BC dating reference is interesting here, as is his belief in the 'settlements of those early men' of obviously an earlier civilization, albeit 'cave-inhabiting'. He was not in a 'scientific' position at that time to speculate with any accuracy on dating and so such reference can be taken with all but casual reliance. But he was correct about the effect of the 'great catastrophes' and as far as Crete is concerned the volcanic eruption causing the destruction of the island of Thera (c.1550 BC or 1627-1600 BC[61]) comes to mind. Although it is disputed that this eruption was the cause of the destruction of Crete due to dating inconsistencies, it is possible the resulting Tsunami may have weakened the island's defences perhaps by destroying its fleet, leading, in later years, to its submission to the Mycenaeans.[62]

Spratt's work as a surveyor proved of immense value, not just in Crete, but throughout the Mediterranean. However, unlike some of his more flamboyant contemporaries of the 19th century, he was reserved in his nature and did not receive the full recognition he deserved. In 1885, Dawson wrote of him:

> Season succeeded season, of excellent surveying work, during which, the classical and geological history of the various ports and islands of the Grecian Archipelago and coasts of Asia Minor received able treatment at his hands. Without any particular interest to push him he reached the highest position of the Mediterranean; and the surveying officers of those days required something more than a knowledge of the sextant and the measuring chain. Spratt had been well educated as a lad, and never failed to turn his early training to account. Had he been less confident of his own powers, less zealous in the use of those powers, more mediocre as a man, he might have proved even more successful; but he could ever stoop to obtain the more marketable description of scientific fame.[63]

In chapter 3 mention was made of an article written in *Lippincott's Magazine* in 1878 by E.S., an otherwise unnamed English naval officer, regarding his journey from Crete to Smyrna and Ephesus. It is not known whether Spratt had read this, but he was certainly alive when it was written, so it is possible. If he had, it would have been interesting to have witnessed his reaction to the officer's comment about Ephesus, 'I do not propose to inflict upon the reader a list of the ruins we saw, some well authenticated, some not. It is not every mind, however well regulated, that will bear the personal inspection of ruins, much less a catalogue of them.'[64] He added a little later in the text:

> It is rather a difficult thing to acknowledge, in face of the great ruins then about us, with all their associations, that the thought of our dinner was by this time uppermost in the minds of nearly all our company. I have generally found, however, in much journeying about this wicked world, the condescension and interest with which one looks upon ancient remains depends very much upon the company in which one finds one's self, the state of the weather and the state of one's stomach.[65]

This relates to the motive behind the travel discussed in chapter 3, but it is highly possible that Spratt may have disagreed with this officer's view.

It must also be remembered that Spratt was writing more or less at the time of the publication of Charles Darwin's

---

[59] Sp II: 273.
[60] Sp II: 305-6.
[61] Still some dispute about this. The 1550 date is based on conventional Egyptian chronology; the 1600 date is based on radiocarbon dating (see Manning *et al.*, 2006: 565-9).
[62] A much debated subject and not a part of this work.
[63] Dawson, 1885: 42.
[64] E.S., 1878: 78.
[65] *Ibid*, 79.

Origin of Species,[66] which opened up the prospect of a lot more time regarding the beginning of man than most people had bargained for until then. Spratt wrote to Darwin (see Appendix E), as the latter had shown an interest in Spratt's illustrations, and in the same letter Spratt suggested to Darwin that his researches in Crete may prove of interest in respect of the 'Eastern Question' and presumably this 'Question' had a bearing on new dating:

> Dear Mr Darwin,
> I shall be very pleased if you find anything in my researches in Crete that will prove of interest to you. I thought they might at this moment, as Crete is in some degree linked with the Eastern Question … I think we have once if not twice met in days past – in the days of poor Edward Forbes - that, and more especially your connection - distinguished connection with the old surveying Branch of the Service, as it was under Beaufort! induced me to desire to offer you a set [of his books] – as you troubled yourself to write, and already shewn that the illustrations have attracted your attention, it has pleased and gratified.
> Yours faithfully,
> T Spratt[67]

This letter gives an indication of a possible belief by Spratt in a new idea of early dating following Darwin's theories, although Spratt made no such direct suggestion himself in his letter to Darwin.

Clearly Spratt carried out some ground breaking work in Crete but received little recognition of it in return. Three and a half years after his letter to Roderick Murchison, the President of the RGS (see chapter 8), regarding Spratt, William Leake wrote again to Murchison:

> Capt Spratt has for a long time been employed under the orders of Sir Francis Beaufort in surveying the coast of Greece and has first completed those in Crete; and I feel persuaded that you will agree with me in thinking that no person living has contributed in a more important degree to the great objects of our Society than Captain Spratt.[68]

In an earlier letter to the RGS, Leake emphasized the importance of Spratt's work 'to ancient literature on Crete …'.[69] This is rightly so and also applies to ancient history in the form of archaeological investigation and is not just limited to the Classical and Hellenistic eras but extends to the Bronze Age and must not be underestimated.

---

[66] Darwin, 1859.
[67] Spratt to Darwin, letter, 2nd January 1877, Darwin Correspondence Project, University of Cambridge, (calendar no 10767) MS DAR.177: 240.

[68] Leake to Murchison, letter, 10th October 1857, RGS, CB 1851-60 although Leake did ask for this note to be withdrawn as being unjust on Graves, Copeland and Admirals Beaufort and Smyth, who had all contributed to the work (Leake to Murchinson, letter, 19th October 1857, RGS, CBS 1851-60), but it shows Leake's high esteem for Spratt..
[69] Leake to Murchison, letter, 19th October 1853, RGS, CB 1851-60.

11. The Labyrinth

Since the demise of the Minoan civilization in the 15th century BC, interest in Crete has evolved around the classical tale of Theseus, the Minotaur and the Labyrinth. It was a myth that has been passed down through time (see chapter 2) but could it bear some relation to the truth? Mention has already been made of Pococke's, Pashley's and Spratt's references to the 'mythical' labyrinth and its possible whereabouts. Spratt in particular appeared to accept that there existed a labyrinth which had been built by the legendary architect Daidalos (Daedalus) on the order of King Minos.[1] Spratt was perhaps inferring that only the likes of Daidalos would have the ingenuity to construct such a complex structure. Based on Spratt's belief, it is worth looking at what is known about a possible labyrinth and whether or not it could be linked with the Bronze Age, or at least an earlier civilization than the Classical period. It is also of interest to look at other early travellers' views on the possible labyrinth.

Whereabouts

If there was such a labyrinth, where could it have been? The mythical position of the labyrinth was Knossos although there is a collection of 'underground' passages similar to a labyrinth actually cut into a hill at Gortyns in the Messara, south of Mount Ida. This latter site has been a 'tourist spot' for several centuries. The labyrinth and its association with a maze held fast during the ancient Greek world and the earliest pictorial example of a maze appears on the reverse of a Linear B tablet from 15th century BC Pylos, 'presumably a doodle by an idle scribe since the drawing has nothing to do with the list'.[2]

Linear B does makes reference to a labyrinth (*da-pu2-ri-to*[3]) by way of a tribute of 'One jar of honey to the Mistress of the ?*Labyrinth*' from the Knossos Gg series of record, Gg 702: *da-pu2 ?-ri-to-jo/ po-ti-ni-ja 'me-ri'* AMPHORA I.[4] This may imply that a labyrinth of some description may have existed at Knossos at the time of the Bronze Age tablets and was important enough to have a female divinity named after it. It may just be that Knossos itself was known as a labyrinth due to its many passages.[5] There

is the labyrinth fresco found by Evans at Knossos,[6] but it resembles more of a pattern (meander) rather than an actual representation of the maze. Pashley found several coins of the 3rd and 4th centuries BC from Knossos demonstrating the Cretan belief in the tale.[7]

Several non-British individuals have visited the 'cave' of Gortyns and pondered on its purpose (see Appendix F), and some have made plans of its intricate passages and its entrance (Figs. 11.1, 11.2, 11.3 & 11.5). Parts of the discussions have been of its actual use, the favourite being a quarry, although Tournefort in 1700 considered there was no evidence for a quarry (see Appendix F). An interesting 1836 report on the subject incorporated Tournefort's belief that similar material for building was much closer to both Gortyns and Knossos, and that the 'labyrinth' was initially a work of nature thereafter enlarged by mankind (see Appendix G).[8]

British visitors

In 1596 the English traveller and writer Fynes Moryson (Fellow of Peterhouse, Cambridge) visited the island and commented (keeping his early spelling):

> We began our iourney in the afternoone, and as we rode, our guide shewed us not farre out of the high way, the monument famous for the love of the Kings daughter *Aridane* to *Theseus*, called the Laberinth of Crete (for so *Candia* was called of old …). Also our guides told us that not far out of the way to the city of Candia, there was a monument of the cave of Minos, which the Candians called the sepulchre of Jupiter: but my adversities had taken from me my woted [want] to see antiquities.[9]

To which place was he referring, Gortyns or Knossos? He did say the city of Candia was 'eight and thirty miles distant',[10] but Gortyns is actually 45 miles from Candia (Herakleion) whereas Knossos is only 4 miles away. He also appeared to see the sepulchre of Jupiter which he later

---

[1] Sp II: 44.
[2] Robinson, 2002: 157.
[3] McArthur, 1993: 128.
[4] Ventris & Chadwick, 1959: 310. The '?' is Ventris & Chadwick's based on a supposed translation of *da-pu2 ?-ri-to-jo/ po-ti-ni-ja* as Λαβυρινφοιο ποτνια although later authors have taken it as read (see Palmer, 1963: 238-9).
[5] Bearing in mind *labrys* in Greek means double-axe and *labyrinthos* is the house of the double-axe (House of Minos?).

[6] See Evans, 1921: 357, Fig 256
[7] Psh I: opp. 208. Although Pashley himself dismissed the existence of a labyrinth as having no 'more real existence than its fabled occupant' (Psh I: 208).
[8] 'The Labyrinth of Crete', *The Penny Magazine of the Society for the Diffusion of Useful Knowledge*, 16 July, 1863: 279 (Appendix G). In the same article, Douglas is fairly dismissive of it being a quarry.
[9] 1617: 255. By his 'adversities' he meant the delays caused by awaiting a 'bill of good health' for clearance to travel across the island.
[10] Moryson, 1617: 254.

referred to as Mount Ida[11] after the Labyrinth, in which case it is most likely that he was at Gortyns.

Shortly after Moryson, George Sandys visited the labyrinth in 1611. He believed it was a quarry supplying stone for both Knossos and Gortyns but was a little vague as to whether it was actually at Knossos or Gortyns, locating them both at the foot of Mount Ida:

> For between where once stood Gortina and Gnossos at the foot of Ida, under the ground are many Meanders hewn out of rock turning this way & now that way ... But by most this is thought to have been a quarry where they had the stone that built both Gnossos and Gortina being force to leave such walls for the support of the roof, and by following of the veines to make it so intricate.[12]

Warren believed that Sandys was the first investigator of the cave when he remarked, 'From this passage ['Meanders ...'] Sandys appears as the first British traveller actually to enter the Labyrinth.'[13] Warren must have assumed that Moryson did not go into the cave and was probably correct as Moryson did not actually say that he went in.

During the 17th century AD there must have been a belief in the maze at Knossos as a picture of it appears in Mallet's book (Fig. 11.4).[14] Did it really exist at this time to be drawn in such a manner? There is no other such evidence to back this up and therefore it must be assumed to be the artist's impression. It also appeared on early maps though sometimes at Gortyns (Maps 8 and 9) and sometimes Knossos (Map 10). At this time the Scot William Lithgow (1582-c.1654) saw the entrance into 'the labyrinth of Daedalus' but did not venture into the cavern: '... I would gladly have better viewed, but because we had no candle-light we durst not enter, for there are many hollow places within it. So that if a man stumble or fall he can hardly be rescued.'[15] He positioned it 'on a face of a little hill, joining with Mount Ida, having many doors and pillars'.[16] This must have been the site at Gortyns which is in the southeast foothills of the Mount Ida range.

As previously mentioned (chapter 4), in the 18th century, Pococke believed the 'famous' labyrinth to have been at Knossos and the Gortyns 'labyrinth' to have been merely a quarry. Also in the 18th century John Morritt aired his opinion in a letter to his Aunt Frances on the 27th August 1795:

> A mile beyond [Gortyns] is what is called the Labyrinth. It is a mountain, large subterraneous range of passages ... You ask what I think about this; to say the truth, neither more or less than a large stone quarry, of which some

passages, where low, are rather choked up ... however, I cannot think it the ancient labyrinth, which built as the one in Egypt, was designed as a subterranean place – a habitation at least. One reason is answerable: the Labyrinth is at *Cnossos* ... and as one reason against the idea is drawn from the difficulty of its access, the lowness of some of the passages ...[17]

Morritt was saying that THE Labyrinth (of Minos) was nothing to do with the 'quarry' at Gortyns but literally a subterranean palace at Knossos. There was indeed a complex of many rooms beneath the earth at Knossos, but he was not able to find any trace of them since he did not excavate.

The 19th century saw varying views. Murray's travel guide, reflecting/copying Pashley's comment on the caverns at Knossos (Makroteikho), was sceptical of such a labyrinth:

> ... there is, however, no sufficient reason to suppose that the Cretan labyrinth ever had a more real existence than its fabled occupant [the Minotaur]. Much as is said in the Homeric poems of Daedalus, Minos, Ariadne, and other Cretan worthies, it is in vain that we search to find in them any evidence of material existence of the monument.[18]

Early in the 19th century Sieber agreed with Pococke and was convinced that there was a labyrinth at Knossos, 'the genuine Labyrinth was undoubtedly at Gnossos',[19] but considered it had been destroyed and so did not visit the site. He did venture to Gortyns to see the so-called 'labyrinth' which existed there, but having surveyed it in detail (see below), agreed with Belon and Pococke that it was merely a stone quarry. The underground development at Gortyns had been identified as a quarry by Belon as long ago as 1548.[20]

The 19th century traveller Charles Rochfort Scott was not so convinced. Having found the south-facing entrance, he set forth through the first passage:

> At its termination, we arrived at a kind of star chamber ... from which passages branch off in all directions, leading to other chambers, where new radii conduct still further into the interior of the mountain, forming, indeed, a very intricate network ...[21]

He then went on to consider its use:

> The purpose for which this labyrinth was formed is yet a matter of conjecture. There is

---

[11] Moryson, 1617: 256.
[12] Sandys, 1615: 176.
[13] Warren, 1972a: 76.
[14] Mallet, 1683: 205.
[15] Lithgow, 1632: 63 (Phelps (ed), 1974 reprint).
[16] Lithgow, 1632: 63.

[17] From Marindin, 1985: 239-40; Stoneman suggested that Morritt's opinion that the Gortyns 'cave' was a quarry 'closed the question' (1987: 92), but this may not be so certain.
[18] Murray, 1854: 361.
[19] Sieber, 1823: 116, relying on the 1st century BC historian Diodorus Siculus (I.16).
[20] Warren, 1996: 15.
[21] Scott, 1837: 273.

not the slightest indication of it having been a place of burial, and the narrow entrance is very much against the supposition of it having been a stone quarry – indeed it is quite unreasonable to suppose that the builders of Gortyna should have come here for stone when they had plenty of the same kind much nearer to hand.[22]

However, he was not convinced that it was the famous labyrinth of King Minos and the Minotaur. One of his concerns was that the account of the 'mythical' structure that had been handed down through the ages stated that it had an opening to the sea which is not the case at Gortyns[23] or Knossos. Although 'an opening to the sea' could mean a river, and both Gortyns and Knossos are adjacent to rivers.

So what was this mass of passages at Gortyns actually built for? Because of its complexity, an underground quarry does not seem practical as its sole purpose. A likely usage would be a place of refuge considering the history of the island, and it must have been used for this purpose during its later years. But what was it originally constructed for? Perhaps a prison in the ancient times. The Greek historian Philochorus (306-260 BC) considered that it was a prison for youths who were given as prizes to victors in the games.[24] It is not clear as to the whereabouts of his reference to the labyrinth, but this explanation ties in to some extent with the mythology.

Spratt supported this hypothesis.[25] Clearly there was a cave consisting of a maze of passages, a real labyrinth, in the mountains behind Gortyns, and the facts, rather than the myth, could be viewed rationally. Spratt was not able to explore the whole underground maze and so was not in a position to estimate its size other than with reference to Sieber's plan (Fig. 11.5). However, relying on its use as a retreat in both history and tradition, he considered that Minos may have had such a contingency in mind on its construction. He speculated that it may also have had other usages but dismissed catacombs because it contained no niches, recesses, or benches. He is assuming particular burial customs at the time it was built. Benches may well have been made of perishable material such as wood and have since deteriorated. He believed a more likely use was that of a prison for the youths of Athens as tributes for the death of Minos' son. They would be detained and cultivated as teachers of Minos' law to the inhabitants of Crete rather than food for the Minotaur. He concluded that the myth had developed from that aspect of fact.[26] There is nothing to say that he is not correct, and again his belief in the existence of Minos is of interest.

Evans very abruptly dismissed Gortyns as a possible labyrinth, believing it to be a quarry similar to the subterranean complex at Hagia Irini about 2 miles above Knossos (and they are similar but the latter has received less attention).[27] He had already convinced himself that the labyrinth referred to the many passages he unearthed at Knossos, '[Of] The Pitaria hill the Myk[enaean] acropolis [Knossos]. We re-examined the mysterious passages & found some more symbols ... I see no reason for not thinking that the mysterious complication of passages is the labyrinth.'[28] He also commented, 'There can be little remaining doubt that this vast edifice, which in a broad historic sense we are justified in calling the 'Palace of Minos', is one and the same as the traditional 'Labyrinth'.'[29] The theory was also supported by Harriet Boyd Hawes:

> Few would deny that he [King Minos] was revered at least as highly as the deified Roman emperors; and the Labyrinth and the Minos-Bull seem actually to have been found on the knoll of Knossos.[30]

One idea that the many rooms of Knossos may represent a labyrinth came from the findings of the 'labyrinth' construction at Caroon in Egypt,[31] as mentioned by Morrit (above). The travelling companion of Pococke, Capt Norden, commented on this Egyptian labyrinth, 'This was an extraordinary building, that Daedalus came on purpose to see it, and built the celebrated labyrinth in Crete, for King Minos, on the same model.'[32] Even though the Egyptian 'labyrinth' may have been utilized as a stone quarry, it may have originally been built for another more formal purpose, as perhaps was Gortyns.

At the end of the 19th century the historian R.A.H. Bickford-Smith believed the labyrinth to be both a quarry and prison:

> The Labyrinth [at Gortyns] is really wonderful, excelling in many ways the Catacombs at Rome. Of course it is in the wrong place, which puzzles the archaeologists a good deal. It ought to be at Knossos where the sweet Ariadne lived with her rigorous father [King Minos], and at Knossos no traces of a labyrinth had been found, though the stratification of rock is suitable, and one may yet be discovered. I think the explanation is that there was a labyrinth near each of the chief old Cretan cities ... Certainly the labyrinth near Knossos is both perfect quarry and perfect labyrinth. There is stone enough – good building stone – left ready to be carted or rolled away, to build a minor capital, and as for a maze, without Ariadne of sorts you would never get out of it. When not

[22] Scott, 1837: 276-7.
[23] Scott, 1837: 277.
[24] From Plutarch's *Lives*, 'Theseus', 16.1: Plutarch was referring to the view of Philochorus (c.319-261 BC).
[25] Sp I: 63
[26] Sp II: 43-54.
[27] Evans, 1921: 532-3.
[28] Diary, 1894: 12 'Knossos' (Brown, 2001: 35, from Evans archive, Ashmolean Museum, Oxford).
[29] 1901: 131; and 'There can be little doubt that it [the Labyrinth] was the great palace itself.' (Evans, 1921: 533).
[30] Boyd Hawes, 1908: 1.
[31] See Herodotus' *Histories*, 2.148-9; also Strabo's *Geographies*, 17.37-8.
[32] From Mavor, 1803: 41.

doing labyrinthe duty it was probably used as a prison. This, indeed, may be the solution of the 'tribute' story, as Spratt suggests.[33]

This was written before Evans' excavations at Knossos, hence Bickford-Smith's reference to no traces of a labyrinth at the site. But he was also suggesting that any such labyrinth would have been used a quarry and a prison.

There appears to be no emphatic conclusion amongst these travellers as to the cave of Gortyns' original intended use or date of construction. However, in support of Scott's contention, it would appear rather elaborate for a mere quarry. Late in the 19th century, Charles Cockerell had dismissed it as a mine due to its insufficient mineral in the walls, but concluded that 'this wonderful excavation was as a secure storehouse for corn and valuables from attack of robbers in the day of Minos'.[34] Looking at the size of the storerooms of the Cretan 'Palaces' of Knossos, Malia and Phaistos, this considered usage would seem rather unlikely (assuming it did date back to 'the day of Minos'). Cockerell's main purpose for visiting the island was to see the labyrinth and Mount Ida, 'To make the best use of our time [on the island], it was proposed that we should make an expedition to see Ida and the famous labyrinth.'[35] In true Thesian style he 'brought a quantity of string for a clue, which we rolled on two long sticks, then lit torches and went in'.[36] He was quite descriptive of the interior:

> At first one enters a vestibule out of which lead
> several openings. Two of the three, perhaps
> four, dark entrances are blocked up, but one
> remains open. This we followed, and for
> three mortal hours and more we groped about
> among intricate passages and in spacious halls.
> The windings bewildered us at once, and my
> compass being broken I was quite ignorant
> as to where I was. The clearly intentional
> intricacy and apparently endless number of
> galleries impressed me with a sense of horror
> and fascination I cannot decide. Every few
> steps one rested, and had to turn to right or left,
> sometimes to choose one of three or four roads.
> What if one should lose the clue [the string]![37]

He added that the work was plainly all done with a chisel and 'the passages were eight and ten feet wide, and four, five, six, eight and ten feet or more high. In many places it

had fallen in.'[38] This obvious danger clearly did not deter him.

Certainly it may have been used as a quarry, but its internal shape and 'rooms' begs a use more than just that. Imogen Grundon reported of a filled-in pit found in Egypt by John Pendlebury and his wife, Hilda, and believed by them to be a tomb. She added, 'though they were aware that it could just as easily prove to be the remains of an ancient quarry as of an ancient tomb'.[39] The reverse could apply to Gortyns, and the lack of finds does not always mean there was nothing of interest going on there.

The Gortyns cave was explored by the Speleological Exploring Group in 1982, and then the Hellenic Speleological Society, led by Anna Petrohilou, in 1984. In 1999 the Cretan department of the Hellenic Speleological Society recorded all the signatures on the walls of the cave. In 2004, following a major investigation of the underground structure at Gortyns, Patroudakis prudently commented:

> From ancient times until now, many guessed
> and argued the position of the labyrinth, but
> none ever proved his/her theory. The labyrinth
> of Gortyne became the biggest tourist scene for
> 600 years, exactly because it was assumed that
> it was the 'true' labyrinth. Furthermore, from
> our knowledge, a clue to prove that this was the
> labyrinth never appeared. However, a clue to
> prove the opposite never arose either.[40]

Obviously Spratt did not discover the caves at Gortyns but he contributed to the debate into its intrigue and possible origin, and, as mentioned at the beginning of chapter 9, he left his mark on an earlier visit in 1843 by way of a graffiti signature, as did his companion, Drummond Hay (Figs 11.6a & b). Clearly the labyrinth was an important reference to an early age of Crete (of Minos), and Spratt's interest in it, particularly in the construction at Gortyns, indicates a possible belief in such an earlier period. Unfortunately, as the dating of the Gortyns' 'labyrinth' is not at all clear (although almost certainly of ancient origin), it is not possible to link it with the Bronze Age with any certainty. However, for possible dating and use, an interesting comparison can be made with the Beer Quarry Caves in East Devon, which date back to the Roman period in Britain.

---

[33] Bickford-Smith, 1898: 109, and Charles Edwardes also supposed this (1887: 179).

[34] Cockerell, 1903: 122 (this book was published after his death by his son, Samuel Pepys Cockerell); see also Matthews, 1922: 27.

[35] Cockerell, 1903: 107.

[36] Cockerell, 1903: 121, as had North Douglas (see Appendix G).

[37] Cockerell, 1903: 121-2.

[38] Cockerell, 1903: 123.

[39] Grundon, 2007: 97.

[40] Patroudakis, 2004: 52 (trans. Efstathios Tamviskos). See also Thomas M. Waldmann's very extensive work on the Gortyns' cave, 2006-2009 (http://www.labyrinthos.com).

12. Other British Travellers

As mentioned in chapter 3, there were other British travellers exploring Crete over the centuries prior to Sir Arthur Evans' excavations and it is worth considering whether they found anything of interest in respect of an early civilization on the island, and if so, whether any such information may have influenced Pococke, Pashley and Spratt. To some extent the same applies to the travellers to mainland Greece, but more particularly their thoughts on the dating of the various monuments that they visited.

Travellers to Crete
William Lithgow (1582-1645)
Although the son of a wealthy burgess and educated at Lanark grammar school, Lithgow was not destined to be a scholar. Possibly to escape the ill-treatment by his brothers, he chose to travel and earn a living from his writings.

He visited Crete in 1609 and recorded his travels in his *Painefull Peregrinations* (Appendix H), but his tales and experiences on the island are mainly of woe. On his very first day he was robbed and nearly killed; he then rescued a French slave only to be chased and nearly slain by the slave's 'owners'; he was nearly bitten by three snakes, having been led to believe that no such venomous reptiles could live on the island; and he was to be the near-victim of an Englishman's desire for the revenge of his brother, killed at the hands of a Scotsman (Lithgow was a Scot).[1] This may be treated with some degree of exaggeration.

He was disappointed with Greece, having believed it to be a land of heroes now subdued by the Ottoman Turks. He commented (keeping his early spelling):

> In all this countrey of *Greece* I could finde
> nothing to answer the famous relations, given
> by auncient Authors, of the excellency of the
> land, but the name onely; the barbarousnesse
> of *Turkes* and Time, having defaced all the
> Monuments of Antiquity: No shew of honour,
> no habitation of men in an honest fashion, nor
> possessours of the Countrey in a Principality.
> But rather prisoners shut up in prisons, or
> addicted slaves to cruell and tyrannicall
> Maisters.[2]

The same could apply to his view of Crete.

It was said of his writing, 'he does not, as they say in creative-writing curricula, bring scenes alive, but instead summarizes, ignores the particulars of the ruins he visits, generalizes, adds historical commentary, and then digresses'.[3] In fact, his description of his fifty-eight days, travelling four hundred miles, is exceedingly brief and uninformative as far as any information regarding the island historically. Of the sites on the island he only mentioned Mount Ida and the Gortyns' labyrinth, but as can be seen from the very first paragraph of his report, a description of the island's historical past was not his intention (Appendix H). Stoneman described his work as entertaining but not offering much to the learned traveller.[4]

George Sandys (1578-1644)
Son of an Archbishop of York, Sandys was educated at Oxford as a gentleman of the University at the age of eleven in 1589, entering St Mary's Hall but soon after transferring to Corpus Christi. He 'grew into a gentleman famed for his learning in Classics and foreign languages'.[5] He was, as were several of his brothers and cousins, admitted to membership of Middle Temple (one of the barristers' Inns of Court) but he was not called to the Bar.[6] He would have had to have trained as a clerk for seven years, but it appears that he left after about a year to marry Elizabeth Norton.[7] His uncle, Myles Sandys, was Treasurer of Middle Temple from 1588 to 1595.

Davis was of the opinion that Sandys did not actually visit Crete, 'the ship did not put into any port on Crete, though Sandys does describe country dancing on the island as though he had seen it'.[8] This does not correspond with Warren's later observation, '... George Sandys, who visited the island in 1611 ...'.[9] Davis possibly took this view because Sandys' brief but stylistic report on the

---

[1] Lithgow, 1632: 81-91 (see also Phelps (ed.), 1974 reprint: 60-66, modernized from Lithgow's 'old' English).
[2] Lithgow, 1632: 71-2 (also Phelps (ed.), 1974: 55-6).

[3] Eisner, 1993: 53.
[4] Stoneman, 1987: 58.
[5] Davis, 1955: 31.
[6] Jones, 1924: 191-2 (from a list of American Members of the Inns of Court, as Sandys had become a Council member of the Virginian and Bermudian Companies on his move to Jamestown, Virginia in 1621, having moved to America probably as result of his disastrous marriage).
[7] Davis, 1955: 34. Trease incorrectly reported that Sandys was unmarried and remained so until his death in 1644 (1967: 69). He certainly remained unmarried after his divorce.
[8] Davis, 1955: 77, but (even if true) that may not detract from his descriptions of the island. Regarding Keos, Bennet & Voutsaki commented, 'Other bona fide travelers did not actually land on the island. Their information ought to be contemporary and reasonably reliable.' (1991: 372), but this must be dependant upon where it came from in the first place.
[9] Warren, 1972a: 74.

island (see Appendix I) made several references to ancient sources but no mention of visiting any sites or actually landing on the island. He was 'much becalmed, and not seldom crossed by contrary winds ... until we approached the South-east of Candy, called formerly Creta'.[10]

However, Warren must be correct as Sandys did describe certain specific areas, such as Mount Ida and Gortyns and its labyrinth (see previous chapter and Appendix I). Even so, as references to sites are rather limited, Warren's comment of Sandys leaving a 'full description of Crete in his book of 1615, packed with Classical scholarship and ancient history ...'[11] is somewhat of an exaggeration. He was certainly interested in Classical literature, having translated Ovid's *Metamorphoses* and Book One of Virgil's *Aeneid*,[12] but of his travels generally Stoneman observed that he 'had little to say of antiquities, being more concerned to reproduce the ancient legends'.[13] This was very true as Sandys talked only of the mythology and some geography.

Fedden considered that Sandys' account of his travels 'revels a well-poised and intelligent mind, a shrewd eye, careful reporting, a respect for accuracy uncommon among contemporary travellers, and also first signs of that preoccupation with archaeology which was to obsess later visitors'.[14] This was very much a generalization and it hardly applied to his visit to Crete.

John Bacon Sawrey Morritt (1771-1843)
Morritt was of the landed gentry and attended St John's College, Cambridge. He was a Lieutenant in the Military Regiment in Lancashire and thereafter became a Tory MP. Having travelled Italy as part of the Grand Tour, he became a member of the Dilettanti Society in 1799 and founder of the Travellers' Club in 1819.

He obviously had a certain belief in the tales of the ancient heroes of Homer as he searched for Troy, believing it to be at Burnabashi[15] before Hissarlick was determined as the more likely site by Schliemann. He visited Crete in 1795 but found no evidence of its former greatness.[16] This is hardly surprising if the following extract from a letter to his sister Ann is indicative of his travelling:

> We set out from Setia at about five o'clock [pm], and as we had a full moon travelled all night, except for about an hour and a half, and got to Girapetra about eight the next morning. I think I hear a certain saucy person observe: "So you travel all night by way of seeing a country!"
> I, in answer, shall observe that a full moon is no bad light to see a pretty country by, and that it

is better to go even in the dark than by the sun, of which really you have not an idea.[17]

However, he did make some observations of interest in mainland Greece. Of the walls of Mycenaean Tiryns he remarked, '... but the striking thing in these is the extreme *rudeness* of the masonry, which carries with it the marks of the very remote and early times of Greece, and one can't help seeing with pleasure and wonder a wall which the Greeks themselves ascribe to the Cyclops (added italics)'.[18] Mention has already been made of both Pashley and Spratt referring to the ancient walls of some of the ruins in Crete they perceived as 'rude' and Cyclopean, perhaps also relating to examples of the Mycenaean Bronze Age on the island.

Morritt was fairly dismissive of the remains of what he perceived to be the ancient palace of Knossos, 'we passed the ruins, or rather the situation of Cnossos ... An old bit of wall is what remains of Cnossos; the tomb of Jupiter and other monuments we inquired for in vain.'[19]

John Antony Cramer (1793-1848)
Cramer was an ordained minister of the Church of England and the Dean of Carlisle. Although born in Switzerland, he was educated at Westminster School before going up to Christ Church, Oxford, in 1811. He graduated with a first in Mathematics and Classics three years later. He was presented with the perpetual curacy of Binsey, Oxfordshire, in 1822, and remained at Christ Church as a tutor and rhetoric reader until 1824. Before long he had proved himself as an ancient historian of great merit and was keen to write up a history of the ancient world (particularly Italy, Greece and Asia Minor). This he did mainly by way of reference to ancient writers rather than by his own travels, although he was more widely travelled than many other academics.[20] In 1843 he was appointed as professor of modern history at Oxford after the death of Thomas Arnold.

Cramer's three volumes on ancient Greece, *A Geographical and Historical Description of Ancient Greece*, were published in 1828, and volume III looked at Crete. Pendlebury criticized this latter volume on Crete as being inaccurate,[21] and Cramer himself said of the whole work, 'I am far from presuming to offer it to the public as the most correct that could be made; but I shall rest satisfied if it be found a material improvement on those which have hitherto appeared ...'.[22] Perhaps one of the main reasons it could be accused of being inaccurate is because Cramer relied too much on Homeric references as historic and on belief in the existence of Minos.

It is certainly not abundantly clear that Cramer had visited

---

[10] Sandys, 1615: 174.
[11] Warren, 2000: 4.
[12] Ellison, 2004.
[13] Stoneman, 1987: 65.
[14] Fedden, 1958: 9.
[15] McConnell, 2004
[16] From Marindin, 1985: 210.

[17] *Ibid.* 229.
[18] *Ibid.* 211-2.
[19] *Ibid.* 232.
[20] Curthoys, 2004.
[21] Pendlebury, 1939: 16, as he did with Pococke (see chapter 4).
[22] Cramer, 1828, Vol. I: vii.

the island. In his preface in the first volume he simply said of the books, '… it will not be necessary to advert here to the method which has been adopted in its composition'.[23] The implication is that he had not visited each and every country he referred to in the three volumes. As far as Crete was concerned, he made his geographical observations of ancient sites by way of references from ancient writers such as Strabo, Herodotus, Thucydides, Diodorus, Pliny, Ptolemy, Pausanias and Stephanus,[24] nearly all of whom also believed in Homer as an historic source. This may account for Cramer's avid belief in Homer. As has been seen in previous chapters, some of these ancient references (particularly Strabo) were repeated by Pashley and Spratt for geographical identification purposes.

Cramer was very much more an historian than a traveller, but both Pashley and Spratt made good use of his work to assist them in their travels of the island and, perhaps not coincidently, most the sites Cramer identified were the very ones sought out by the two travellers because they too believed in Homeric references as evidence of an early civilization.

Sir John Gardner Wilkinson (1797-1875)
Wilkinson was born in 1797 and of learned parentage. His father was a clergyman and a Fellow of the Society of Antiquaries, and his mother was a Classical scholar. He was educated at Harrow and Exeter College, Oxford. From 1817 he spent his life travelling, including the 'Grand Tour' of Europe. He met Sir William Gell (see below) in France, who introduced him to Egyptology after having persuaded him to leave the army.

He visited the islands of the Mediterranean and sketched a plan of Crete in about 1833 (see Map 11). This is much the same time as Pashley's visit to Crete but they do not appear to have met and Pashley did not mention Wilkinson. Thompson's otherwise interesting biography of Wilkinson[25] made no mention of his time in Crete. It must have been a short visit and, apart from the map and some notes and sketches which are catalogued in the Bodleian collection in Oxford, of little historical interest.

Charles Rochfort Scott (d. 1872)
Scott, a Captain in the Royal Staff Corps, also visited Crete in the early 1830s and wrote up his findings in the second volume of his *Rambles in Egypt and Candia*.[26] His trip was brief and he only travelled from Candia (Herakleion) to Gortyns and onto Retimo (Rethymnon) and Canea (Khania). He made no reference to ancient sites other than Gortyns but made some interesting observations about the 'labyrinth' near the old town (see previous chapter). Surprisingly he did not go to Knossos as he was more interested in the political state of the country than its ancient history.

Edward Lear (1812-88)
Lear was born in 1812 and one of twenty children of Jeremiah and Ann Lear. Due to this large family he did not receive any formal classical education, although, before leaving for school at eleven, he had been tutored by his sister Ann, who read to him many of the tales of Greek mythology.[27] She was also very keen on Byron and read Byron's poetical autobiography, *Childe Harold's Pilgrimage*, to her young brother which instilled within him the romanticism of Greece and later the need to learn the modern Greek language.[28] At the age of fifteen, following his father's fall into financial ruin, he left school to earn his own living as an artist and later as a writer of 'nonsense' poems. This led him on to become an ardent traveller, recording his discoveries by way of pictures and poetry.

Lear visited Crete with his servant, George Kokalis (from Suli in Epirus), in 1864, but the trip was relatively brief, only six weeks (April to May), and its purpose was to sketch and paint pictures of various sites he encountered. He arrived at Khania and based himself initially at Khalepa. He travelled west to Kisamos, then back eastwards only as far as Herakleion. Then he went south to Phaistos, before turning north back to Khania via Rethymnon.

Lear was not an antiquarian but he had read Pashley's book.[29] Spratt's had not then been published as it came out the year after Lear's visit to Crete, but Spratt's map was available to Lear.[30] He did make the occasional remark about seeing ancient vestiges, particularly the Roman remains at Gortyns[31] and walls 'like Tiryns' at Aptera.[32] He produced some two hundred drawings/sketches/paintings which unfortunately did not include many ancient sites of Crete. The majority were of intact architecture and landscapes. He was not very impressed with the island mainly due to the bad weather and general discomfort. After a month he noted in his diary:

> I and George both think it better that I should give up farther journey in Crete: first, the advanced season and increasing heat; second, the little picturesqueness gained by so much toil; third the bad food and dirt and the little rest – are all good reason for leaving Crete.[33]

Of the ancient site of Knossos he stated, 'but except scattered masses of brickwork, little remains'.[34] He commented that Crete's 'antiquities are so old as to be invisible',[35] but he really did not look that hard because the search for

[23] Cramer, 1828, Vol. I: iii.
[24] Cramer, 1828, Vol. III: 356-95.
[25] Thompson, 1992.
[26] Scott, 1837.
[27] Noakes, 1979: 22-3.
[28] *Ibid.*
[29] 'I sit writing, or read Pashley …' (from diary entry, 8th May 1864 (Fowler 1984: 62 – 31. Lear's actual diary is in the Houghton Library at Harvard).
[30] Diary entry, 16th April 1864 (Fowler, 1984: 31).
[31] Diary entry, 17th May 1864 (Fowler, 1984: 82).
[32] Diary entry, 3rd May 1864 (Fowler, 1984: 52), following Pashley's view (see chapter 6).
[33] Diary entry, 14th May 1864 (Fowler, 1984: 74).
[34] Diary entry, 11th May 1864 (Fowler, 1984: 66).
[35] From Noakes, 1979: 204.

antiquities was not his motive. This is unfortunate as his drawings/paintings, had they been of ancient sites, might have proved most interesting. Lear's friend and fellow traveller to Greece, Franklyn Lushington, a Cambridge Greek scholar, commented that the eminent geologist, Sir Roderick Murchison, President of the Royal Geographical Society, had said he could always tell the geology of a country from one of Lear's sketches.[36] High praise indeed, but there is no evidence that his sketches assisted in the discovery of a Bronze Age Cretan civilization.

Lear wrote many letters in his life but, again, the Cretan period is not so well recorded. The more renowned of his biographers, Vivien Noakes, revealed (to the author) that as far as she knew there was only one letter written from Crete, to Chichester Fortescue, dated the 24th April 1864, but it says nothing at all about his actual visit.

Lear's work is therefore somewhat disappointing as far as the discovery of any antiquities of Crete is concerned. It had great potential if he had been particularly interested in the early ancient archaeology as any sketches of the sites would have been most enlightening in relation to what would have been visible during the 19th century. Even so, Eisner commented, 'Nevertheless, he saw and painted what others have not, and what is no longer there for anyone to see – a pre-liberation, underpopulated, unexcavated, untouristified Crete …'[37] But generally Lear was not too impressed with Crete, comparing only favourably with the Sussex sunset, '… I have never seen any sunset here [Crete] warmer in colour that those of Hastings [East Sussex]: a sort of pearly silver mist involves all the isle.'[38]

Charles Edwardes (19th century, exact dates unknown)
Edwardes' tour of Crete was somewhat limited as he tended to return to a base each night. He arrived in Crete in the Spring of 1886 and took up residence in Khalepa, just outside Khania. In Khania he met the Governor-General of Crete, Savas Pasha, but the more interesting meeting was with the Pasha's secretary (who remained nameless). Edwardes reported that the secretary showed him a manuscript that he had been working on for many years which incorporated descriptions of about 100 ancient cities of Crete,[39] and Edwardes urged him to get it published, but:

> … he is one of those scholarly men who finds faults in their work whenever they glance at it, and in course of time become so diffident about their abilities that they persuade themselves it is not worth the while to publish after all.[40]

Needless to say the book was not published, which is unfortunate, as clearly it would have proved a useful insight to the known archaeology at that time. It would

also have been of interest to see if, and how, the secretary may have dated the sites.

From Khalepa Edwardes headed west to Kisamos where he was to temporarily stay. He ventured upon Platanias, a site, he observed, '… too commanding to have been overlooked by the city-builders of pre-Homeric times, and there can be little doubt that it sent representatives in the eighty ships which were Crete's contingent in the grand Hellenic force of Troy'.[41] Clearly a belief in a pre-Classical period.

Of the Bay of Kisamos he commented, '… the small mole, of big stones and rocks piled one upon another, which Cretans of two or *three thousand years ago* made for the security of their men-of-war …' (added italics).[42] Of the bazaar at Kisamos, he commented, 'Coins in gold, silver, and bronze, with a range of *three thousand years in date*' (added italics).[43] Coins of that age may be somewhat inaccurate, but Edwardes was in no doubt about the existence of an early Cretan power which existed 'three thousand years' ago - during the Bronze Age.

Edwardes credited Spratt with the discovery of ancient Polyrrhenia at Palaiokastron[44] and referred to it himself as 'the prehistoric city, with its huge untrimmed blocks of squared stone …'.[45] He also made reference to the 'Cyclopean' masses of stonework.[46] These are a description of Mycenaean stone. Likewise he reported that Phalasarna has 'huge grey walls … they were ten and twelve feet thick'.[47]

Edwardes was very disappointed in Knossos and said of it, 'Not that it has eventuated in anything important archaeologically.'[48] Little did he know what lay beneath his feet. He was only to refer to it as a name to conjure with, it having vanished completely beneath green barley and great red poppies.[49] Edwardes added that his 'guide was very ignorant about Cnossos, naturally enough. It was to him a mere field of barley, with something queer underneath.'[50] At that time a field of barley was much more important and useful than anything an old ruinous site could produce.

Edwardes, when talking of the archaeological exploits in Crete of the British Consul Alfred Biliotti, observed that

---

[36] Chitty, 1989: 7; see also Lehmann, 1977: 96-7.
[37] Eisner, 1993: 164.
[38] Diary entry, 29th May 1864 (Fowler, 1984: 102).
[39] Referring to Homer's reference in the *Iliad*: 'Krete of the hundred cities', 2.649.
[40] Edwardes, 1887: 63-4.

[41] Edwardes, 1887: 219-20. The eighty ships coming from Homer's *Iliad*, 2.652, and his reference to 'pre-Homeric builders' reflected his writing after the finds at Troy and Mycenae by Schliemann.
[42] Edwardes, 1887: 236. He added, 'But the mole is a stout achievement, and will probably last for another two or three thousand years…unless… later improvement in steam communication make these glorious bays of the Aegean as favoured of the people as are Margate and Hastings and Brighton' (1887: 275) - which, unfortunately, it did.
[43] Edwardes, 1887: 243.
[44] Edwardes, 1887: 253.
[45] Edwardes, 1887: 254.
[46] Edwardes, 1887: 263.
[47] Edwardes, 1887: 279 and 281.
[48] Edwardes, 1887: 361.
[49] Edwardes, 1887: 362.
[50] Edwardes, 1887: 365.

one of his and his workers' tasks would be to explore the labyrinth of Gortyns, 'and it will be through no lethargy on his part if they do not make some discovery'.⁵¹ So some finds of ancient interest were always to be expected. Edwardes hopefully thought that King Minos' 'labyrinth' might have been a subterranean connection between Gortyns and Knossos,⁵² but this was rather an extreme view considering the distance between the two sites.

Finally Edwardes' enthusiasm was dampened with his search for Mount Iouktas. As with Pashley, he was keen to discover the cave on Mount Iouktas where Zeus was believed to be buried. However, the Cretans were not so intrigued and he was horrified to discover that none of the locals had heard of the deity.⁵³ He did come upon a cave complete with bones and pottery, but classed the contents as rubbish⁵⁴ rather than the burial place of a god. Edwardes seemed unaware that the 'tomb of Zeus' would have been on the summit of one of the peaks of the mount.

Travellers to Greece
Certain important Bronze Age sites, such as Mycenae and Tiryns, were always visible in the Peloponnese on mainland Greece during the 19th century. Accordingly it is important to see what British travellers during that century considered was the age of these monuments. This may have some bearing on what Pashley and Spratt may have been thinking regarding the age of their 'cyclopean' remains in Crete. As mentioned in chapter 3, the idea of a Bronze Age was 'introduced' by Thomsen in the 1830s although no specific dates were attributed to it as far as the Aegean was concerned. George Grote's idea of Greek history beginning in 776 BC⁵⁵ was beginning to be eyed with doubt. Mycenae and Tiryns are particularly relevant to this dating. With regard to this, four British travellers deserve attention: William Gell, Edward Dodwell, Colonel William Leake and William Clark.

William Gell (1777–1836)
Gell visited the mainland of Greece at the beginning of the 19th century (1801-6) and was in no doubt about the dates of the Mycenaean sites:

> Everything at Mycenae is of the most
> ancient date, for the city was destroyed and
> depopulated by the Argives soon after the
> Persian invasion (Strabo) about 466 years
> before Christ, having existed about 913 years

from its foundation by Perseus in the fourteenth century [BC].⁵⁶

Of Tiryns he said, 'Tiryns is the best specimen of the military heroic age now existing. There can be no doubt that the present ruins are those of the citadel which existed in the age of the poet [Homer]. It was built by Praetus, about the year 1379 BC ...'.⁵⁷ It was clear to him that a civilization existed prior to that of the Classical Greeks.

Edward Dodwell (1776/7–1832)
Dodwell was also travelling the country at the same time as Gell and made many drawings of the ancient sites. He certainly considered that Tiryns was earlier than the Classical 5th century BC, and he was actually correct about his dating:

> Appollodorus and Strabo assert that it [Tiryns] belonged to Proetus ... Proteus is supposed to have reigned over the kingdom of Tirynthia about one thousand three hundred and seventy-nine years before our era. This computation would give an antiquity of nearly thirty-two centuries [c.1400 BC] to the walls of Tiryns, and even this long series of revolving years does not appear too vast a period to assign the duration, when we consider the gigantic masses of which they are composed, and the impenetrable strength which they display.⁵⁸

Dodwell was not quite so specific with dating Mycenae, although it is likely he considered it much the same date as Tiryns based on the cyclopean construction:

> Sixteen centuries ago that traveller [Pausanias] was not less bewildered in the dark labyrinth of Mycenaean antiquities, than we are at the present day; history throws no light upon their construction, and all that we can know for certain is, that the architects of those distant days were possessed of science and of genius that have not been surpassed in later times!⁵⁹

William Leake (1777–1860)
Leake visited Mycenae in March 1806 and commented on the ruins, 'The later reparations of the walls may easily be recognized; with this exception everything left at Mycenae dates from the heroic ages...'⁶⁰ Again no dating of these 'heroic ages', but it would imply a pre-Classical era of Homer. He then referred to the solar worship, 'most common in Greece at that *distant period*' (added italics).⁶¹ This 'distant period' was pre-Classical. Of Tiryns he remarked, 'we find a great resemblance, not only to

⁵¹ Edwardes, 1887: 179.
⁵² Edwardes, 1887: 362.
⁵³ Edwardes, 1887: 370. This had not changed in the 1940s when Moss commented, 'The Cretans, though sometimes showing surprising ignorance of mythical stories reputed to have taken place on their island...' (1950: 50). This may have something to do with the teaching of the Orthodox church, with ancient paganism contravening this teaching, particularly during the Venetian and Ottoman occupations, but I also found that this ignorance still remains today with many non-academic Cretans I spoke to during my travels.
⁵⁴ Edwardes, 1887: 379. Pashley referred to an unexplored cave he encountered descending the mountain (about half-way down), with an entrance of 12 feet in width and a depth of some 90-100 feet leading to a cavern (Pshl: 220), and this may have been the same one.
⁵⁵ Grote, 1846-56.
⁵⁶ Gell, 1810: 29. In his *Narrative of a Journey in the Morea* (Morea being the Peloponnese), he dismissed Mycenae in two line, 'From Argos we went to Mycenae, or Krebata, where we remained several days, and visited Nemea' (1823: 397), but he may have considered he had dealt with it sufficiently in his 1810 publication.
⁵⁷ Gell, 1810: 54.
⁵⁸ Dodwell, 1834: 3 (published posthumously).
⁵⁹ Dodwell, 1834: 8.
⁶⁰ Leake, 1830, Vol. II: 369.
⁶¹ Leake, 1830, Vol. II: 370.

Mycenae, which was built by the same engineers, but to several other Grecian fortresses of *remote antiquity*' (added italics).[62] He continued, 'According to ancient history of Argolis, Tiryns was founded by Proetus about 1400 years BC, and Mycenae, a generation later by Perseus.'[63] He did not comment on this dating reference with belief or disbelief, but clearly of 'remote antiquity'.

One other comment is worth a mention with regard to Leake's observations of the massive walls of Tiryns:

> The rudeness of the Cyclopean work, the magnitude of the masses, and the firmness with which their weight keeps them together, have preserved the ruins from the hands of the barbarous masons of modern Greece, who have found more manageable materials in Hellenic constructions of a later date.[64]

By the 'Hellenic constructions of a later date' he meant the Classical period, and the 'Cyclopean work' of a remoter antiquity was of 1400 BC, the Bronze Age. In fact, in the first volume of his *Travels in the Morea*, Leake distinguished 'Hellenic masonry' into two eras of first and second orders, the first being the earlier:

> The first or most ancient manner, as exemplified in the walls of Tiryns, consists in the accumulation of large masses of stone rudely hewn, the intervals of which are filled with smaller stones of the same kind. In the second order, no less than in the first, the stones were of various shapes, but the sides were all right lines, and so accurately fitted to one another by previous labour, that no interval remained between the large masses to be filled up with small stones, so that the whole wall may be said to form a single course of masonry.[65]

Leake gave an example of the second order of the Classical ruins at Khaiaffa (Samikon),[66] and so the first order is clearly pre-Classical and perhaps of the Bronze Age. These orders could be similar to Pashley's first and second style cyclopean walls (see chapters 6 and 7).

William Clark (1821–78)
In 1858 Clark wrote of Mycenae:

> Thus seventeen centuries ago – nay, six centuries before that, at the birth of history – these walls were of a fashion which was left so completely without record, that, in belief of the men who dwelt beside them, they had been piled by fabulous monsters for a mythic king. A story which no more contains any fruitful germ of truth ...[67]

The no 'fruitful germ of truth' referred to the monster and mythic king, not the people 'without record' that lived there. This is another example of a belief in a pre-Classical or pre-historic ('without record') civilization as inhabitants of this cyclopean architecture. Clark also referred to Mycenae as the city of the 'heroic age' which was different from the city of 'later times',[68] later times being the Classical period. This is further emphasized when he commented, 'Those who inhabited Mycenae in *historic times* were probably in no way lineally descended from those who built the walls ...' (added italics).[69] His reference to the Classical period being the 'birth of history' is his 'historic times'.

This 19th century belief in the existence of a pre-Classical civilization on mainland Greece could not have escaped Pashley and Spratt when they encountered what they perceived to be cyclopean remains in Crete.

Importance of these travellers
The motives and/or achievements of the early travellers to Crete appear not to be very helpful with regard to the discoveries of ancient sites of any particular age. Lithgow was just looking for adventure and his report on his activities make little mention of ancient sites and are not to be relied upon. Sandys, although a scholar, again made no real identification of ancient ruins. Morritt, another scholar, was a little more interested in the ancient world of Crete, although he did not spend a great deal of time looking for evidence of it. This may have been because he seemed to be doing most of his travelling at night. Cramer was more of an historian than a traveller/antiquarian, and his writings, although informative, are reliant upon ancient sources which is not entirely safe for accuracy. Wilkinson certainly had the credentials of an antiquarian but his reporting on Crete is rather disappointing. Scott really did not spend enough time on the island to make any significant contribution to its ancient history. Lear could have contributed so much more had he sketched the ancient ruins, but they were not of interest to him. Edwardes appears to have had the interest and met the right people, but his actual reports were very limited.

These travellers are interesting not so much for what they discovered but for what they did not discover. They discovered very little in relation to the island's ancient history, and so this gives more importance to the achievements of Pococke, Pashley and Spratt in that it shows they were following an archaeological purpose.

The date references of Gell, Dodwell and Leake on mainland Greece are vitally important as they actually referred to the Bronze Age period. Pashley and Spratt must have been aware of this dating, having almost certainly read their work (Clark would have been later). This is perhaps the 'earlier' period to which both Pashley and Spratt kept referring.

---

[62] Leake, 1830, Vol. II: 352.
[63] Leake, 1830, Vol. II: 354-5, only a discrepancy if Dodwell's 'before our era' is not interpreted as 'before our Christ'.
[64] Leake, 1830, Vol. II: 355.
[65] Leake, 1830, Vol. I: 53 fn. a.
[66] Leake, 1830, Vol. I: 53.
[67] Clark, 1858: 67.
[68] Clark, 1858: 75.
[69] Clark, 1858: 81.

13. Discussion

Discovery of Bronze Age Crete

Interpreting and piecing information together can be a personal trait, the results of which not everyone will possibly agree with. When a particular goal is in mind, care must be taken not to force the pieces to fit. The 19th century American traveller J.L. Stephens, when searching for the 6th century BC Temple of Diana/Artemis at Ephesus in Asia Minor, commented:

> As a traveller I would fain be able to say that I have seen the ruins of this temple; but unfortunately, I am obliged to limit myself by facts. Its site has of course engaged the attention of antiquarians. I am no sceptic in these matters, and am disposed to believe all that my cicerone [guide] tells me … but I am sorry to say, in spite of his authority and my own wish to believe him, that the better opinion is, that now not a single stone is to be seen.[1]

This is reminiscent of the finding of Homeric Troy as Heinrich Schliemann wanted to believe he had found it at Hissarlick in northwestern Anatolia (Turkey), and was very convincing. He was possibly correct with regard to the actual site[2] but he was clearly incorrect in his belief that he had found Homer's Troy in level II of the mound.[3] It turned out to be 1000 years too early for Homer's Trojan War,[4] if we want to believe in Homer's tale. One has to be very careful in making the archaeology fit the myth.

This work has attempted to retrace the footsteps of Pococke, Pashley and Spratt to establish whether or not they might have seen the ruins of the Bronze Age of Crete before Sir Arthur Evans' findings. If this is the case, then they contributed to the discovery of the island's Bronze Age archaeological heritage, for which Evans appears to have taken most of the credit. It has not been an easy task as the terrain in Crete has obviously changed over the last two centuries and not all the sites seen by Pococke, Pashley and Spratt are still visible today.[5] Between 1947 and 1977 the archaeologist George Bean examined many sites around the coast of Turkey and made a pertinent observation about Spratt visiting Corydalla in Lycia, which certainly applied to the author's experiences in Crete:

> Spratt in 1842 saw quite considerable ruins, including a theatre and aqueduct and remains of many buildings of varying antiquity covering two low conical hills; of all this nothing whatever survives … when the writer was there in 1952, he found a constant stream of lorries carrying away stones (quite illegally, but a blind eye was evidently turned), and Kumluca itself, and the neighbouring villages of Haciveliler, Callea, and Hizirhaya, were full of the dismembered remnants of Corydalla.[6]

Both Pashley and Spratt used the words 'Cyclopean' and 'Hellenic' to describe the differing styles of architecture that they encountered. Having both been classically educated, albeit briefly in Spratt's case, they would have read Homer's *Iliad* and been aware of his reference to 'Tiryns of the huge walls' and 'Mykenae, the strong-founded citadel',[7] from whence the term 'Cyclopean' was later adopted by Strabo and Pausanias for this style of immense walling. Even if Pashley and Spratt did treat Homer's Trojan War as mythology,[8] they may have had Homer's 'world' in mind when they used the 'Cyclopean' term themselves to describe the style of architecture that they had seen. This would have been to distinguish it from the very different and more refined later 'Hellenic' style of the Classical/Hellenistic period. This is not withstanding Gell, Dodwell, Clark and Leake's dating references (previous chapter). Even Evans, when he travelled/explored the island between 1894-99 before he began his excavations, referred to sightings of Cyclopean ruins of the Mycenaean civilization.[9] So they were there to be seen by Pococke, Pashley and Spratt.

As mentioned in chapter 6, Pashley made references to Homer's *Iliad* being composed 'three thousand years

---

[1] Stephens, 1840: 202-3.
[2] Easton perhaps summed it up when he said that there was no proof for the historicity of the Homeric Trojan War, but added, 'for those who wish to believe – faith is once again possible' (1985: 195).
[3] Schliemann commented, 'The excavations made this year [1873] have sufficiently proved that the second nation [level II] which built a town on this hill, upon the debris of the first settlers…are the Trojans of whom Homer sings.' (1875: 16).
[4] See Blegen, 1995 (originally published in 1963).
[5] See Rackham & Moody, 1996: 118-22, on changes in the Cretan landscape (vegetation) over the last 150 years.
[6] Bean, 1978: 146.
[7] Homer's *Iliad*, 2.559 and 2.569 respectively.
[8] Although, in the 19th century, there was a belief in the Homeric tales which led to searches for Homeric cities, 'in the first decade of the nineteenth century European researchers in Greece were stimulated by an interest in topographical studies. The then current European fascination with the identification of 'Homeric sites' was only one aspect of a new concern for the authentication of classical antiquity' (Tsigakou, 1981: 25).
[9] Evans, 1901: 119. The style of mainland Mycenaean architecture was known to him from the work of Schliemann mentioned in the introduction.

ago'. Although it is not clear where he came upon this timescale, it is most likely from Herodotus' references.[10] It was within the correct bounds of the Bronze Age to which Homer was possibly referring. Accordingly, Pashley certainly had an earlier civilization in mind when referring to 'ante-Homeric' and other sites he considered relevant to the Homeric heroes.

Sir Arthur Evans
Professor Richard Dawkins (Director of the BSA, 1906-14) said, 'Here I allude to the archaeological discovery of Minoan Crete, which will always be associated with Knossos and its excavator, Sir Arthur Evans.'[11] This observation is very true as the discovery of the archaeology of 'Minoan' Crete has always been associated with Evans at Knossos. However, this is a generalization in relation to a specific civilization of the Bronze Age of Crete and not entirely correct. Sir Arthur Evans' achievements were, without doubt, of immense value, but some credit is due to earlier travellers.

Mention has already been made of the Cretan archaeologist Minos Kalokairinos and his findings of the walls at Knossos in 1878. Professor John Papadopoulos of University College Los Angles recently pointed out, unfortunately correctly:

> When [Arthur] Evans finally began
> his excavations at Knossos [in 1900],
> Kalokairinos's name and legacy were relegated
> to virtual obscurity ... and Evans quickly
> assumed the mantle of excavator and, in many
> contexts, discoverer of Knossos.[12]

Professor John Bennet also observed, 'In the wake of his [Evans'] persuasive influence, it is easy to forget, however, that Evans was not the first to explore the site ... the first serious excavations at Knossos were carried out in 1878 by ... Minos Kalokairinos.'[13] Dr Yannis Hamilakis also gave Kalokairinos the credit for discovering the site before Evans: '... and he [Evans] falsely claimed for himself the discovery of the site *first spotted* and initially systematically excavated by a local, amateur archaeologist, Minos Kalokairinos ...' (added italics).[14] Kalokairinos may have been the first to carry out 'serious excavations' of the site but he was not the first to 'spot' or 'explore' it, and exploration is all part of archaeology. Knossos was spotted and explored, albeit to a small extent, by Pococke, Pashley and Spratt (amongst others), and so, borrowing Bennet's phrase, 'in the wake of his [Evans'] persuasive influence it is easy to forget' *about all of his predecessors who explored the site* and many other parts of the island. Such predecessors include Pococke, Pashley and Spratt.

Even at the end of the 19th century the importance of the

work of these three travellers had not been recognized. In his commentary on Pausanias, Sir James Frazer, once a student of the British School at Athens, said, 'The great island of Crete, though it has hitherto been little explored, is said to swarm with relics of the Mycenaean age.'[15] He was referring to Evans' investigation in 1894, not his later excavations. But some of these 'swarms of relics', which include walls, were referred to by Pococke, Pashley and Spratt during their travels, even if not identified as Minoan/ Mycenaean by name. Also, they had explored the island, contrary to Frazer's belief.

Certainly Evans gave a name to Crete's earliest civilization and revealed the 'Minoan' civilization to the public. However, to some extent Evans was further developing Pococke's, Pashley's and Spratt's reports. They had recorded what they had seen but made no specific suggestions as to dating other than Cyclopean, Hellenic and Roman. The question that they left unanswered was: who were these people who had built these Cyclopean walls? With excavation Evans was able to reveal an ancient Cretan civilization otherwise unknown.

Archaeologists Dr Louise Hitchcock and Paul Koudounaris commented, 'It can be said that Minoan civilization was created in the twentieth century by Sir Arthur Evans ...'.[16] Evans did 'create' a 'Minoan civilization' based on his own excavations (and imagination), but how much of it is indicative of the real Bronze Age Cretan civilization is a matter still under dispute.

Evans did not limit his excavations to Knossos but his work there was paramount to anything else on the island, hence the use of an enormous amount of his own money on the site. The American archaeologist Richard Seager had visited Evans in Oxford and was somewhat annoyed that Evans judged all Crete from Knossos.[17] Seager had been making great headway with excavations at Gournia with fellow American Harriett Boyd Hawes and with his own excavations at Mochlos shortly afterwards.[18] He obviously considered that Evans was receiving all the 'limelight' for the discovery of Knossos and this was out of proportion to the many other sites appearing around the island at the time due to the work of others.

Admittedly the full consequences of the Cretan myth of King Minos were not made apparent until Evans excavated Knossos in 1900 and opened up the Bronze Age world of the Minoans. However, Pococke, Pashley and Spratt had been there before him and tantalized academics with references to this world for which Evans was to later revel in. Interestingly, Sir John Evans (father of Sir Arthur), in his address to the Royal Archaeological Institute in 1891, referred to the immense advances made within the last quarter of a century, particularly by Heinrich Schliemann

---

[10] Herodotus (c.450 BC) told us that the Trojan War was not more than 800 years before his own time (*Histories*, 2.145).
[11] Dawkins, 1930: 13.
[12] Papadopoulos, 2005: 96.
[13] Bennet, 2002: 214.
[14] Hamilakis, 2002: 2.

[15] Frazer, 1898: 146.
[16] Hitchcock & Koudounaris, 2000: 42.
[17] From a letter from Seager to Gisela Richter, 9th January 1916 (in Becker & Betancourt, 1997: 149).
[18] Boyd Hawes, 1908, on Gournia and Seager, 1912, on Mochlos.

at Troy and Mycenae, his own Hellenic Society and the explorers of Cyprus,[19] but made no specific mention of the work of Pococke, Pashley or Spratt. This was an uninformed or simply a neglectful omission.

In 1909 Edith Hall remarked, 'Ten years ago, when the island was *first* opened to scholars [by Evans], the most promising sites, like that of Knossos palace, were already known from reports of peasants and the notices of travellers (added italics).'[20] Assumingly she was referring to the ability to visit and excavate sites once free of Ottoman rule, but arguably Pococke 170 years previously 'first' opened the island to scholars if they had taken an interest. Professor Peter Warren suggested Pococke was the first to establish 'the tradition of learned exploration'.[21] Certainly Pashley's book, published 75 years before Hall's comment, was a scholarly work, as was Spratt's book, published over 40 years before Hall's comment.

Professor Bennet was of the view that Minoan archaeology was 'born in the year 1900 … One hundred years ago it scarcely existed. Evans' excavations at *tou Tselevi I Kafala* [Knossos] inaugurated the field…'.[22] The name 'Minoan' may have been 'born' (see chapter 2) and 'One hundred Years ago' the archaeology may have 'scarcely' existed, but due to the work of earlier travellers it did exist. Again, Evans' work 'inaugurated the field' only in so much as it put the ancient archaeology of Crete into the public eye for the first time and his publications certainly led the way for defining the nature of the civilization.

Archaeologists, antiquarians or historians?

Archaeology as a social science had certainly taken root by the middle of the 19th century even if it had not developed into an education until the 20th century. But did Pococke, Pashley and Spratt fit into this archaeological category? It may be argued that these early travellers were not investigators and therefore not archaeologists at all. They were simply amateur antiquarians whose 'techniques' detracted from the true purpose of archaeology. This would be unfair because they were investigating and recording sites, even though not by today's standards. The same could apply to 19th century 'enthusiasts'. Can Pococke, Pashley and Spratt be accused of amateurism? They were certainly professionals in their own right, and new interests and a skill in them can be attained from outside those of one's own speciality.

Yet treasure seekers they were not. Pashley in his own words admitted this when being told of possible buried 'statutes' and 'idols' at Kutri or Phalasarna, northwest Crete, which he accepted with great scepticism and reluctance:

Captain Manias [Pashley's guide], whose antiquarian zeal shews itself daily in the

alacrity and indefatigableness with which he aids me in making inquiries for ancient remains, and for coins or other antiquities, is very anxious that I should not suffer all these hidden treasures to continue buried beneath the earth … At length, although the assertion that the "idols" are small and golden, makes me fear that it will end in nothing, for the form assumed by the story bears a slight resemblance to that of buried treasure, which, of course, no European in his sense would ever search for …[23]

John Pendlebury remarked of Pashley's and Spratt's books:

For Crete Pashley and Spratt are both good reading and excellent companions. They are, however, more in the nature of an archaeological survey of the island. Nor do they give many details of their routes. They lived in the times when there were fresh trails to blaze; fresh identifications of famous sites to make.[24]

An 'archaeological survey', even if not excavation, is still part of the archaeologist's remit, and coming from someone such as Pendlebury the comment is revealing with regard to a positive view of the two as archaeologists. Also, the 'famous sites' to which he referred would most likely have been of the Bronze Age, his specific interest in Crete.

Pashley and Spratt were of an era when archaeology was still under definition. Their purpose was not commercially motivated but inspired by the ideal of knowledge. At that time historians did not appear to be particularly concerned with anything of the pre-historic era, nor in physically searching out the truth. It required another 'group' to embark upon such investigation. This group was the antiquarians whose members, by the very nature of their investigation, became archaeologists, as did Pashley and Spratt.

As far as discovery is concerned, it really does not matter what Pococke, Pashley and Spratt were called when they travelled Crete, as labels are misleading. Labelling individuals as archaeologists does not necessarily give them the full rights/qualifications as discoverers of ancient pasts. Evans' work in Crete made him into an archaeologist, but prior to that he had been a journalist/correspondent to the *Manchester Guardian*, and he went to the island with no previous archaeological 'qualifications' other than a keen eye and yearning for knowledge. Likewise with Schliemann who had been a highly successful trader prior to his discovery of the Bronze Age of Mycenae and Tiryns on the mainland of Greece and Troy in Turkey.

---

[19] Evans, 1891: 10.
[20] Hall, 1909: 779.
[21] Warren, 1972a: 80.
[22] Bennet, 2002: 214.

[23] Psh II: 76 (see also 'Dr Schliemann in Crete' below), although Pashley agreed to the excavation to appease his host, nothing was found.
[24] Pendlebury, 1948: chapter on 'Travelling hints', 3-4 (this was printed for limited private circulation).

Contribution to the discovery of Crete's Bronze Age past

As mentioned in chapter 12, during the 19th century the historian George Grote had insisted on Greek history beginning in 776 BC.[25] This date was based on the first writing of ancient Greek by way of the first recorded Olympic Games. Clearly Pashley and Spratt were not of this view due to their many references in Crete to early architecture, ante-Homeric periods, times of Minos and other such factors previously referred to in this work. This was of course before Sir Arthur Evans.

On a comparable note it has been argued that it was not Schliemann who discovered the Bronze Age of mainland Greece but Christos Tsountas, and that it is he (Tsountas) who 'properly deserves the title Father of Greek Bronze Age …'.[26] Certainly Tsountas carried out important and extensive excavations at Mycenae shortly after Schliemann (between 1884-1902),[27] and, unlike Schliemann, he was able to relate proper chronology to the site. Schliemann may have been an adventurer, a charlatan and even a liar[28] but his travels and enthusiasm certainly led to the discovery of the Bronze Age of 'Greece' and Troy,[29] even if he was unable to date sites with any accuracy at the time. Accordingly he must be given some credit, even though, like Pococke, Pashley and Spratt, he had no idea what he was looking at. Dating, actual excavation and even correct identification are not the only issues, as the groundwork or legwork that leads to the discovery is also an important contribution.

Pashley and Spratt were recognized by the press in the United States of America in 1881:

> DR. SCHLIEMANN IN CRETE
> From the Pall Mall Gazette
> Dr Schliemann is expected to be in Crete by April. The harvest ought to be plenteous in a field which has lain fallow so long for want of laborers. There have been two English explorers of modern days – Robert Pashley, a Fellow of Trinity, Cambridge, in 1834, and Admiral Spratt, in 1851-65. Pashley, who is exemplary as a travelling scholar, judicious, business-like, and modest, was only an occasional excavator. Once he excavated under pressure of his Cretan guide who was suspicious of "a buried treasure, which, of course, no European in his sense would ever search for." Admiral Spratt, who was [a] surveyor for the Admiralty charts, shows more versatility and vivacity than scientific scholarship. He seems to have made a rule of keeping to the surface…[30]

Pashley and Spratt have not been totally ignored in Great Britain. One of the most eminent investigators of the Minoans, Sinclair Hood, said, 'During the nineteenth century the sites of the Greek and Roman cities [of Crete] were successfully identified by two Englishmen, Robert Pashley … and Captain (later Admiral) Spratt, commanding HMS Spitfire.'[31] This is, in itself, testament to their contribution to the archaeological research of the island, although admittedly not necessarily to the Bronze Age. It does not matter that these travellers were unaware of the dating of the site, and to quote Mee regarding Alfred Biliotti in Rhodes:

> It could be said that Mycenean [sic] archaeology began, not in 1876 with Schliemann's discoveries at Mycenae, but in 1868 when Sir Alfred Biliotti excavated the first Mycenean chamber tombs on the hill of Moshou Vunar below the acropolis of Ialysos. His achievement would have been the more remarkable had he not thought that the tombs were Archaic [c.750-480 BC].[32]

This could also apply to Pashley and Spratt with regard to the Bronze Age archaeology of Crete.

As a final testimony to support the argument, reference is made to a recent comment by the Cretan archaeologist Dr Eleni Hatzaki, whose 'later systematic work' must mean (or certainly include) the Bronze Age 'Minoans' by Evans and his successors:

> British interest in Crete can be traced long before the establishment of the BSA [British School at Athens, in 1886] and is rooted in the tradition of British and Irish early travellers. Robert Pashley and Thomas Abel Brimage Spratt, whose work exhibits a strong interest in ancient topography and archaeology … can be viewed as the forerunners of later systematic work on the island.[33]

---

[25] Grote, 1846-56.
[26] Gere, 2006: 96.
[27] See Tsountas & Mannat, 1897.
[28] See Traill, 1995.
[29] Although it was the Englishman, Frank Calvert, who first identified the site of Hissarlick as possibly Troy, but he has received little credit (see Allen, 1999).

[30] Printed in *The New York Times*, 27th March 1881.
[31] Hood, 1971: 12.
[32] Mee, 1982: 1.
[33] Hatzaki, 2005: 69.

14. Summary and Conclusion

Summary
Terminology
Since the time of Strabo (63/64 BC–AD 24) and Pausanias (2nd century AD) the term 'Cyclopean' has been used in reference to the large walls of the Bronze Age of mainland Mycenae and Tiryns. It is no coincidence that both Pashley and Spratt used this term to describe the early architecture of Crete seen by them. The fact that they were unable to put an exact date to this style of walling does not detract from their belief in it being earlier than the Classical 'Hellenic' period of the 5th century BC.

Difficulties have arisen throughout this research as to what Pashley in particular may have been describing as 'Cyclopean'. Was it Bronze Age, Archaic or even Hellenistic? It would appear certainly pre-Classical. Pashley also referred to the pre-Classical period as 'crude' or 'rude' or 'high antiquity', and also used the term 'cyclopean' but he did confuse matters by referring to a 'first and second cyclopean' style without explaining what he actually meant. He also used the term 'ante-Homeric' (before Homer) and he had a timescale for Homer of around three thousand years ago - the Bronze Age period about which Homer was composing.

Both Pashley and Spratt used the term 'Hellenic' for anything that they believed to be of the more refined Classical and Hellenistic periods, and what they considered earlier, but with no specific date, was Homer's 'Cyclopean' world, to be labelled the Bronze Age by later scholars.

Pococke
Pococke's contribution was very small and this is really reflected in his motive for travelling to the island. He has been credited with geographical information by the 19th century traveller James Augustus St John, but criticized for inaccurate information by the 20th century archaeologist, John Pendlebury. However, in his favour he did find the cave on Mount Ida and the port of Amnissos, both identified at a later date to be of the Bronze Age. He even referred to Amnissos as a port in the time of Minos. This recognition of the possible historical acceptance of Minos was raised again with his comment that Knossos was famous as the residence of King Minos. He did not say when this might have been but it implies his belief in the existence of an early civilization under Minos.

So Pococke's contribution to Crete's archaeological heritage should be accepted as limited but not non-existent.

His references cannot be ignored totally without some consideration by him of a possible belief in a period earlier than the Classical in the island's ancient history.

Pashley
Pashley became involved in the discovery of ancient Crete by way of the naval hydrographer Francis Beaufort. The latter was determined to investigate the antiquities of the island, if not directly by visiting the place himself, then through others. One of these 'others' was Pashley. Beaufort's letters indicate a keenness for such investigation and he made it clear to Captain Richard Copland of HMS *Beacon* that Pashley was to be given every assistance and encouragement in his investigations of this ancient land.

However, Pashley did not need much encouragement as he was already keen to search the island's past. From a letter to Beaufort, Pashley stated that he had a belief in a society in Crete in a time before Troy and therefore he must have had some notion of a timescale prior to the Classical era.

His travels were reasonably extensive and he was certainly intent upon discovering the whereabouts of as many ancient cities as he could. This he achieved and so it must be concluded that he came upon sites of the Bronze Age, even if he was not aware of their actual dating. His reference to the walls of Aptera being similar to the Cyclopean walls of Bronze Age Tiryns is an indication of a belief that the two places were of similar age, regardless as to how old the walls of Aptera actually were. Again, this is a belief in an earlier age prior to the Classical.

In the first volume of his book he came upon the Melidoni cave which has subsequently been identified as of the Bronze Age, and Pashley investigated it in some detail and even had a 'room' in the cave named after him. He also came across Axos, south of the Melidoni cave, which has Bronze Age origins. The same must apply to the Bronze Age site of Tylissos (see Appendix C for full list of sites).

Knossos itself must be disregarded as one of Pashley's discoveries as it was well known as being of ancient origin prior to his arrival. What is more important is his reference to the dancing youths he saw who were preserving the city's chorus, he said, of *three thousand years ago*. This must be evidence of a belief in a civilization those many years ago. He then came upon the Bronze Age mount of Iouktas which he described as having massive walls of his early *first cyclopean style*. This is a comparison with his later *second cyclopean style* of the Classical period. None of the locals knew anything about this site and so Pashley may be regarded as having discovered it himself.

In the second volume of his travels, Pashley visited Phalasarna, another site that was to prove to be of the Bronze Age. Further south he discovered and drew some very interesting walls at places such as Elyros, Hyrtakina, Khadros, Vlithia and Kalymides. These were very similar in style to the rough cut of the Bronze Age. However, the sites themselves appear to have been identified by modern scholars as existing between the Archaic and Hellenistic periods. The former is still pre-Classical, and Khadros (Kantanos) was possibly occupied in the Bronze Age period as may be seen by its mention in Linear B. It is certainly not clear that the walls Pashley drew have ever been seen in the 20th or 21st centuries, and so identification of their age cannot be confirmed one way or the other for certain.

Pashley's emphasis on Cyclopean walls, his *first style*, and his references to pre/ante-Homeric, are recognition of an earlier activity to the Classical era. Whether or not he was correct in these recognitions, and whether or not what he saw was actually of the Bronze Age is immaterial. The point is that he believed in them and that these references result in a belief in an earlier civilization which may well have been the Bronze Age.

Spratt

Spratt's involvement in the antiquities of Crete came about through his work as a Royal Naval hydrographer. His keenness to understand the Cretan landscape was as a result of advice from his former captain, Thomas Graves, to survey the land adjacent to the sea he intended to chart. This led to a study of the ancient sites of the island. He already had an interest in the ancient world which can be seen from his published travels in Turkey seeking out ancient Troy and his tour of Lycia.

Spratt finding 'his Cretan gems' and identifying them as being similar to those found by Heinrich Schliemann at Bronze Age Mycenae is of interest, particularly as he referred to them as 'archaic' rather than Classical. I suggest that in the 19th century the term Archaic was more of a generic reference to a non-specific age that was simply earlier than the then known Classical period rather than a specific reference to 750-480 BC, as is excepted today.

Spratt made it clear at the commencement of volume I of his travel book that he had intended to collect information about the ancient cities of Crete. Some of their relics, Spratt believed, would go back thirty centuries (the Bronze Age). He began, as had Pococke, by recognizing Amnissos as a port to ancient Knossos and the port was of the Bronze Age. Although there was very little to see at Knossos, he did have a belief in the existence of the labyrinth and compared the catacombs at Makryteichos (nearby to Knossos) with the Gortyns labyrinth which he linked with Minos by querying

whether was it was 'originally or subsequently to Minos'. As this mythical king is clearly not part of Classical ancient history, Spratt must have been thinking of an early civilization to which Minos had been a part. Spratt also recognized several cites such as Lyttos, Lycastus, Gortyna and Phaistos, all of which he said belonged to the period of Minos, and which have all now been identified as being of the Bronze Age.

As with Pashley, Spratt identified two different styles of architecture in Cyclopean and Hellenic. He compared these two styles at Smari which has both Bronze Age and Hellenistic connections. As can be seen from the gazetteer (Appendix C), Spratt visited many sites referred to in his first volume that have since been dated to the Bronze Age. In particular, Malia and Kato Zakros, both of which he has been credited with discovering by the renowned Cretan archaeologists, Adonis Vasilakis and Nicholas Platon respectively.

In volume II of his travels Spratt visited Phaistos which he believed to have been founded by Minos. It has since turned out to be one of the major Bronze Age 'palace' sites. Although the remains of Gortyns were predominantly Roman when Spratt was there, the city does have Bronze Age origins and the same may apply to the Labyrinth just beyond the city of Gortyns which intrigued Spratt (see below). He went in search of Tylissos and Axos, both of which have important Bronze Age links. At the latter he found cyclopean walling of 'a rude and early age' and terracing typical of the Bronze Age. He then followed Pashley's route to the western end of the island where his potential Bronze Age discoveries were a little limited.

Although not a scholar like Pococke and Pashley, Spratt had researched his ancient authors and his references to the works of the 16th century Venetian physician, traveller and artist Onorio Belli show that he had prepared for his investigation of the island and its ancient sites.

His interest in Darwin's theories may imply a realization of the possibility of an earlier pre-Classical history in Crete, so much so that he felt the need to write to Darwin on the subject. Clearly Spratt was not limiting his thoughts to the Classical era as being the first period of time that Crete was inhabited. His various references to Minos and cyclopean walls bear witness to this but he remains in the shadows of contributors to the history of the island's archaeology. His contemporary and fellow traveller Colonel William Leake recognized his true worth and wrote to Roderick Murchison, the President of the Royal Geographical Society, accordingly. Since then very little has been written about Spratt and his discoveries.

The Labyrinth

Spratt's fascination with the labyrinth at Gortyns makes it a topic worth investigating, particularly as Spratt was convinced it was the work of King Minos' architect, Daedalus. Yet again, this is an indication of a belief in an early period, albeit one linked to mythology. In this respect it does not really matter that the date of the construction of the 'labyrinthian' cave at Gortyns cannot be established. The fact that it has been a tourist spot for many other inquisitive travellers over the centuries merely adds to its intrigue, if not to its true purpose. It certainly fits the myth if one wished to believe in the existence of an early civilization of Minos.

Other travellers

The most important factor of other travellers during the 19th century is the recognition of those visiting mainland Greece of the dating of the mainland Bronze Age sites of Mycenae and Tiryns. Gell, Dodwell and Leake are important for this purpose. If their fairly accurate dating could be recognized by them, then such dates could have been in the minds of Pashley and Spratt when they were looking at some of the cyclopean walls in Crete. They both must have been aware of these travellers writings and so why they did not refer to this early dating is not clear other than their simply being unsure. However, emphasis must be given to the fact that lack of knowledge of a site's dating should not preclude credit for its discovery.

Conclusion

Conclusions can be based on matters of opinion, interpretation or fact. In this work fact has been a little difficult to come by. It was hoped that some of the walls seen by Pashley and Spratt in Crete would still have been clearly visibly identifiable and have proved to be obviously of the Bronze Age. Time and the elements have prevented this to be the clear case with many of their sightings.

Following Pococke's, Pashley's and Spratt's footsteps around the island was of immense value in bringing their journals to life. Unfortunately most of what does remain of the ancient sites that they saw is mainly identifiable as belonging to the later Hellenistic period of the 4th century BC. However, all three of them certainly visited sites with Bronze Age origins and some of the Bronze Age remnants of walling which can still be seen today could represent what was found by them.

The architecture of Classic/Hellenistic Crete clearly differed from that of its Bronze Age. Pashley and Spratt talked of two different styles of architecture as seen by them and they identified the Classical/Hellenistic as Hellenic but referred to another style – 'Cyclopean'. This style was of an earlier period and was possibly evidence of the buildings of the Mycenaean and Minoan Bronze Age.

Pococke, Pashley and Spratt were initially travel writers, but they were also important as historical recorders. They recorded a landscape that has long since disappeared under modern advancement. They recorded what may not be seen today other than what has survived through natural consequences or from excavations. Such records included the exploration and investigation of ancient sites. Unlike Evans, the fact that they were not specifically searching for an ancient civilization does not detract from the importance of any of their potential Bronze Age finds. Nor does it matter that they were unable to identify them as such. Evans found Greek sealstones by chance in a 'flea' market in Athens, but was unable to understand what they meant other than that they were a form of early hitherto unknown writing. Nor was he able to say exactly how old they were, and he was not the only scholar to collect them. Even so he is still credited with their discovery, and rightly so.

Without doubt Pococke, Pashley and Spratt were essential to the development of the archaeology of Crete, yet they have been practically ignored (with the occasional brief exception) even as antiquaries. Research usually involves a certain amount of speculation, but these three individuals did 'brush shoulders' with the ancient Cretan world of around the 2nd millennium BC, yet their names are virtually unknown outside the academic world of travellers.

Sir Arthur Evans may rest easy with regard to his remarkable achievements in relation to the discovery of the 'Minoan' Civilization as his work has certainly had the most impact. However, it is clear that Pashley and Spratt, and to some extent Pococke, have contributed to the discovery of the island's Bronze Age, or at least pre-Classical, archaeological heritage and they should be recognized within their rightful place in the history of the archaeology of Crete.

APPENDIX A

Maps

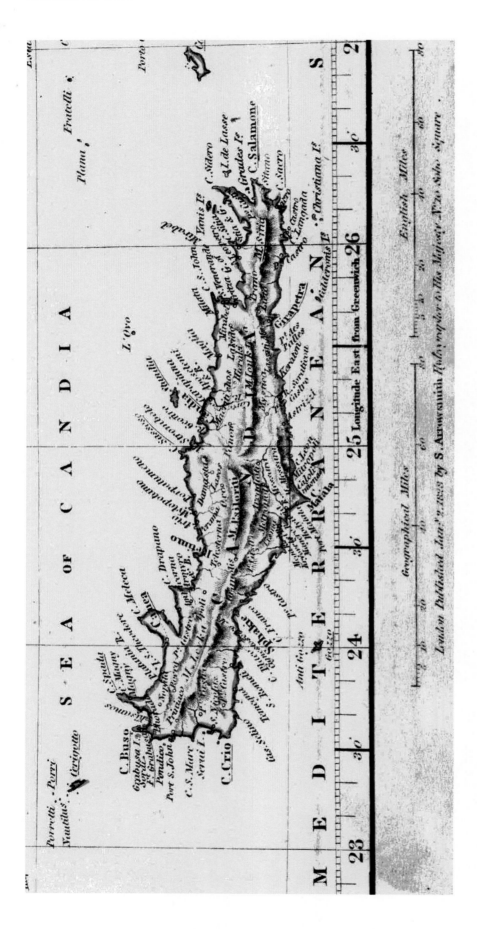

Map 1: Arrowsmith's map of Crete (1828) – available to both Pashley and Spratt (although Spratt would have had the advantage of Pashley's observations)

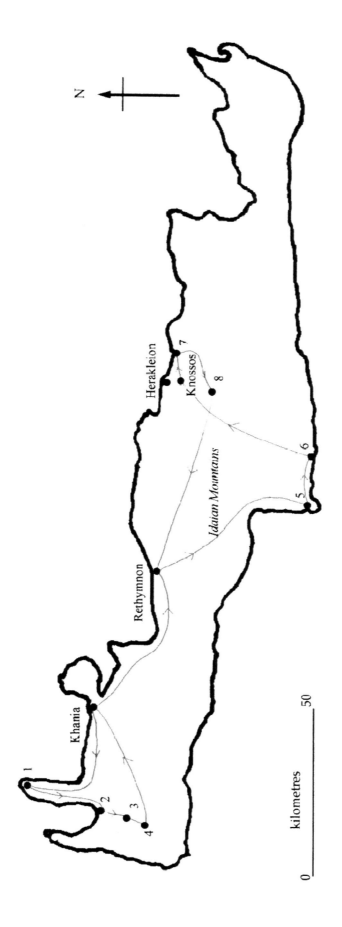

Map 2: Ancient Sites (referred to in text) visited by Pococke

Key (arrowed travel lines are not representative of exact route travelled by Pococke but simply directional guidelines):

1. Cape Spada/Dyctnnaeon; 2. Kisamos; 3. Aptera (Pococke's); 4. Artacina; 5. Matala (Pococke's); 6. Lasea; 7. Amnisso(s); 8. Iouktas

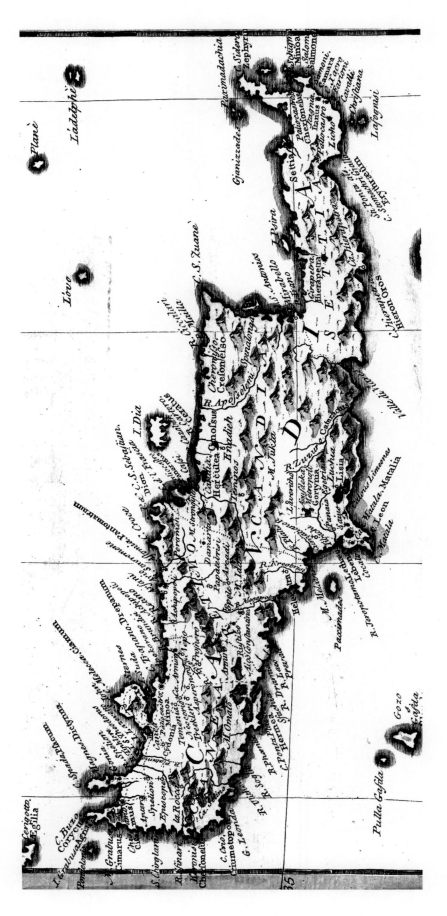

Map 3: Pococke's map (Pococke, 1745: 236-237)

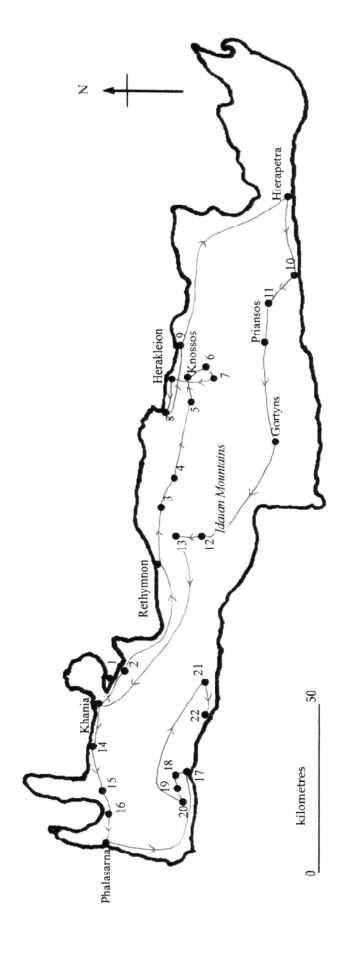

Map 4: Ancient Sites (referred to in text) visited by Pashley

Key (arrowed travel lines are not representative of exact route travelled by Pashley but simply directional guidelines):

1. Sudha Bay; 2. Aptera; 3. Melidoni Cave; 4. Axos; 5. Tylissos; 6. Iouktas; 7. Khani Kasteli; 8. Palaekastron (Cytaeum); 9. Amnissos; 10. Arvi; 11. Viannos; 12. Eleutherna; 13. Sybrita; 14. Gerani/Platanias/Pergamus; 15. Rocca; 16. Kisamos; 17. Lyssos; 18. Elyros; 19. Hrytakina; 20. Khadros/Vlithia; 21. Anopolis; 22. Tarrha

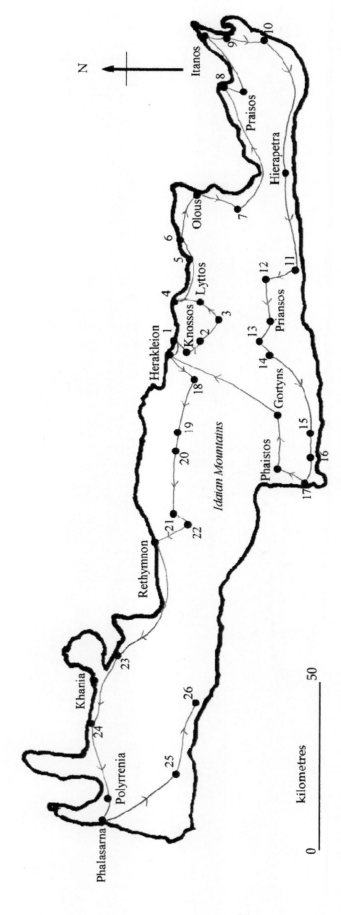

Map 5: Ancient Sites (referred to in text) visited by Spratt

Key (arrowed travel lines are not representative of exact route travelled by Spratt but simply directional guidelines):

1. Amnissos; 2. Iouktas; 3. Astritzi; 4. Khersonesos; 5. Malia; 6. Milatos; 7. Latos; 8. Sitia (Petras); 9. Palaikastro; 10. Kato Zakros; 11. Keraton; 12. Biennos/Inatos; 13. Stelae; 14. Rhyton; 15. Lebena; 16. Lisea; 17. Matala; 18. Tylissos; 19. Anoya; 20. Axos; 21. Eleutherna; 22. Sybrita; 23. Aptera; 24. Gerani/Platanias/Pergamus; 25. Hyrtakina; 26. Tarrha

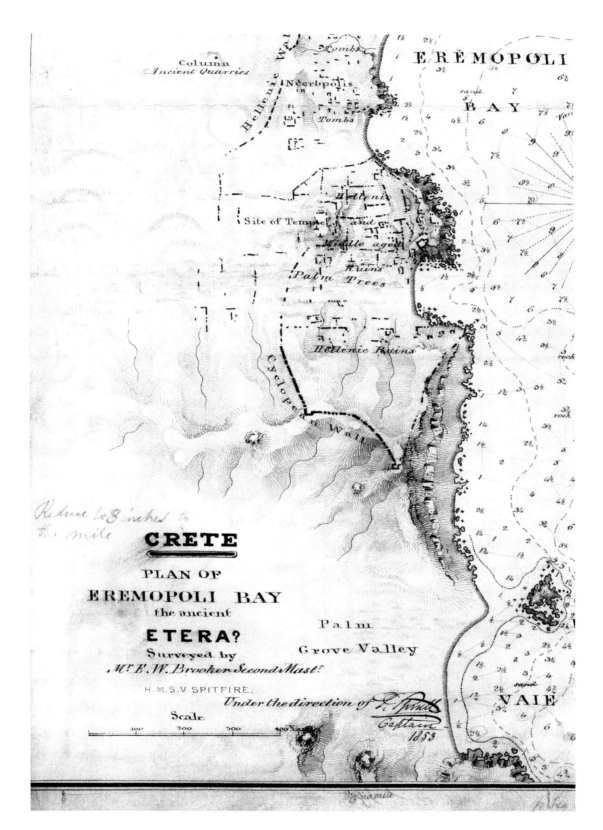

Map 6: Cyclopean Walls seen by Spratt at Eremopoli – signed by Spratt, 1853
(by kind permission of Hydrographic Office, Taunton, ref. D4070, Med Folio 2)

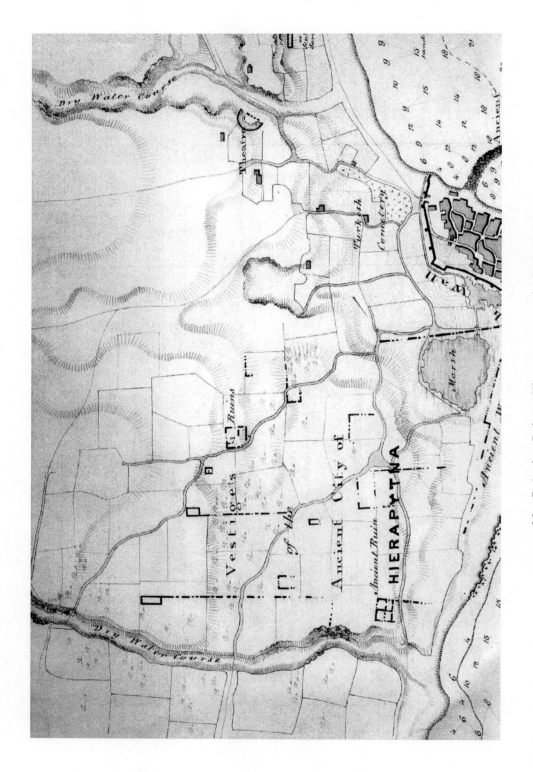

Map 7: Ancient Ruins at Hierapetra as seen by Spratt
(by kind permission of Hydrographic Office, Taunton, ref. D4069, SW)

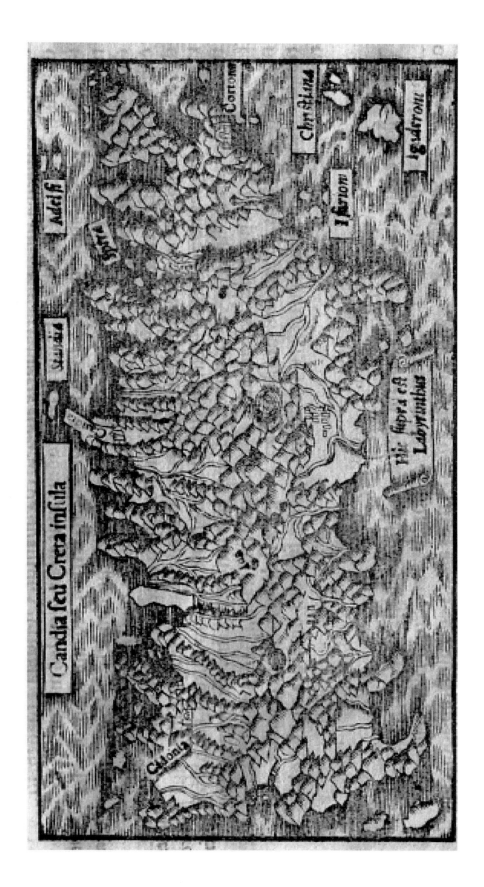

Map 8: 'Candia seu Creta Insula' (Crete), 1572, by Sebastian Muenster (1488-1552)
Hic supra est Labyrinthus (below centre): 'above here is the Labyrinth'
– looking at possibly Gortyns rather than Knossos

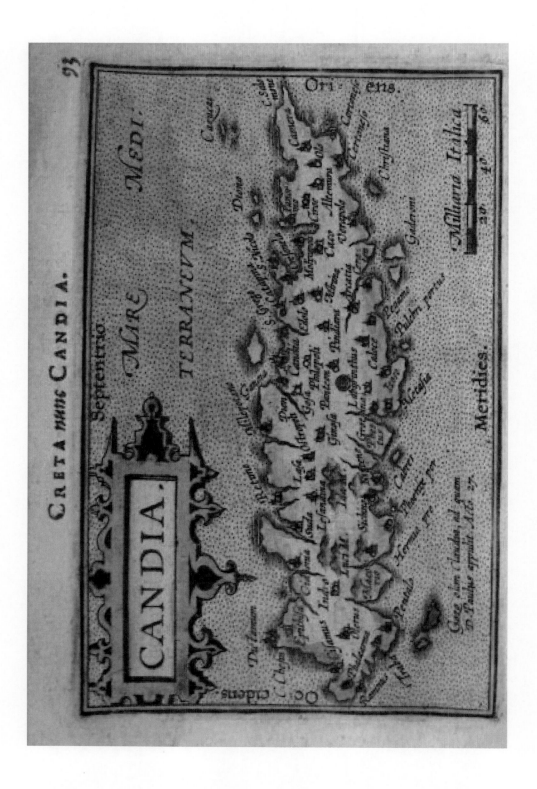

Map 9: Abraham Ortelius' map of 1570 with the labyrinth ('Labyrinthus' - centre) also nearer to Gortyns ('Grotina' - below left of 'Labyrinthus')

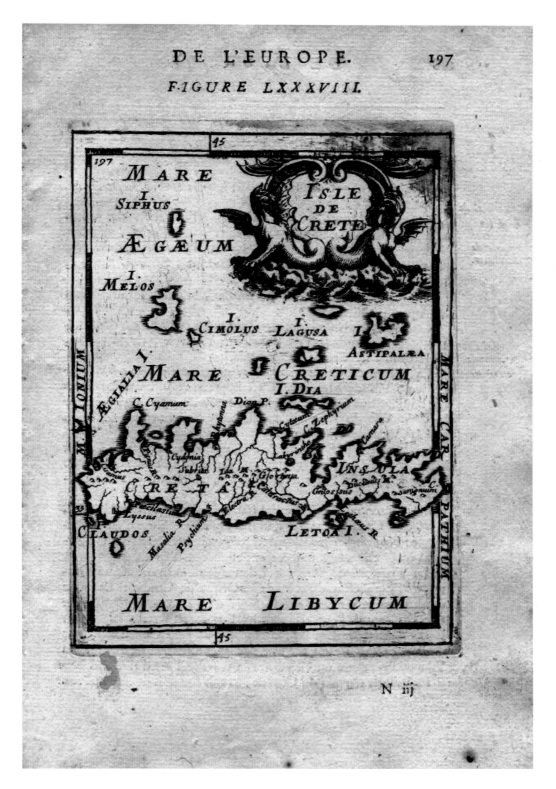

Map 10: Crete showing position of 'Labyrinth' at Knossos
(below 'Cytaeum' – centre north)
(Mallet, 1683, Vol. 4: 197)

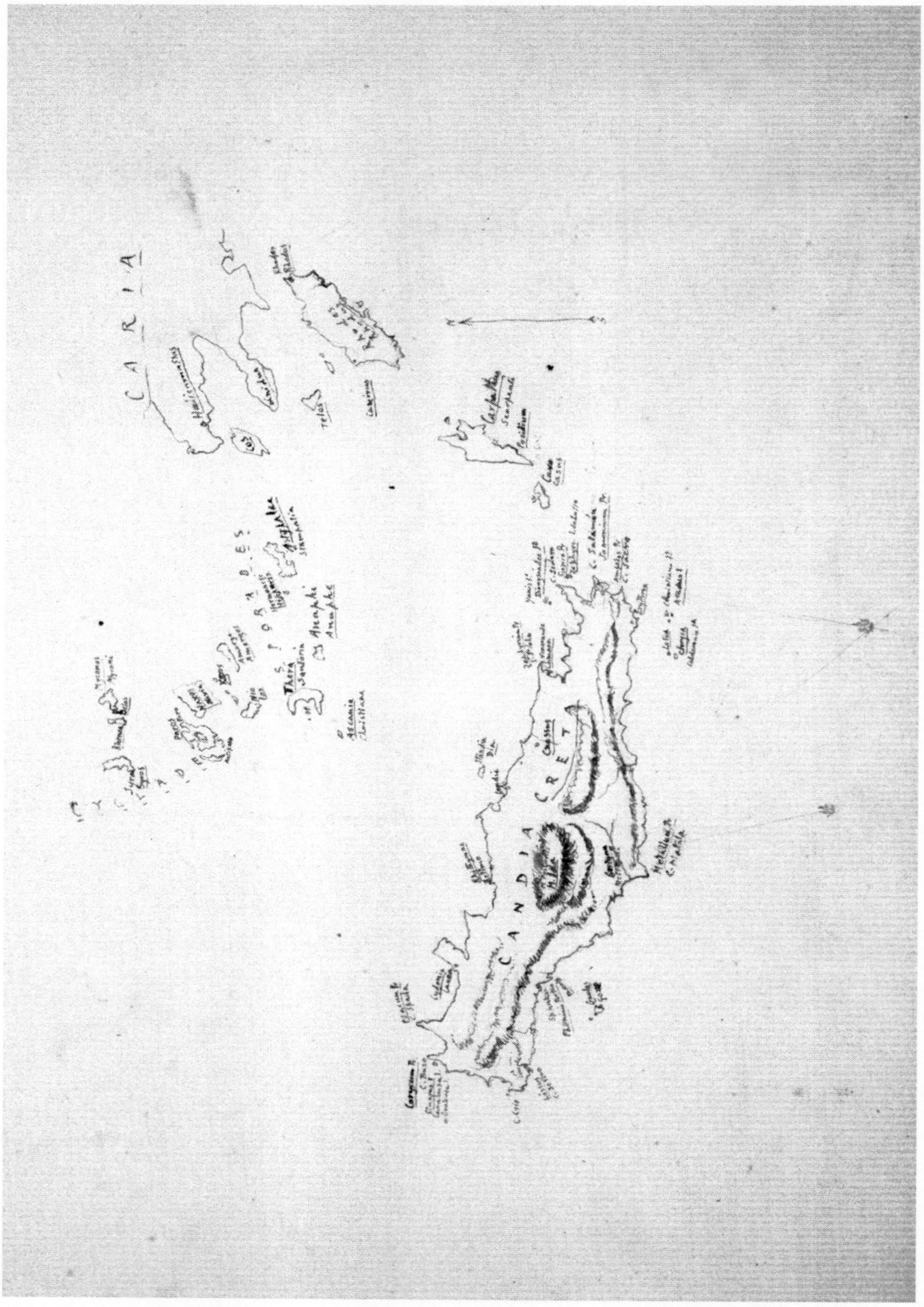

Map 11: Drawing of Crete by John Gardner Wilkinson, *c.*1833
(by kind permission of the National Trust, Bodleian Library/Gardner-Wilkinson Collection, dep a.2. fol 48v)

APPENDIX B

Figures

1. Introduction

Fig. 1.1: Person (5'2") shows scale of larger 'Cyclopean' stones at Mycenae's Lion Gate (photo: D. Moore (hereafter DM), 2006)

Fig. 1.2: 'Cyclopean' wall at 13th century BC Tiryns, mainland Greece – main stones filled with smaller ones (person represents scale) (photo: S. Green, 2005)

Fig. 1.3: 'Cyclopean' walls of the 13th century BC Treasury of Atreus at Mycenae (person represents scale) - stones are not representative of the largest but are still of 'Cyclopean' character even though not 'roughly hewn' (photo: DM, 2006)

Fig. 1.4: Compare, again large, but much neater and more uniform 5th century BC 'Hellenic' stones and columns of Classical Greece (highlighted by the lighter reconstructed ones) – the Erechtheum on the Acropolis at Athens (see people to right for scale) (photo: DM, 2005)

Figs. 1.5a and b (above and below): 'Cyclopean' wall blocks at the Minoan palace of Malia
(person represents scale) (photos: DM, 2006)

3. EARLY TRAVELLERS

Fig. 3.1: Cartoon about the 'Powers' intervention in Crete
(from *Punch, Or The London Charivari*, 6th March 1897)

Fig. 3.2: Cartoon about the 'Powers' intervention in Crete
(from *Punch, Or The London Charivari*, 13th March 1897)

4. RICHARD POCOCKE

Fig. 4.1: Pococke, *c.*1738-9, by Jean-Étienne Liotard
(by kind permission of the Musée d'Art et d'Histoire, Geneva)
In 1887, Kemp reported, 'There was an admirable whole length of Dr Pococke in Turkish dress, by Liotard, in the possession of Dean Milles of Exeter, his first cousin. It is not known where it is now'(1887: lx). In fact, it was reportedly sold by the family in 1947 for £577 and presented to a museum in Geneva (Hegarty, 1989: 30)

Fig. 4.2a: Entrance to Ideion Andron cave (person represents scale) (photo: DM, 2006)

Fig. 4.2b: Looking into the cave from the entrance (the truck rail line in the middle foreground gives an idea as to scale) (photo: DM, 2006)

6. ROBERT PASHLEY
Travels in Crete, Vol. I

AN EVENING IN A PEASANT'S COTTAGE.

Fig. 6.1: No image of Pashley has been located, but could this be a sketch of him (on right) in Crete from his own book? (Psh I: 306 – probably by his companion and illustrator, Antonio Schranz, but not acknowledged)

Fig. 6.2a: Aptera (Psh I: 38) - 'Their massiveness gives them almost as good a claim to admiration as those of Tiryns itself' (Psh I: 38)

Fig. 6.2b: 'Tiryns itself' (scale: the thickness of the entrance is 25 ft, approx. 8m)
(photo: DM, 2006)

Fig. 6.2c: Polygonal wall at Aptera today (person represents scale) – the 'massive' wall seen by Pashley perhaps? (photo: DM, 2007)

Fig. 6.2d: Continuation of the same wall (photo: DM, 2007)

Fig. 6.3a: Aptera (Psh I: 36) -'the ruins of Palaeokastron [Aptera] shew that its
establishment belongs to the very earliest period of civilisation'
(Psh I: 47) – in fact Hellenistic

Fig. 6.3b: Hellenistic ruins at Aptera – the ones seen by Pashley in Fig. 3a perhaps?
(photo: DM, 2007)

Fig. 6.4a: The Melidoni Cave entrance today (the pigeon inside the gateway gives an indication of scale) (photo: DM, 2006)

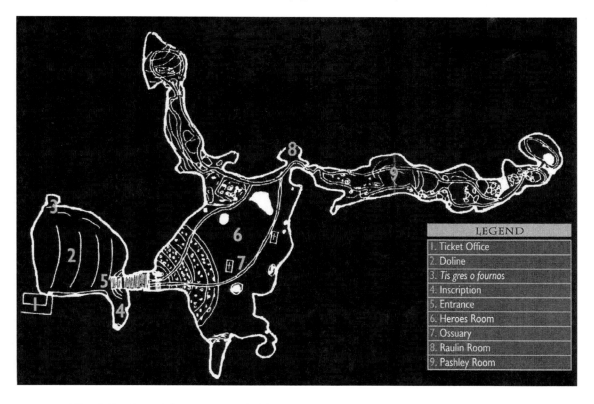

Fig. 6.4b: Plan of the cave (Gavrilaki, undated pamphlet) – note 9, 'Pashley's room', as discovered by him (but not open to the public today as too dangerous for access)

Fig. 6.4c: Drawing of the inside of the cave by Antonio Schranz, Pashley's illustrator (Psh I: opp. 136)

Fig. 6.4d: Inside the cave today – 'Heroes Room' with 'Ossuary' at foreground right
(6 and 7 respectively on the plan in Fig. 6.4b) (photo: DM, 2006)

Fig. 6.5: 'Cyclopean' walls of Iouktas peak sanctuary
(person represents scale) (photo: DM, 2005)

Fig. 6.6: Pashley's sketch of the ancient walls of Iouktas (by Schranz) (Psh I: 210)

- Altar

- Fissure

Fig. 6.7: Altar 'to Zeus' at Iouktas (4.7 m long, 50 cm high) with deep fissure (chasm) in the foreground (photo: DM, 2005)

Fig. 6.8 Two of the five rooms below the altar at Iouktas (looking east - town of Archanes below background) (photo: DM, 2005)

7. ROBERT PASHLEY
Travels in Crete, Vol. II

Fig. 7.1a: Pashley's drawing of the 'great chair' from Phalasarna (Psh II: opp. 64)
Scale: height of arms above seat is 2 ft, 11ins (Psh II: 64)

Fig. 7.1b: The 'Great chair', still in situ today (person represents scale)
(photo: DM, 2007)

Fig. 7.2: The 7th century BC (Archaic) 'curious compartment' (hearth?) at Kommos
(the 'seat' is only just above the ground and smaller than the above (Figs. 7.1a and b)
(photo: DM, 2005)

Fig. 7.3: Hyrtakina (Psh II: 111) - 'cyclopean masonry' and 'length of which is 11 ft 6 ins,
its height being 8 feet 6 inches' (Psh II: 112 and fn 1)

8. THOMAS SPRATT
The Traveller

ADMIRAL T.A.B. SPRATT. C.B. F.R.S. &c.

Fig. 8.1: Studio portrait of Vice-Admiral T.A.B. Spratt
(by kind permission of the Royal Geographical Society, ref. X195/021356)

109

Fig. 8.2: HMS *Spitfire* (by kind permission of the National Maritime Museum Greenwich, ref. C 1875, MTN/107)

Fig. 8.3: Flooded north-east annexe rooms of the palace of Kato Zakros in July (looking southeast) (photo: DM, 2005)

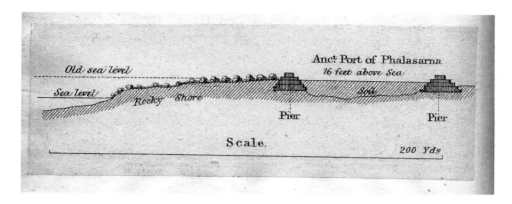

Fig. 8.4a: Spratt's plan of the Phalasarna harbour with old (pre-5th century AD)
and 19th century sea levels (Sp II: 232)

Fig. 8.4b: View to coast from the now 'inland' harbour at Phalasarna (photo: DM, 2007)

Fig. 8.5: Spratt's gems from Crete (Spratt, 1879: opp. 120;
now in the British Museum)

9. THOMAS SPRATT
Travels and Researches in Crete, Vol. I

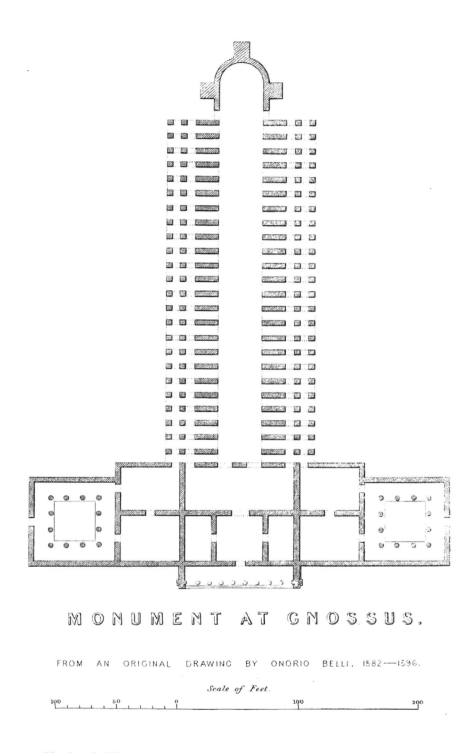

MONUMENT AT GNOSSUS.

FROM AN ORIGINAL DRAWING BY ONORIO BELLI, 1582—1596.

Scale of Feet.

Fig. 9.1: Belli's monument at Knossos 1582-96 (Falkener, 1854: opp. 24)

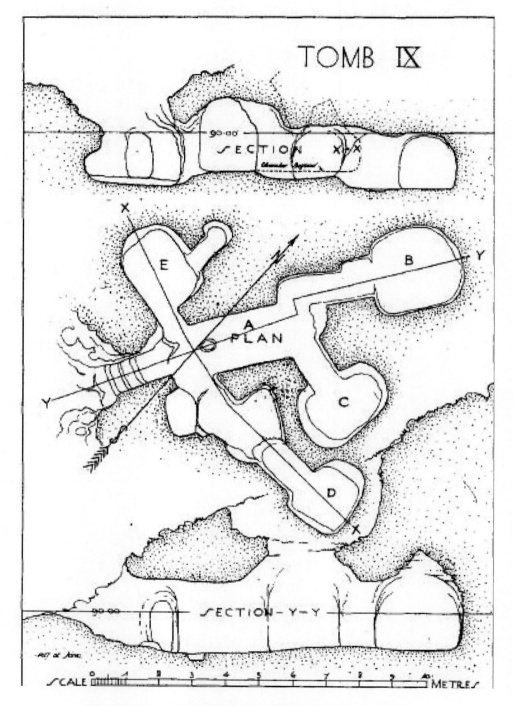

Fig. 9.2: Plan of 'labyrinthian' Tomb IX, from the cemetery
at Mavro Spelio(Forsdyke, 1927: 265)

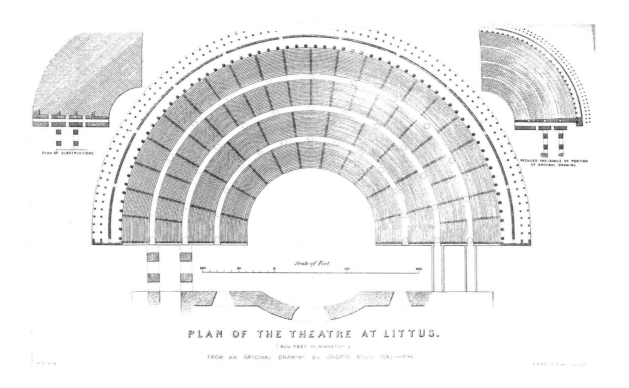

PLAN OF THE THEATRE AT LITTUS.

Fig. 9.3: Belli's theatre at Lyttus, 1582-96 (Falkener, 1854: opp.18)

Fig. 9.4: Khersonesos, the small chapel in the cave beneath the basilica – note the cave roof referred to by Spratt (photo: DM, 2005)

Fig. 9.5: Khersonesos, ruins of Basilica (looking northwest) with the mosaic remains in foreground (photo: DM, 2005)

Fig. 9.6: Khersonesos, tessellated fountain with four triangular sides – this side showing fish, seabirds and a fisherman (photo: DM, 2005)

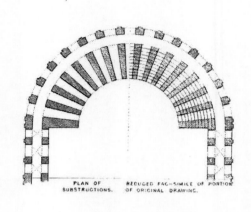

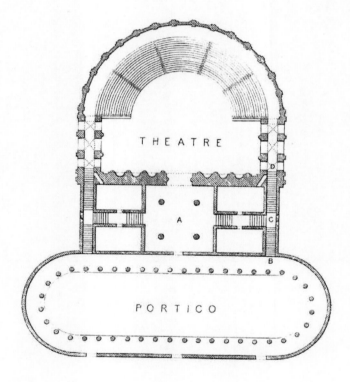

Fig. 9.7: Belli's 16th century plan of the theatre at Khersonesos, 1582-96, (Falkener, 1854: opp.16)

CYCLOPEAN HOUSE AT OLUS.

Fig. 9.8a: Spratt's 'Cyclopean' wall of 'Olus' (Lato) (Sp I: 141)

Fig. 9.8b: 'Cyclopean' walls of Lato (person represents scale) – wall to left similar
in style to Spratt's drawing above (photo: DM, 2005)

Fig. 9.9a: Narrow and high entrance to Lato (person represents scale) (photo: DM, 2005)

Fig. 9.9b: Compare similar narrow and high entrance and walling to Mycenaean Midea
on the mainland of Greece (photo: DM, 2004)

Fig. 9.10: 'Cyclopean walls' of Itanos 'ascending into the hills' - Spratt's Eremopoli/ancient Etra
(person represents scale) (photo: DM, 2005)

Fig. 9.11: Typical Minoan buildings of Palaikastro with the Spratt's 'flat-topped hill'
in the background (photo: DM, 2005)

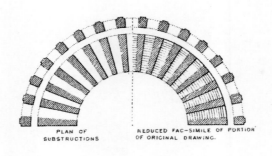

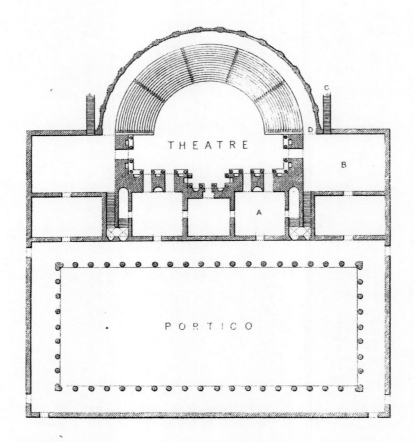

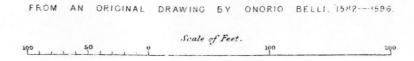

Fig. 9.12: Belli's smaller theatre at Hierapetra, 1582-96 (Falkener, 1854: opp. 12)

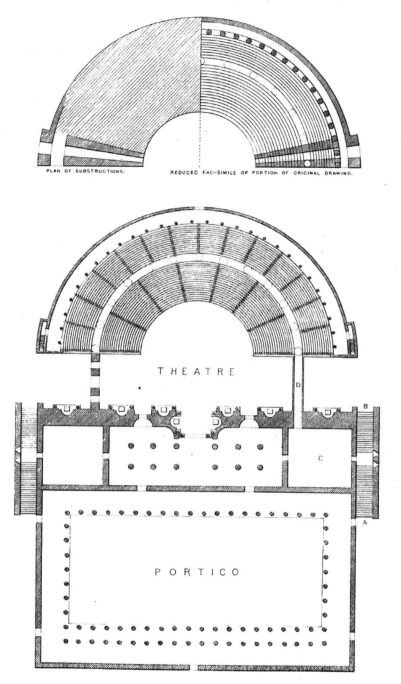

Fig. 9.13: Belli's larger theatre at Hierapetra, 1582-96
(Falkener, 1854: between 12 and 13)

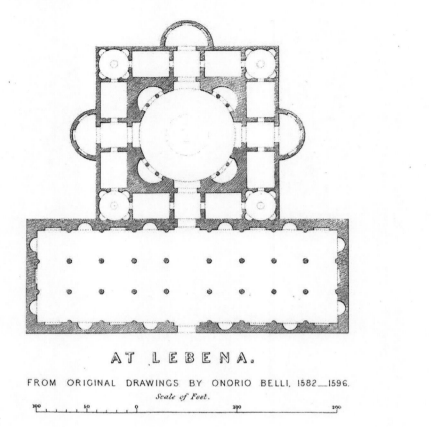

Fig. 9.14a: Belli's 'Temple of Aesculapis' at Lebena, 1582-96
(Falkener, 1854: between 18 and 9)

Fig. 9.14b: Remains of Hellenic Temple of Aesculapis (Asceplios)
at Lebena today (photo: DM, 2006)

10. THOMAS SPRATT
Travels and Researches in Crete, Vol. II

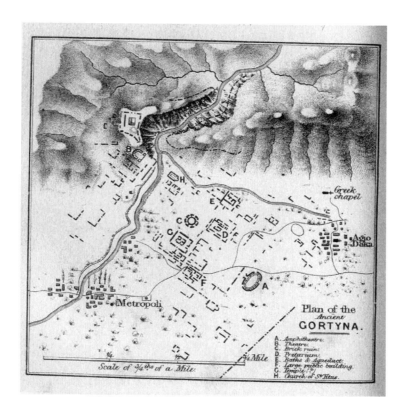

Fig. 10.1: Spratt's plan of city of Gortyns (Sp II: 28) - towards the top left is
Belli's larger theatre marked B (see Fig. 10.2 below)

Fig. 10.2: Spratt's drawing of the large theatre at Roman Gortyns (left)
– note the seating built into the hill – very little remains today; the
6th century AD ruins of the basilica of Ayios Titos is to the right (Sp II: 28)

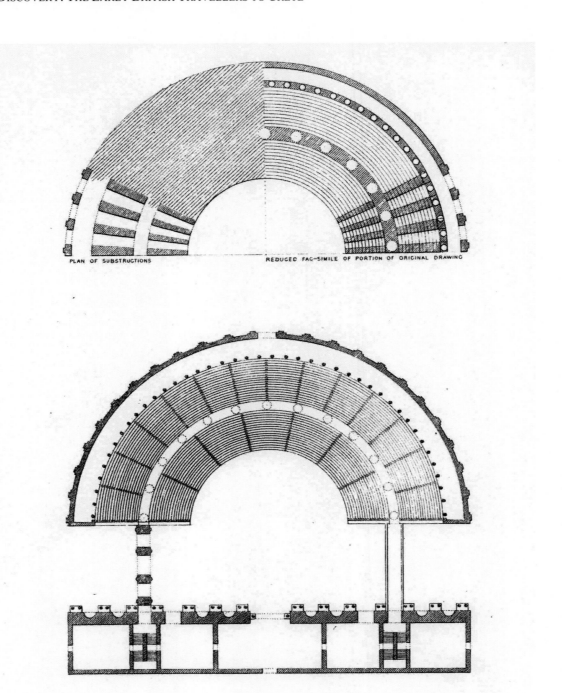

PLAN OF THE LARGER THEATRE AT GORTYNA.

FROM AN ORIGINAL DRAWING BY ONORIO BELLI. 1582---1596.

Scale of Feet.

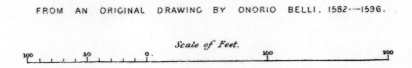

Fig. 10.3: Belli's larger theatre at Gortyns, 1582-96 (Falkener, 1854: between 20 and 21)

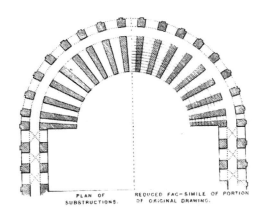

PLAN OF
SUBSTRUCTIONS.

REDUCED FAC-SIMILE OF PORTION
OF ORIGINAL DRAWING.

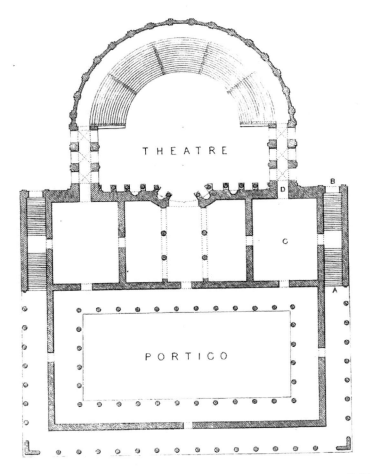

PLAN OF THE SMALLER THEATRE AT GORTYNA.

FROM AN ORIGINAL DRAWING BY ONORIC BELLI. 1582 —1596.

Scale of Feet.

Fig. 10.4: Belli's smaller theatre at Gortyns (Falkener, 1854: opp. 20),
not seen by Spratt

127

Fig. 10.5: The smaller theatre being excavated
(photo: DM, 2006)

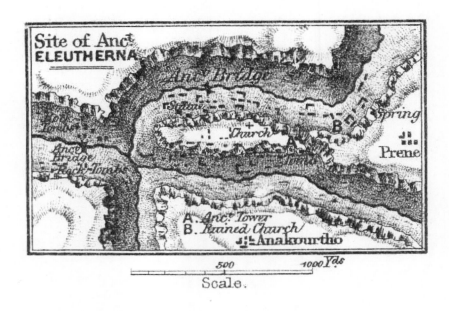

Fig. 10.6: Spratt's plan of Eleutherna (north to the left)
(ancient acropolis is the light area at centre incorporating '+ Church')
(Sp II: 90)

Fig. 10.7: Hellenistic part of the ancient acropolis at Eleutherna (person represents scale)
(photo: DM, 2006)

Fig. 10.8: The Medieval tower ('A' on Spratt's plan, Fig. 10.6 above) as Spratt
would have seen it in the 19th century (person represents scale) (photo: DM, 2006)

Fig. 10.9a: Cisterns at Eleutherna as seen by Spratt – below the acropolis
(person represents scale) (photo: DM, 2006)

Fig. 10.9b: Inside one of the large cisterns (person represents scale)
(photo: S. Green, 2006)

Fig. 10.10a: Spratt's drawing of the 'Hellenic' (Hellenistic) bridge (northwest side)
Eleutherna, Crete – rock tombs top left (Sp II: 95)

Fig. 10.10b: The bridge today (northwest side) – the circular arch drawn (and referred to)
by Spratt has been filled in (to the left) (person under main arch represents scale)
(photo: DM, 2007) - the rock tombs that Spratt referred to are up to
the left (see Fig. 10.11 below)

Fig. 10.10c: Clearer picture of the bridge from southeastern side (person represents scale)
(photo: S. Green, 2007)

Fig. 10.11: One of the rock tombs above the bridge referred to by Spratt
(photo: DM, 2007)

Fig. 10.12: Hellenistic wall of 'lagoon' at Phalasarna (person to right represents scale)
(photo: S. Green, 2007)

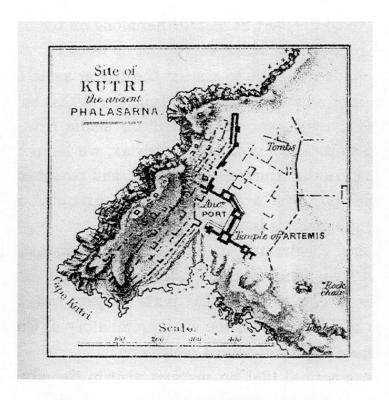

Fig. 10.13: Spratt's plan of Phalasarna (Sp II: 229)

Fig. 10.14: Spratt's drawing of the 'bema' (Sp II: 234) – marked bottom right in
Fig. 10.13 above (Pashley's 'great chair/throne' – see chapter 7 and Figs. 7.1a and b)

11. THE LABYRINTH

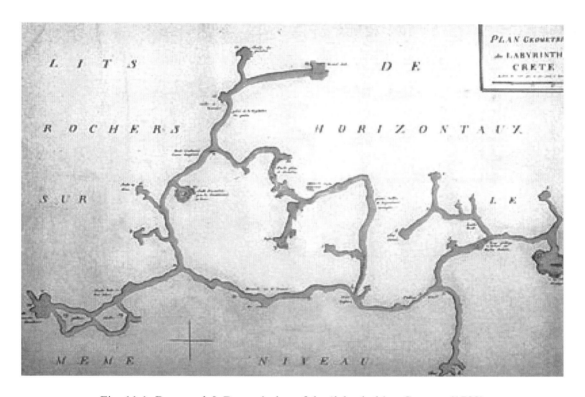

Fig. 11.1: Bonneval & Dumas' plan of the 'labyrinth' at Gortyns (1783)

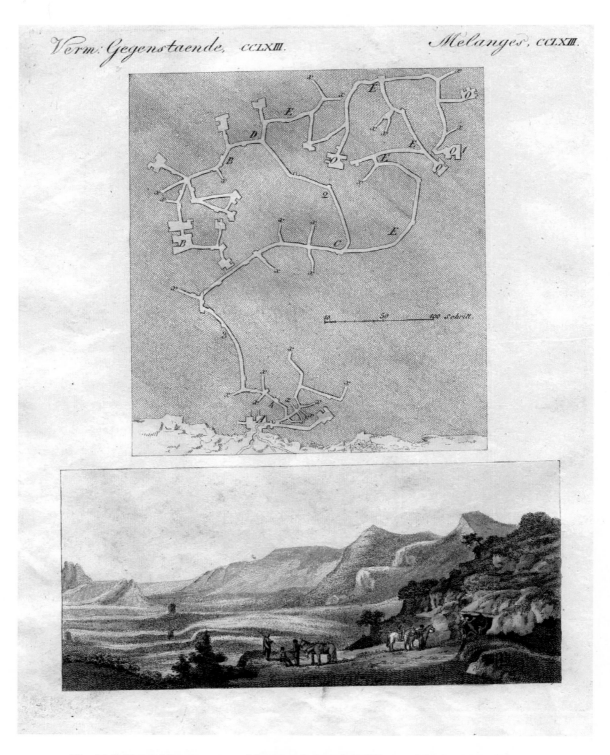

Fig. 11.2: Bertuch's engraving of the plan (somewhat different to Bonneval & Dumas')
and entrance of the 'labyrinth' at Gortyns (1821)

Fig. 11.3: Entrance to 'labyrinth' engraved by Etherington after a drawing by Therond,
from *Magasin Pittoresque* (1854)

Fig. 11.4: 17th century artist's impression of the maze/labyrinth at Knossos
(Mallet, 1683, Vol. 4: 205). Knossos is not mentioned in the text
to this figure, but see Map 13 (from the same book). In this plan the maze
appears to be in the centre of a river – probably the River Kairatos

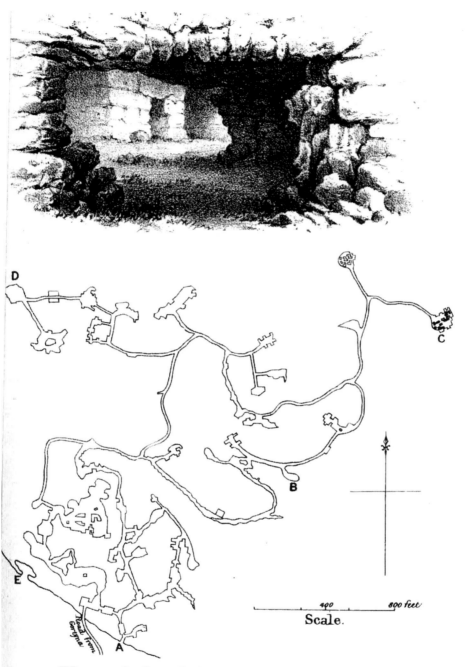

Plan of the Labyrinth of Gortyna.

A.B. *Entrances to the quarry, now filled up.*
C. *The corridor here is obstructed by blocks of stone and chips: an entrance must have existed in the vicinity.*
D. *A communication with the exterior must have existed here.*
E. *A small excavation by the side of principal entrance.*

Fig. 11.5: Spratt's drawing of the entrance to the 'labyrinth' and Sieber's plan (different again to Bonneval & Dumas' and Bertuch's) (Sp II: 49)

Fig 11.6a: Spratt's graffiti signature on the wall of the Gortyns labyrinth
It reads: T. Spratt HMS Beacon 1843 (Photo: T. Waldmann, 2006/7, http://www.labyrinthos.ch)

Fig 11.6b: Drummond Hay's graffiti signature on the wall of the Gortyns labyrinth (Drummond added his wife's family name, Hay, to his when he married in 1859) (Photo: T. Waldmann, 2006/7, http://www.labyrinthos.ch)

APPENDIX C

Gazetteer

Gazetteer of main Bronze Age sites visited by Pococke, Pashley and Spratt and by Evans prior to his excavations at Knossos

Site	Pococke	Pashley	Spratt	Evans
Amnissos (Matium)		√	√	
Aptera (Palaekastro west)	√	√	√	
Aradena		√		
Armyros		√		√
Arvi		√	√	√
Axos		√	√	√
Berecynthos		√		
Chersonessos		√	√	√
Dictynnaeaon	√		√	
Eleutherna		?	√	√
Elyros		√		
Eremopoli (Itanos)			√	√
Gonia		√	√	
Gortyns	√	√	√	√
Herakleion		√		√
Hierapetra		√	√	√
Ierami	√			
Inatos		√		
Iouktas	?	√	√	
Kalamydes		√	√	
Kalepa		√		
Kato Zakros			√	√
Khadros		√		√
Khamaleon		√		
Khani Kasteli (Rhokka)		√	√	√
Khania	√	√		√
Kissamo	√	√	√	
Knossos	√	√	√	√
Kopra Kefali			√	
Kytaeon (Rhogdhia)		√		
Lassea		√	√	
Lato (Kritsa)			√	√
Lebena			√	
Limenes			√	√
Lissos	√		√	
Lutro (Phoenix)		√	√	
Lycastos (Astritsi)			√	√
Lyttos		√	√	√
Malia			√	√
Melidhona		√		
Methymna		√	√	
Milatos		√	√	√
Minoa	√			
Mount Ida	√	√	√	
Murnies		√		
Olous			√	√
Palaekastro (east)			√	√
Perama		√		√
Pergamos		√		
Phaistos			√	√
Phalasarna		√	√	
Polyirehimna		√	√	
Praesos	√		√	√

Priansos			√	
Rhithymnos	√	√	√	√
Rhokka (west)		√	√	
Rhytion/Rotassi (Stelae)		√	√	√
Sidero	√			
Sina			√	
Sitea (Petras)			√	√
Suda Bay		√	√	
Sybrita			√	√
Tarrha (Tripiti)		√	√	
Temnos	√			
Thenae		√		
Tylissos		√	√	√
Viannos (Biennos)		√	√	√

APPENDIX D

Pococke's footnote identifying ancient sites
(Pococke, 1745: 250, 251)

' I found myself misled by Ptolemy to search for Lebena, the other port of Gortynia further to the east; for Metalia being to the south south east of Gortynia, and sixteen miles and a quarter from it, and Gortynia being but eleven miles and a quarter from the sea, and from Lebena, according to Strabo Lebena could not be farther east, but must have been where the sea approaches nearest to Gortynia, consequently somewhere in the bay at which the plain ends, and probably at the mouth of the old river; they told me there was formerly a town about a castle near it, which they now call Mouriella. The Tables also place Ledena twelve miles from Gortynia, which confirms Strabo's authority, who was well acquainted with Crete. I should have thought that Leon promontory, which Ptolemy places in the same longitude as Lebena, was the point at Matala, and that both might be well corrected to 55. 0; and the river Lethaeus to 54. 16. and then as to the other places Ptolemy may be corrected in this manner, as to the order and the longitudes: Le-

thaeus 54. 16; Lebena 54. 16; Leon promontory 54. 20; Metalia 54. 20; Cataractus river 54. 50, which probably is the river Luzuro in Homan; but if that geographer has reason for calling a point of land much further west than Matala cape Leonda, that seems to be the point, which in sailing by it we took to be four or five leagues to the west of what I found afterwards to be Matala; then Leon promontory ought to be put after Matalia, with the longitude which Ptolemy gives it nine minutes west of the river Cataractus.

" I do not find that Lisia is mentioned by any authors under this name; but Strabo speaks of Prasus as near the Lebenii, and as twenty two miles from Gortynia; so that it is very probable that Prasus and Lasea were the same city, where there was a temple to Jupiter Dictaeus; for Phaestus was destroyed about this time, which must have been near Lebena, five miles to the north west of Metallum, and seven miles and a half to the south east of Gortynia, the rival city that destroyed it, and two miles and a half from
. . . . . . the

the fea, and does not fo well agree with the diftance of Lifia in the Tables, though indeed Strabo fays, that the Hierapytnii had deftroyed Prafus. The poet Epimenides was a native of Phæftus, who gave that character of the Cretans, which is quoted by St. Paul. The next place mentioned by Ptolemy, after the river Cataractus, is Inatus, about ten miles more to the eaft, which might be at the river Coudre, where Homan has a place called Litina. The Tables place Inato thirty two miles from Hiera, which was an inland town, and gives title to a bifhop, who refides at Hierapetra, and probably it was where Epifcopi is placed in the map: Ten miles more eaftward is Hieronoros, and about five miles eaft of it Hierapetra, and five further the promontory Erythræum. About the point which I took to be this promontory a town was feen, which we judged to be Hierapetra, there being a large opening between the mountains to the north of it; this cape is five miles weft of Hierapetra. To the fouth eaft of that city we failed by the iflands Gaidurogniffa, called by mariners Calderoni, they are two leagues from the land, the larger is about two miles long: Half a furlong eaft of it is the other, about half a mile in circumference; and two leagues to the eaft there is a point called by Homan Santi Ponta, which we judged to be eight leagues to the eaft of the laft point, which Homan calls Leonda, and muft be Ptolemy's promontory Erythræum, which he places five miles eaft of Hierapetra, which is the fame as Hierapytna, and is called alfo by Ptolemy Hierapolis. Ptolemy mentions only two more places on the fouth of Crete, the first is Ampelus, ten miles eaft of cape Erithræum: This I take to be a little to the eaft of the ifland Chriftiana, where we faw a port, and judged there was a town, or village, opening to the weft of a fmall point, which is what Homan calls cape Stomachri Giallo. We had a plain view of the three iflands of Chriftiana, the largeft is about a league in extent every way: To the fouth of it are two very fmall ones. The laft place on the fouth is the city Itanus, ten minutes more to the eaft, and only ten to the weft of Samonium promontory, now called cape Salomone. Homan, who doubtlefs muft have had his inftructions from fome Venetian charts, feems to have laid down thefe places very exactly as to their diftances, though as to the bearing of the ifland, he fhapes it in fuch a manner here that thefe places are rather to the eaft, than to the fouth fide of Candia; he puts the rocks, or ifles Cavallus and Farioni to the weft of cape Xacro, and placing the river Xacro to the north eaft of it, he calls it the promontory of Itanum, and a little beyond it to the north eaft he puts down Palio Caftro, or the old city, where doubtlefs there are ruins of the antient

city Inatus. If cape Salomone were brought out further eaft, as it ought to be, Homan's map would agree very well with Ptolemy's eaft end of Crete. He puts the port and cave Minoa eleven miles fouth, and thirty minutes weft of the cape, which probably was at Porto Schigma, and if that bay fet in a little more to the fouth, the latitude would agree better. He places Camara ten minutes more to the weft, and five minutes further north; I fhould have inclined to have fixed it to point Trachila, if there were not a Paliocaftro in the bay to the north weft of it, which bay might be five miles more north than that in which Minoa is; for the ruins of an antient city there, are a great argument in favour of this fituation; we may fuppofe it was in the fouth corner of the bay, and that Olus was between it and Cherfonefus, which is in the middle of that bay, as Homan makes a peninfula there; and the longitude and latitude of Olus, ought to be corrected thus, 55. 5. 35. 20. The laft place to the eaft promontory Zephyrinum is plainly cape Sidero. Strabo fays, that from Minoa of the Lychi to Hierapytna, from one fea to the other, it was only feven miles and a half: This Minoa muft have been another place of that name, at the bottom of the gulf of Mirabello. On the north part of Crete Ptolemy's longitudes are fo falfe, that they are not to be regarded, for he makes but one degree and fifteen minutes of longitude, from the promontory Zephyrinum to Rhitymna, though it is two thirds of the ifland, and it is computed to be fixty miles only from Retimo to Candia, though, doubtlefs, the miles are very fhort. The account of Ptolemy alfo feems to be imperfect; for the firft place he mentions is Heraclea, which was the port of Cnoffus, to the eaft of which was Cherfonefus, the port of Lyctus; which was fixteen miles from Cnoffus, and is now called Cherronefo; it is a bifhop's fee, where there are fome ruins, and here was a temple to Britomartis, or Dictynna. The Tables make it fixteen miles to Licium, probably Lictus; but if a place called Toxida, where there are ruins, four miles to the eaft of Candia, be Lictus, which is two hours from Cherronefo, it ought to be rather put fix miles; Arcade is fixteen miles further, from that place to Blenna thirty, and to Hiera twenty, and fo ends the northern rout of the Tables from Gortynia; there being another more to the fouth from Hiera to Gortynia, in which there are fome omiffions, Inato only being mentioned in it. Strabo computes Lictus to be only ten miles from the fea, and fifteen from Cnoffus; it was one of the flourifhing cities, when Cnoffus loft its privileges, before the time of Strabo; but afterwards, as he obferves, Cnoffus recovered its antient dignity.

APPENDIX E

Letters from Spratt

1. Copy of extract of a letter from Capt. Spratt to Col. Leake, 18th September 1853, forwarded by Leake (with alterations) to the Royal Geographical Society for a reading on 13th March 1854.
The letter relates to the rising of the western end of Crete and the submerging of the eastern end (Royal Geographical Society, JMS 15/33)

2: Copy of letter from Spratt to Darwin, 2nd January 1877, written as a result of Darwin showing an interest in Spratt's findings in Crete (*Darwin Correspondence Project*, University of Cambridge, DAR.177: 240)

1. Copy of letter from Spratt to Leake

Extract of a letter from Capt. Spratt, R.N.
on Crete.
Smyrna, Sep. 18 1853
by Col. Leake, F.R.S.
"Read March 13 - 1854"

I made an interesting discovery in the western part of the Island (Crete) — viz. that it has been subject to a series of elevations amounting at the maximum to 24. 6 in which occurs at this coast near Pœkilassos & Suia. At the Messara & Fair Havens it is nothing, nor at Megalo Kastro. The eastern end of the Island has dipped a little. The upheaving towards the western end I had observed to be ab.t 7 ft in Suda Bay, many years ago interesting fact. But supposed it to be of a time prior to history, although there was a freshness in these markings which might have induced me to suspect they were of a more recent date. When at Kissamo I observed, that the ancient Mole was remarkably high out of the water the port almost choked by sand. This latter is so common, that it did not open my eyes, although the height of the naked unhewn rocks which formed the Mole ought to have done so. On going to the caserna I looked for its ancient Port, mentioned by Scylax, and in the Stadiasmus, as the Emporium But I could find no artificial work in the sea there

there is, however, a long ledge of rocks, or rather an Islet which lies off it, helping to form a natural but not an artificial harbour. This satisfied me in fact, till on examining the ruins, I saw in the plain a square place enclosed by walls and towers more massive & solid than those of the city. Pashley describes them without having been sensible of their purpose object – I was instantly impressed for several reasons, that here was the Ancient or artificial Port, although full 200 yards from the Sea and nearly 20 ft above it. My first idea was, that the Ancients had a means of hauling their vessels into it as a dry dock; but at last the coast elevation was remembered and on measuring the sea mark at its upper level here I found that the bed of this ancient Port is now 3 or 4 ft below that level; so that I had only to imagine the coast again let down 22 ft 6 the amount it has been elevated here and at Gra busa and the sea would immediately into the ancient Port and float any small craft within it. Geologically the recognition of this ancient Port has another interest, by establishing the recent origin of this remarkable upheaving of the western end of Crete, without there being any record of the event; which however is not surprising, as elsewhere Ancient harbours have been lifted into the air, Rocks have become Islets

maritime
and cities or buildings placed many yards from
the shore. These facts will enable me to reconcile
the ancient geography with the Modern and thus
to verify points otherwise very difficult. For example,
Suia is noticed in the Stadeasmus as a town with
a good port (πόλις ἐτι καὶ λιμένα καλὸν ἔχει) and
as following next to Pakilassos is easily recognized
There are so few of the Ports of Crete in the Stadeasmus
so designated that I naturally looked for a well
sheltered harbour. Pashley says nothing about it
and to look at the locality, few would hope to find
a port. A straight & steep shingle beach off which
there is no anchorage stretches across the mouth
of the valley of Suia, & beyond the points of the hills
on either side. These points however were sea cliffs form-
ly rising out of the beach, at ab.t the height of 23 f.t
On these cliffs the old Sea level is thrown distinctly
by the appearance of the rocks as well as by a line of cylindri-
cal holes the cells of sea boring shells, in some of which
the shells still remain. Pashley speaks of the town
& ruins of Suia as lying on the east side of the torrent
or valley, but takes no notice of the west, where there is
a little plain within a long ridge of ruined buildings
running parallel to the shore & nearly 300 y.ds
60 or 70 broad. This was undoubtedly the to[wn] of
land which sheltered the port, lying between it
position of the port
indicated by a hollow or flat depression of the place
but which depression is? even now be overflowed by

the Sea, if the island was again let down to its old
level. The recognition of this fact here therefore was a
confirmation of the view that this great elevation of
the coast must be looked upon as subsequent to the
existence of these amphitheatres, and subsequent to the
decline of the Roman Empire"

2 Copy letter from Spratt to Darwin

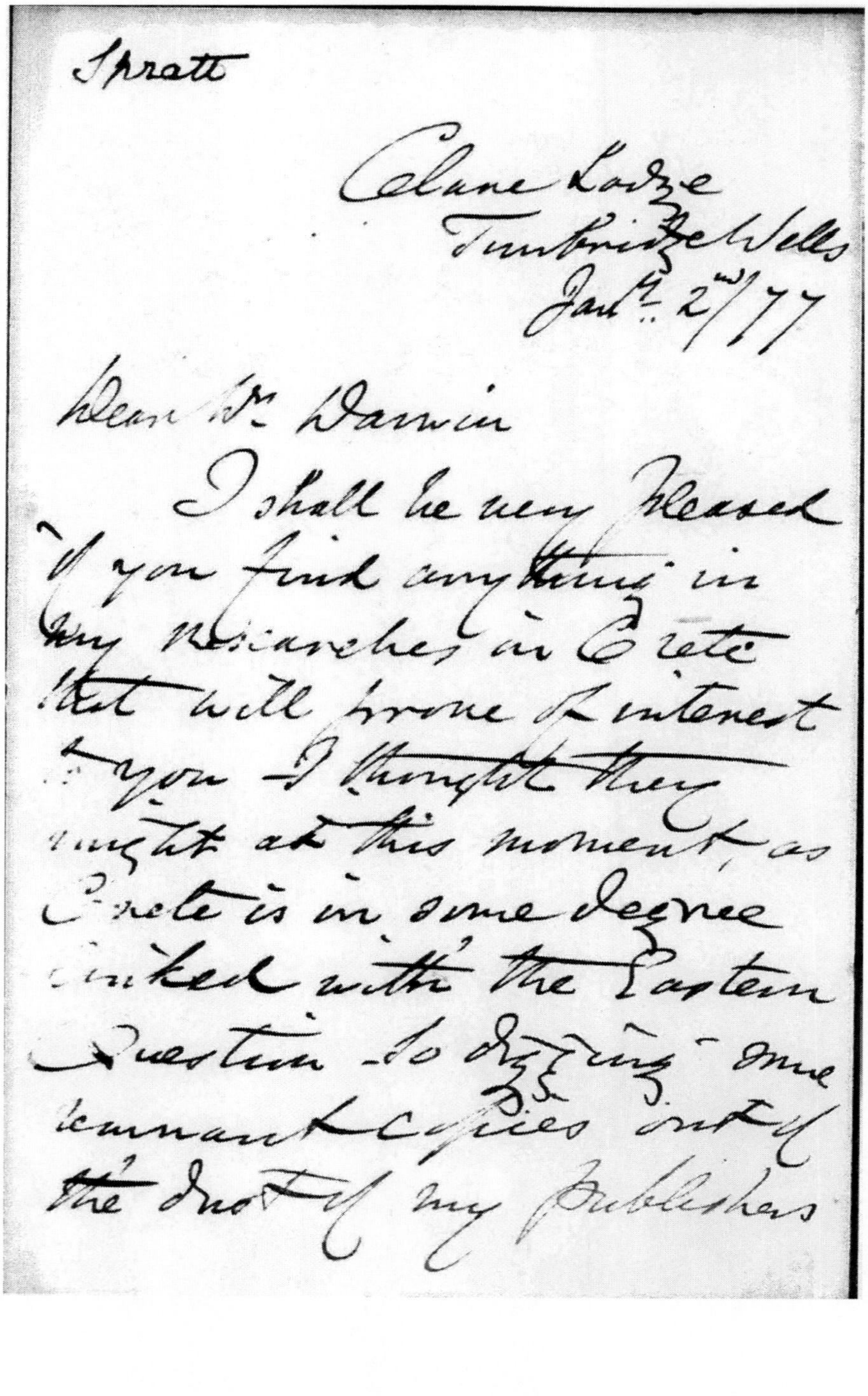

Spratt

Clane Lodge
Tunbridge Wells
Jan.y 2.nd/77

Dear M.r Darwin

I shall be very pleased
if you find anything in
my researches in Crete
that will prove of interest
to you — I thought they
might at this moment, as
Crete is in some degree
linked with the Eastern
Question — So digging some
remnant copies out of
the dust of my publishers

Stones I asked our
Secretary Mr. White
to be kind enough
to distribute them to
the Fellows, as they came
to the Royal Society, whose
names I had selected,
or to send them by Post
if they did not put in
an appearance — Therefore
I told White to say
as they were presented
that I neither expected
thanks nor acknowledge-
-ment under the
circumstances — Merely

wanting a place for
the volumes upon the
shelves of those among
acquaintances or friends
however slight, who I
thought would thus
give them room — I think
we have once if not twice
met in days past — In
the days of poor Edward
Forbes — That, and
more especially your
connection — distinguished
connection with the
old surveying branch
of the Service, as it was
under Beaufort!

induced me to desire
to offer you a let – as
you troubled yourself
to write, and already
shewn that the illustration
have attracted your
attention, it has pleased
and gratified

Yours faithfully

T. Pratt

APPENDIX F

Early foreign travellers' observations of the 'labyrinth' at Gortyns

All from Patroudakis, 2004: 53ff (trans. Efstathios Tamviskos):

Cristoforo Buondelmonti (1415)

Above the water there is a long passage, which few, or maybe none, will risk to go through. The signs and the names of the visitors are written everywhere. There are many bats as well. It is very dangerous for someone to follow these caves, because occasionally big stones fall and block the passage. You, Nicolas, that you know everything, you won't believe that this is the real labyrinth. The stones that come out here are alike the stones of the ancient city. In many places of the island you can find this kind of underground caves. These are quarries. I did seek for you an artificial construction named Labyrinth, but I didn't find it anywhere.

Joseph Pitton de Tournefort (1700)

We are able to see many inscriptions with carbon, e.g. P. Francesco Maria Pesaro Capucino, Frater Tadeus Nicolaus and all these beside the year 1539. Another year, 1444. In another place we read: Qui fu el strenuo Signor Zan de Como Cap de la Fanteria 1526. There are many other messages in the cave, between of which one of them seems to be made from a Jesuit. We observed the next years: 1495, 1516, 1560, 1579, 1699. We wrote as well with a black stone "1700" in three different places. Some of the inscriptions are magnificent and prove the system which I have shown of the growth of rocks (Tournefort thought that the phenomenon which rocks increase in caves was a proof that rocks grow as plants…). With careful measurements it was very easy to leave the depths of the labyrinth. When we studied carefully its structure we all agreed that there is no evidence that it was an ancient quarry, from which they took stone to build the cities of Gortyne and Knossos, as Bellon and some others of that age believed. There was no point of moving out stones from a cave that has 1000 steps depth and is parted from infinite other caves, which anyone could be lost anytime.

We have to mention that the stone of the labyrinth is neither pretty, nor strong, but it has a pale-white color, and is very close to the stone of the mountains, in the beginning of which Gortyne is built.

This creation is not of lesser importance for its kind than the labyrinth of Crete. However, it should not become a belief that the labyrinth that we described is the one that the Ancients mentioned. Diodorus from Sicily and Plinios say that no clues of the ancient labyrinth existed in their times and that it was constructed with prototype the labyrinth of Egypt, which was one of the most famous buildings in the world, 100 times bigger than the one of Crete and with its entrance designed with many pillars. Furthermore, it can be seen from the ancient coins that the labyrinth of Knossos was a part of the city. It is possible that the labyrinth of Knossos was familiar to some writers. Kerdinos writes that, when Theseas had gone to Crete with an invitation by the MPs of Gortyne, Mynotaurus, by seen that was left alone and understanding that they were ready to turn him in, went to hide in a cave that was named 'Labyrinth'. The writer of the Great Hellenic Dictionary writes that the labyrinth of Crete was only a mountain full of caves, and the episcope of Crete, George Alexander, which Volateran mentions, describes the labyrinth not only as an "empty" mountain, but dig from human hands, which none should try to walk through it without someone who knows it well and with enough light, if he doesn't want to wander in an eternity of caves.

Ph. De Bonneval – M. Dumas (1783)

Due to the remembrance of the myth and the several mentioning of the travelers who visited this labyrinth, our curiosity was so intrigued that we decided to please it by not leaving the labyrinth before we examine all of its caves one by one to the most secret and deep hidings of Minotaurus.

There were travelers which wrote that the big number of bats is dangerous and that they are very aggressive, biting and injuring the visitors. We did not face this danger and the amount of bats was much smaller than mentioned. However, it would be a mistake to continue entering deeper grounds without measuring the deep beyond us.

It is really fascinating how careful the construction is, with all these complex and different destinations and rest points.

We were highly interested in finding the tracks of the previous visitors. We hadn't found any tracks, when we observed the initials of Mr. Tournefort. A bit further we found more initials written on the walls, which are mentioned by the former in his descriptions of the labyrinth.

Not only have the letters that Tournefort mentioned grown, but other points as well. They have begun to cover with a white substance, which is neither salty, nor has any kind of smell. This substance seems to be the same with the stone that it comes from. There is only one place of the labyrinth that this phenomenon can be observed.

We thought that it was a quarry which was used to build the ancient cities of Gortyne and Knossos. We cannot completely deny this possibility, as Mr. Tournefort did, nor accept it, because it is not impossible that they had opened other exits as well. We believe that some parts of this cave are a game of nature and that they existed before humans hands added anything to it. The human interference was easy due to the horizontal zones which make it easy for stones to be taken out. The skilled Cretans completed this magnificent work and used it as a shelter in the period of the national wars.

Their dictators used the labyrinth as prison. The true Minotaurus is the grief and the pain of the anguished, which were left in the labyrinth, forgotten in oblivion.

We won our battle with Minotaurus. Afterwards, finding again the 9th crossing, we exited the labyrinth and saw again the light of our Ariadnes.

F.W. Sieber (1817)

I have no doubt that the real labyrinth was in Knossos and its construction was based on a drawing of Dedalos following a command from Minoas, as it is mentioned by Diodoros and it is clear that it is demolished. The one that we are going to examine now, is introduced by Bellon and later by Pococke as a quarry under a sand-hill, which forms some passages, caves, etc. and its walls restrain the evidence of stones that have been taken off. Most of its visitors have given it the name, Labyrinth.

We examined it carefully, marking everything with the use of a compass and forming a drawing mentioning every single passage, corridor and chamber with names given by the French ambassador. The results of our observations made clear that this is rather a stone quarry, agreeing with Belon's opinion, against to the opinions of Tournefort and Savary.

APPENDIX G

1836 Report on the 'Labyrinth of Crete'
The Penny Magazine of the Society for the Diffusion of Useful Knowledge
16th July 1836: 278-79)

(With mention of Tournefort and North Douglas)

now is singularly imposing; and the observer feels satisfied that it is a monument of antiquity, and that it must, at some period, have been the scene or the object of religious veneration.

In the neighbourhood, this remarkable fragment is known by the name of the "Hemlock Stone." It, I have no doubt, was originally called the "Cromlech," or "Crumlech Stone,"—a name which at once points out its original use. The provincial pronunciation of *hemlock* is *humlock*: the transition from *crumleck* to *humlock* is natural and easy; but, as if to divest it of vulgarity, and confine to the plant its distinct appellation, it is now universally called, as before mentioned, the "Hemlock Stone."

This stone lies about five miles from Nottingham; and the ridge on which it stands is of the same conformation as the rock on which Nottingham Castle is built,—as that in which the various caves are scooped in the park, and, in fact, similar to the ground on which the town itself is situated. It is a huge piece of a reddish rock, of perhaps fifty feet high, presenting on one side a broad flattish face, and at each end an appearance not much dissimilar to the Cheesewring of Cornwall. It is full of seams and crannies, but yet appears to be one connected, if not entirely compact, stone. The top projects over the sides and ends very considerably, and has a gentle slope of its plane summit towards the east. This, if it does not prove it to have been a cromlech, shows at least its possessing one of its most distinguishing properties. It is evidently a work of Nature; and in its present state, independently of whatever may have been the use to which it has been put to, is an object not devoid of picturesque beauty.

It appears highly probable that it has been a druidical altar; for it stands on the sloping side of a hill, commanding an extensive view of a plain in which thousands might assemble, and was overlooked by two other hills of something greater altitude, not unlikely at the time, covered with a wood of native oaks; and it was within a little distance of the druidical residence in Nottingham Park: besides, as there was not a place of sacrifice nearer than those on the Peak Hills, in the neighbouring county of Derby; such a place would of necessity be wanting. It seems therefore natural to conclude that it has been used for such a purpose.

It is singular that none of our tourists and few of our topographers have so much as mentioned this cromlechstone: perhaps its lying at a little distance from the road, and not being in sight, except at three or four miles' distance, may have been one reason; yet I feel convinced that, had such a monument stood on the summit of one of the hills of Wales, or Cornwall, or Devonshire, it would long ago have attracted the notice of our travelling antiquaries.

The stone itself is entirely void of verdure, except having on the top a small straggling sloe-bush, and, a little below, a few small tufts of polypodium. It is not much enriched with lichens and weather-tints; but from its dark enormous mass projecting against the light horizontal sky, and the well-wooded distance contrasting with the flowers of the luxuriant furze-bushes in the fore-ground, it forms a picture to which its singularity adds an interest.

THE LABYRINTH OF CRETE.

IN a recent article, while treating of Grecian dresses and dances, we had occasion to allude to this extraordinary excavation, which was once classed among the wonders of the world, and was supposed to be of the remotest antiquity. A short description of the labyrinth, or at least of the excavation which is generally supposed to be the ancient and famed work (for there are some doubts on the subject), may amuse our readers, and give them an excellent field for conjecture as to the uses and object of a work of such labour and extent.

In the island of Crete, which is now called Candia, upon the side of a mountain forming one of the roots of Mount Ida, and at the distance of four miles from the town of Agiosdeka (the ancient Gortyna), there is an opening somewhat in the shape of a mouth, of a man's height, and no way distinguishable from many apertures in the neighbourhood. But this common-looking entrance leads to passages beautifully cut out in the rock, which twist and turn, diverge from, and intersect each other in so puzzling a manner, that, without a clue, or great precaution, it seems almost impossible for a person once engaged in them to find his way out again. Nearly the whole of the mountain is cut through and through by these subterranean mazes, which, from their irregularity, appear rather as the effect of chance than the designed work of man. When the old French traveller Tournefort visited the place, every one of the party carried a torch: at every difficult turn they stuck up, on the right-hand side, pieces of paper marked with numbers; one of the guides lighted faggots made of the branches of the pine-tree, and left them to burn at certain distances from each other, and another guide scattered pieces of straw on the ground as they went along. And yet, with all these precautions, it should appear that Tournefort was able to explore only a part of the labyrinth. A more recent traveller (the Honourable F. S. North Douglas) undertook the task with a great many guides, furnished with torches and lanterns, and 1300 yards of packthread; but he too was obliged to leave many of the windings unexamined, and to abstain from entering some high and broad passages that seemed calculated to entice and then bewilder him.

Immediately beyond the entrance to these caves there is a small chamber, to the right of which there runs a passage which is 3300 feet long, and on an average 12 feet wide and 10 feet high, though Tournefort says that in some places he was obliged to stoop a little, and that at one point, about the middle of the road, they found the passage so low and so narrow, that they were obliged to crawl on their hands and knees, one by one. This passage neither ascends nor descends very much; the floor is smooth and level from side to side; the walls or sides are perfectly perpendicular, and formed of the solid rock, except here and there, where they are cased with masonry most carefully executed. At every ten or twelve paces new passages of the same sort present themselves, and they, in their turn, either break off into other passages, or return to the original passage from which they had diverged. After an apparent progression in this subterranean puzzle of nearly an hour, Mr. North Douglas's party, who thought themselves in the very heart of the mountain, came back upon their packthread at the very place whence they had started. This gentleman remarked as a striking peculiarity, that, instead of finding any close or unwholesome air in these narrow recesses, they breathed as freely when they were nearly a mile from its mouth as when they first entered the labyrinth. He also observed that all the angles in this singular excavation were as sharp as if they had just been cut. In one of the passages he, with great difficulty, discovered, through a narrow aperture, a small octagonal room, remarkable for the elegance of its form. Tournefort speaks of two small chambers, almost round (*presque rondes*), cut in the rock, at what he considered the most distant or innermost part of the labyrinth. On the walls of these rooms he found several names of visiters, which had been written with charcoal during the time that the Venetians were masters of Candia. He copied two or three of these; for example:—"Qui fu el strenuo Signor Zan de Como, Cap.º dela Fanteria, 1526." (Here was the bold Signor Zan de Como, a captain of infantry.) "P. Francesco Maria Pesaro, Capucino (a Capuchin friar); Frater Taddeus Nicolaus (another friar), 1539." In these rooms, and in the passages leading to them, were several other dates (written or cut out by the chisel), ranging from the year 1495 to 1579, and Tournefort added 1700, the year of his visit. According to this correct old traveller, the most tortuous and difficult part of the labyrinth is that which branches off to the left, at about thirty paces from the entrance, where an infinitude of passages, some crossing each other, and some having no outlet, perfectly bewilder the explorer. Sandys, who visited the island of Candia more than two centuries ago, but whose curiosity did not lead him to the labyrinth, tells us, that he "had heard an English merchant (who hath seen it) say, that it was so intricate and vast, that a guide which used to show it unto others for twenty years together lost himself therein, and was never more heard of." There is no water dripping through the rocks, no congelation of any kind, but, throughout, the labyrinth is dry, and the air of an equal and pleasant temperature.

According to the early part of Grecian history or tradition, where fable is mingled with fact, or nearly everything is to be taken in an allegorical sense, the key to which we have lost, the labyrinth was made, in imitation of a similar work in Egypt, by Dædalus the Athenian, for the second Minos, King of Crete, who flourished some thirteen centuries before the Christian era. The story of the monstrous Minotaur that ranged through these recesses, and of Theseus who was shut up in them to be devoured, and of the fair Ariadne who extricated her lover by giving him a clue of thread, belongs to the most imaginative part of mythology, and will hardly assist us in conjecturing what the place was really intended for. It has been called a catacomb, but no remains of any kind, indicating that it was put to such a use, have ever been found in it or about it. "The labyrinth," says Mr. North Douglas, "could never have been intended for a burial place, as we find none of those recesses in the walls which were used as sepulchres in the catacombs of Italy and Malta, nor indeed any other place fitted for the reception of a corpse." Belon and other old travellers concluded it was merely a stone quarry. Sandys says, "but by most this is thought to have been but a quarry where they had the stone that built both Cnossus and Gortyna; being forced to leave such walls for the support of the roof, and by following of the veins, to make it so intricate."

A modern traveller, Monsieur Sonnini, who, however, like Sandys, never visited the labyrinth, adopts this opinion, and unnecessarily refers the quarry to a much more modern date. Mr. North Douglas who, Theseus-like, explored the passage with a clue of thread in 1812, objects to these conclusions. He says, "Independently of there being no city nearer to it than Gortyna, which in comparatively modern times could never have required so large a quantity of materials, is it likely that there would have been such extreme regularity of design, such handsome chambers and entrances, and above all, such artful intricacy, so evidently intended to mislead, if the object had been a mere stone quarry? The traditions of the country-people, among whom it still bears the name of Ο Λαΰρινϱος, (the labyrinth) seem to confirm its antiquity; but its precise object, though it clearly enough appears to have been in-

tended, generally, for purposes of concealment, must yet remain a matter of doubt."

Tournefort had already rejected as an absurdity the idea of the place being a quarry. He says the stone has nothing peculiar to recommend it—that precisely the same material is found in the hill directly above Gortyna, and close to Cnossus. Was it then probable that people would seek at a distance across rude mountains and deep valleys for what they had close at hand? Would they make a choice of all kinds of difficulties, rather than cut the stone on the spot they wanted it, and where there were no difficulties at all? After a good deal more to the same purpose, Tournefort concluded that the labyrinth was originally the work of nature,—a *lusus naturæ*, but that man, whose handiwork is everywhere visible in it, had taken delight, or had found some advantage in enlarging it where it was narrow, and in giving regularity to its sides, roof, &c. "The ancient Cretans," he continues, "a people highly civilized and much attached to the fine arts, were disposed to finish what nature had only sketched out. Without doubt some shepherds having discovered these subterranean passages, gave room to greater men to make out of them this marvellous labyrinth, which might serve as an asylum to many families, during civil wars or the reigns of tyrants, although they now only serve as a retreat to the bats." He might have added that in ages when robbery and violence were held to be heroic virtues, and the seas of Crete swarmed in an especial manner with pirates, the people flying from the coast at times would be happy to have so excellent a hiding-place for themselves and their goods.

He conjectures that the ancient Cretans did not touch that part of the passage where it is necessary to crawl on hands and knees, because they wished posterity should know, by seeing it, how all the rest was made originally by nature, and how much their art and industry had done to improve it. Beyond that narrow passage the labyrinth is as regular and beautiful as it is before reaching that point. In support of Tournefort's hypothesis it should be mentioned, that many natural grottoes and long caverns exist in this volcanic island, and that Mount Ida, close by, is in many places quite honey-combed with them.

We will offer no conjecture of our own, but leave that pleasant field open to our readers. One thing is certain, that whether it be the labyrinth so often referred to by ancient writers (and we are inclined to think it is) or whether it be wholly, or only in part, the work of man, the labyrinth visited and described by Tournefort and Mr. North Douglas, is an exceedingly curious and interesting place.

The latter gentleman was of opinion that the primitive meaning of "labyrinth," which he thought was a word of Phœnician origin, might assist us in discovering something of its history and uses.

CAPACITY OF THE CHEST, AND ITS CONDITION DURING BODILY EXERTION

(From Sir C. Bell's Dissertations in the new edition of 'Paley's Natural Theology.')

SUPPOSE a machine formed of two boards of equal diameter, and joined together by leather nailed to their margins like a pair of bellows: a hole is made in the upper board into which is inserted a tube. Now if a person mount upon this apparatus when it is filled with water, and blow into the tube, he can raise the upper board, carrying himself upwards by the force of his own breath—indeed by the power of his cheeks alone. It is on the same principle that, when a forcing pump is

APPENDIX H

The 'woeful' start of Lithgow's report on his trip to Crete incorporating his attack by bandits (Lithgow, 1632)

Lithgow (1632: 78-81) (Crete begins at the twelth line, 'This [Crete] is the chiefe Dominion ...')
Note: he mentions right from the start his intention of only a brief reference to the island 'in general'

78   *The 19. yeares Trauels of William Lithgow*,   Part. j

Greece and *Cyrene* in *Affrick*, not being distant from the one, nor from the other, about two dayes sayling: It is a most famous and auncient Kingdome: By moderne Writers, it is called Queene of the Iles *Mediterrene*: It had of olde an hundreth Citties, whereof it had the name *Hecatompolis*, but now onely foure, *Candia*, *Canea*, *Rethimos*, and *Scythia*, the rest are but Villages and Bourges. It is of length, to wit, from *Capo Ermice* in the West, called by *Pliny*, *Frons arietis*, and *Capo Salomone* in the East, two hundreth and forty Miles, large threescore, and of circuit sixe hundreth and fifty miles.

The antiquity of Creet.

This is the chiefe Dominion, belonging to the *Venetian* Reipublique: In euery one of these foure Citties, there is a Gouernour, and two Counsellors, sent from *Venice* euery two yeares. The Countrey is diuided into foure parts, vnder the iurisdiction of the foure Citties, for the better administration of Iustice; and they haue a Generall, who commonly remaineth in the Citty of *Candy* (like to a Viceroy) who deposeth, or imposeth Magistrates, Captaines, Souldiers, Officers, and others whatsoeuer, in the behalfe of Saint *Marke* or Duke of *Venice*. The *Venetians* detaine continually a strong guard, diuided in Companies, Squadrons, and Garrisons, in the Citties and Fortresses of the Iland: which doe extend to the number of 12000. Souldiers, kept, not onely for the incursion of *Turks*, but also for feare of the *Creets* or Inhabitants, who would rather (if they could) render to the *Turke*, then to liue vnder the subiection of *Venice*, thinking thereby to haue more liberty, & lesse taxed vnder the Infidell, then now they are vnder the Christian.

This Ile produceth the best *Maluasy*, *Muscadine*, and *Leaticke* wines, that are in the whole Vniuerse. It yeeldeth Oranges, Lemmons, Mellons, Cytreons, Grenadiers,

159

Part.3   By 3. voyages in Europe, Asia, and Affrica.   79

ers, *Adams* Apples, Raisins, Oliues, Dates, Hony, Sugar, *Vua di tre volie*, and all other kindes of fruite in abundance. But the most part of the Cornes are brought yearely from *Archipelago* and *Graece*. The chiefe Riuers are *Cataracho*, *Melipotomos*, *Escasino*; being all of them shallow and discommodious for shipping, in respect of their short courses, and rocky passages: And the principall Citties of olde, were *Gnossus*, where *Minos* kept his Court, 2. *Cortina*, 3. *Aphra* and *Cydonia*. This Countrey was by *Marcellus* made subiect to the *Romanes*: It was afterward giuen by *Baldwin* Earle of *Flanders*, the first Latin Emperor of *Constantinople* to *Boniface* of *Montferrat*, who sold it, *Anno* 1194. to the *Venetians*.

The Riuers of Creta.

This much of the Ile in generall; and now in respect of my trauelling two times through the bounds of the whole Kingdome, which was neuer before atchieued by any Traueller in Christendome; I will as briefly as I can in particular, relate a few of these miseries indured by me in this Land, with the nature & quality of the people.

This aforesaid *Carabusa*, is the principall Fortresse of *Creta*, being of it selfe innincible, and is not valike to the Castle of *Dumbertan*, which standeth at the mouth of *Clyd*; vpon which Riuer the ancient City of *Lanerke* is situated: For this Fort is enuironed with a Rocke higher then the wals, and ioyneth close with *Capo Ermico*: hauing learned of the theeuish way I had to *Canea*, I aduised to put my mony in exchange, which the Captaine of that strength very curteously performed; and would also haue disswaded me from my purpose, but I by no perswasion of him would stay. From thence departing, all alone, scarcely was I aduanced twelue miles in my way, when I was beset on the skirt of a Rocky Mountaine, with three *Greeke* murdering *Renegadoes*, and an *Italian Bandido:*

The old and famous City of *Lanerke*.

dido: who laying hands on me, beate me most cruelly, robbed me of all my clothes, and stripped me naked, threatning me with many grieuous speeches.

At last the respectiue *Italian,* perceiuing I was a stranger, and could not speake the *Cretan* tongue, began to aske me in his owne language, where was my money? to whom I soberly answered, I had no more then he saw, which was fourescore Bagarines: which scarcely amounted to two groats *English:* But he not giuing credit to these words, searched all my clothes and *Budgets,* yet found nothing except my linnen, and Letters of recommendations, I had from diuers Princes of Christendome, especially the Duke of *Venice,* whose subiects they were, if they had bene lawfull subiects: Which when he saw, did moue him to compassion, and earnestly entreated the other three theeues to grant me mercy, and to saue my life: A long deliberation being ended, they restored backe againe my Pilgrimes clothes, and Letters, but my blew gowne and Bagarines they kept: Such also was their theeuish courtesie toward me, that for my better safegard in the way, they gaue me a stamped piece of clay, as a token to shew any of their companions, if I encountred with any of them; for they were about twenty Rascalles of a confederate band, that lay in this desart passage.

Leauing them with many counterfeit thankes, I trauelled that day seauen and thirty miles, and at night attained to the vnhappy Village of *Pickehorne:* where I could haue neither meate, drinke, lodging, nor any refreshment to my wearied body. These desperate *Candiots* thronged about me, gazing (as though astonished) to see me both want company, and their Language, and by their cruell lookes, they seemed to be a barbarous and vnciuill people:

161

Part.3. *By 3. Voyages in Europe, Asia, and Affrica.* 81

people : For all these High-landers of *Candy*, are tyran-
nicall, blood-thirsty, and deceitfull. The consideration *Cruell*
of which and the appearance of my death, signed to me *Candiots*
secretly by a pittifull woman, made me to shun their villa-
ny in stealing forth from them in the darke night, and
priuatly sought for a secure place of repose in a vmbragi-
ous Caue by the Sea side, where I lay till morning with
a fearefull heart, a erased body, a thirstie stomacke, and a
hungry belly.

APPENDIX I

George Sandys' report on Crete (1615)

174   *Creete.*   L I B. 4.

Much becalmed, and not seldome crossed by contrary winds, for divers days we saw sea, and air onely-(yet once within ken of a Promontory of *Lycia*, called the seven Capes) untill we approached the South-east of *Candy*, called formerly *Creta*,

Creta Jovis magni nutrix veneranda feraxque Et frugum & pecoris——— Dionys.	*Creet sacred nurse to Jove, a fruitfull ground With corn and cattell stor'd———*

and to make up the distich with that of *Homers*,

———pulchra, pinguis, circumflus. Hom Odyss.l.19.	———*faire, fat, sea-bound;*

It lieth an hundred miles South-west from the lesser *Asia*, as many South-east from *Peloponesus*, and North of *Africa*, an hundred and fifty: wherefore aptly saith *Homer*,

Creta quidem terra medio est in nigro ponto. Idem.	*Creet in the midst of the dark Sea doth stand,*

imitated by *Virgil*,

Creta Jovis magni medio jacet insula ponto. Vir. Æ 1. l.3.	*Creet seated in the midst of seas, Joves land,*

lying neither in the *Adriatike*, *Ægean*, *Carpathian*, nor *Libyan* seas; which on each side environ it. It stretcheth two hundred and fifteen miles from East to West; containing forty five in breadth, and in circuit five hundred and twenty. Full of mountains, yet those not un-profitable, affording excellent pasturage: the highest is *Ida*,

Ida frequens piceis & quercubus optima mater. Dionys.	*In pitch rich above other, Of Okes the pregnant mother:*

seated almost in the midst of the Island, now called *Psilotriti*; from whose lofty and spiny top both seas may be discerned. Where standeth a little Chappel; compact of great square stones without lime, in form of an arch: being there so exceeding cold in the heat of the Summer (at which time goats and sheep can onely graze there) that the shepheards are glad to descend before night into the valley. From thence issue many springs. Some part of it is a plain descent, some precipitate, some clothed with trees of severall kinds, but by the Cypresse especially graced. It fostreth nothing that is wild, but hares, red deer, and fallow; and is the inheritance of the *Calergy*: a family that for this thousand yeers have retained a prime repute in this Island. Two other mountains of fame there be; the one at the West end, called anciently *Leucaore*, now *la Spachia*: and other at the East-end now called *Sethia*, and anciently *Dicta*, which received that name from *Diana*, to whom this Island was greatly devoted; it signifying nets: she being an huntress & patroness of hunters:

Ades en comiti Diva Virago Cujus regna pars terrarum Secreta vacat——— ———tua Creteas Dextra——— Sequitur cervos: nunc veloces Figis Damas leviore manu. Senec. in Hipp.	*Virago, thou that soveraign art Of woods, and wastes; the Cretan Hart Thy hand pursues, and with quick cunning Strikes thorow the swifter Fallow running.*

The story goes, how one *Britomart* a Nymph of this Island eagerly following the chase, and over-thrown ere aware in a toile, not able to free her self, the beast now rushing upon her; she vowed a Temple to *Diana*, if so be she escaped that danger; who forth-with set her on her feet; and of those nets was called *Dictynna*: *Diana* also assuming that name for the love which she bare her. The ancient Geographers do jointly affirm with *Virgil*, that the *Cretans*

Centum urbeis habitant magnas. Virg. Æn. l.3.	*Did in an hundred ample Cities dwel:*

which were not so many in the days of *Homer*:

——— in hac nonaginta civitates, Inter has Gnossus magna civitas ubi Minos. Per novem annos regnavit Jovis magno contabulator. Odyss. l. 19.	*With ninety Cities crowned. Of those most great. High Gnossus; for nine years the royall seat Of Minos, he that talks with Jove.*

This

163

LIB. 4.   Creete.   175.

This City long held the Regality; seated in a plain, not far from the East extent of the Island, and from the North shore not above six furlongs; where it had a convenient haven: long since having nothing left but a sound of the name; a little village there standing, called *Cinosus*. The next in dignity was

Gortina strongly wall'd ——	Gortina bene cincta mœnibus. Hom. Od l. 19.

seated not far from the Southern basis of *Ida*: who sheweth what she was by her ruines; there yet remaining an Aquaduct entire, supported by a number of arches, certain stragling houses possessing the place, now named *Mataria*. The third *Cydonia*, now next to the greatest, and called *Canea*: seated towards the West, and on the North-shore; enjoying a large and safe harbour. These three were all of those hundred that remained (or at least retained their repute) in the days of *Strabo*, who was of this countrey. Four onely it hath at this day: *Candy* and *Canea* fortified by Art, *Rhetymo*, and *Sitia* by nature. *Candy*, that now giveth a name to the Island, standing upon the North-shore (as doe all the rest) is a strong and well inhabited City, accommodate with an excellent harbour; of which the elder *Scaliger*:

An hundred Cities finely wall'd (if trew *Fame sings) Times waste hath now reduc'd to few.* *Small towns I judge they were. Yet what destroy'd* *In all; alone by Candy is supply'd.*	Centum olim cinctas operosis mœnibus urbes Reddidit ad paucas imperiosa dies. Oppida parva tamen reor illa fuisse, sed aucta Quod deest ex reliquis Candida sola refert. J. C. Scal.

The whole Island is divided into the Provinces of *Canea*, *Rhetimo*, *Candia*, and *Sittia*, lying furthest East-ward: strengthned both by the shore in few places approachable, & by the many fortresses. It hath no navigable rivers. It aboundeth with grain, oil, and fruits of all kinds: amongst the rest with the apples of *Adam*; the juyce whereof they tun up and send into *Turkie*, much used by them in their meats. The mountains afford diversity of Physical herbs: as Cistus (& that in great quantity) from whence they do gather their Ladanum, Halimus, that resisteth famine, and Dictanus so soveraign for wounds; whose vertue was first found out by stags and bucks, that by eating thereof ejected the arrowes wherewith they were wounded. Used by *Venus* in the cure of her *Æneas*.

With her white hand she crops from Cretan Ide' *The fresh leav'd stalk, with flower in purple di'd,* *A soveraign hearb well known to fearfull Dear,* *Whose trembling sides the winged arrows bear.*	Ipsa manu genetrix Cretea carpit ab Ida Pulveribus caulem foliis, & flore comantem Purpureo, non illa feris incognita capti Gramina cum tergo volucres hæsere sagitta. Virg. Æn. l. 11.

But that which principally enricheth this countrey is their Muscadines and Malmsies, those kinds of grapes brought first hither from *Arvisia*, a mountain of *Chios*. Wines that seldome come unto us uncuted, but excellent where not, (as within the straights) and compared unto *Nectar*.

Creet I confesse, Joves fortresse to be: *For Nectar onely is transferr'd from shee:*	Vera equidem fateor Jovis incunabula magni: Nam liquor haud alibi Nectaris ille venit. J. C. Scal.

The ancient inhabitants of this Island are related by *Homers Ulysses*:

Infinite people of mixt speech here dwell: *Achaians, Eteocretans, who excell* *In valour; Cidons, Dorians, Trichaites,* *Divine Pelasgians.*	—— In hac autem homines Multi infiniti —— Alia alio non lingua mixta, in ipsa quidem Achivi, Ibi autem Eteocretes magnanimi ibique Cidones, Dorensesque, Trichaites, divinique Pelasgi. Hom. Odyss. l. 19.

But the naturall people hereof were the *Cidonians*, and *Eteocretans*, or *Curetes*; so ancient that thay are fained even in this place to have their creation. The last named Inhabited *Ida*, *Cretas* their first King, of whom the Island was so named. They lived in caves (for houses then were not) and used no other coverture then nature afforded them. They found out many things usefull for life; as the taming of certain beasts, whom they gathered first into flocks & herds; & brought civility amongst men, by instituting laws, and observing of discipline. They taught how to direct the voice unto

unto harmony, possessing the mind with the awe of Religion, initiating with orders and ceremonies. They found out the use of brasse, & iron, with the sword, & head-piece: the first inventers of shooting, hunting, & dancing in armour. Being called *Idæi Daktili*, either in regard of their numbers or observed measures: but according to *Diodorus*, of their ten *Ephori*. The progenie of the *Painim* gods were born in this Island to whom divine honours were ascribed: to some for their beneficial inventions, to others for in-troducing justice amongst men, repulsing of injuries & violence, cherishing the good, deterring the bad, suppressing by force of armes the tyrants of the earth, & relieving the oppressed. But that they were no other then mortals the *Cretans* themselves do testifie, who affirm that *Jupiter* was not onely born & bred in their countrey, but buried, and did shew his Sepulchre (though reproved by *Callimachus*)

Cretes mendaces semper Rex alme sepulchrum   (*Still lying Cretans, sacred King, dare rear*
Erexere tuum; tu vivis semper & usque es.   *Thee a tombe: thou ever liv'd, and art each where.*)

on the mountain *Lassia*: and that he was fostered by the *Curetes* in *Æginus*, which lieth on the South of *Ida*; concealed and delivered unto them by his mother, to prevent his slaughter. For *Saturne* resolved to destroy his male children: either having so compacted with his brother *Tytan*, or to prevent the Prophecie, which was that his son should depose him. A cruelty used amongst the *Grecians* it was (& therefore this not to be held for a fable) to expose the infants whom they would not foster, unto the mercy of the Desarts. Long after the death of these reputed Gods lived *Minos*, and *Rhadamant*: who for their justice upon earth were fained after to have been Judges in hell. Notorious is the adultery of *Phasiphae* with the Generall *Taurus*; which gave unto Poets the invention of their *Minotaur* (so called they the bastard)

Destinat hunc Minos thalami removere pudorē,   *To hide his marriage shame, him Minos doomes*
Multiplique domo cæcis includere tecti.   *To durance in un-explicable roomes.*
Dædalus ingenio fabræ celeberrimus artis   *The work of witty Dædalus; confounding*
Ponit opus, turbatque notas & lumina flexu.   *Th' direct by resemblance: abounding*
Ducit in errorem variarum ambage viarum.   *With winding wayes, the Maze of errour rounding:*
    Ovid. Met. l. 8.

made in imitation of that in *Egypt*, as afore-said. But no tract thereof remained in the dayes of *Pliny*, although at this day the inhabitants undertake to shew it unto strangers. For between where once stood *Gortina*, and *Gnossus* at the foot of *Ida*, under the ground are many Meanders hewn out of the rock, now turning this way, & now that way: insomuch that it is not without a conductour to be entred, which you are to hire at the adjoyning village. I have heard an English Merchant say (who hath seen it) that it was so intricate, and vast, that a guide which used to shew it unto others for twenty yeers together, lost himselfe therein, and was never more heard of. Within are little turrets which over-look the walls that make the divisions, in many places not reaching to the top. But by most this is thought to have been but a quarry where they had the stone that built both *Gnossus*, and *Gortina* being forced to leave such walls for the support of the roof, and by following of the veines to make it so intricate. *Metellus* first made the *Cretans* stoop to the *Romanes*. After they were under the *Greek* Emperours, untill *Baldwin* the *Latine* Emperour of *Constantinople* bestowed the Island upon *Boniface* Marquesse of *Monteferrato*: who sold it to the *Venetians* in the yeare 1194. But in the time of Duke *Dandalus* they rebelled, and were again in the yeare 1343 reduced to their obedience. So remain they at this day: the *Greeks* being permitted the free exercise of their Religion, by whom it is for the most part inhabited. And although in many things they imitate the *Venetians*, yet still retain they their old vices; Liers, evill beasts, slow bellies, whereof formerly up-braided by Saint *Paul*, out of their Poet *Epimenides*. They still exercise shooting; wherein throughout all ages they have excelled,

—— Gnossasque agitare pharetras   *Gnossians good Archers are, the use of bowes,*
Docta, nec Eois pejor Gortina sagittis.   *Not Parthia better then Gortina knows't*
   Lucan. l. 3.

using the *Scythian* bow, but much better then the *Scythians*. The countrey people doe dance with their bows ready bent on their armes, their quivers hanging on
their

their backs, and their swords by their sides, imitating therein their ancestors, (a custome also amongst the *Lacedæmonians*) called by them *Pyrricha*: and as of old, so use they to sing in their dancings; and reply to one another. The better sort of men are apparelled like the *Venetians*, and so are the women, who seldome stirre abroad, except it be to the Church, but in the night time. The common people are clothed like the *Greeks* of *Simo*, of whom we have spoken: the women onely wearing loose veils on their heads, their brests and shoulders perpetually naked, and died by the Sun into a loathsome tawny.

Now our of sight of *Candie*, the winds both slack and contrary, wee were

BIBLIOGRAPHY

Primary Sources

Diodorus Siculus, *The Library of History,* Vol. III, trans. C.H. Oldfather (Loeb Classical Library, Harvard University Press, Cambridge, Mass., 1939).

Herodotus, *The Histories*, trans. G. Rawlinson (Wordsworth, Ware, Herts., 1996).

Homer, *The Iliad*, trans. R. Lattimore (Chicago University Press, Illinois, 1961).

Homer, *The Odyssey*, trans. R. Lattimore (Harper Perennial, New York, 1991).

Pausanias, *Guide to Greece*, 2 vols., trans. P. Levi (Penguin Classics, Middlesex, 1971).

Plato's *Hippias* Major, trans. T.J. Saunders (Penguin Classics, Middlesex, 1987).

Pliny (the Elder), *Natural History*, trans. J. Healey (Penguin Classics, Middlesex, 1991).

Polybius' *Histories*, trans. W.R. Paton (Loeb Classical Library, Harvard University Press, Cambridge, Mass., 1989).

Strabo, *Geography*, Books 1-2, trans. H.L. Jones (Loeb Classical Library, Harvard University Press, Cambridge, Mass., 1997).

Strabo, *Geography*, Books 10-12, trans. H.L. Jones (Loeb Classical Library, Harvard University Press, Cambridge, Mass., 2000).

Strabo, *Geography*, Bk 14 trans. H.L. Jones (Loeb Classical Library, Harvard University Press, Cambridge, Mass., 1989).

Thucydides, *The Peloponnesian War*, trans. S. Lattimore (Hackett, Indianapolis, 1998).

Virgil, *The Aeneid*, trans. C. Day Lewis (Oxford University Press, Oxford, 1991).

Secondary Sources

Adkin, R. (2004) *Trafalgar: The Biography of a Battle*, Abacus, London.

Akurgal, E. (1983) *Ancient Civilizations and Ruins of Turkey*, Hasat Kitabevi, Istanbul.

Alexiou, S. & Warren, P. (2004) 'Early Minoan Tombs of Lebena, Southern Crete', *Studies in Mediterranean Archaeology* Vol. XXX.

Allen, S.H. (1999) *Finding the Walls of Troy*, California University Press, Los Angeles.

Altick, R. (1962) 'The Social Origins, Education, Occupation of 1100 British Writers, 1800-1935', *Bulletin of the New York Public Library* 55 vi, 389-404.

Bakker, J. de (2001) *Across Crete, Part One: from Khania to Herakleion*, Logos Tekstproducies, Amsterdam.

Bann, S. (1994) 'Travelling to collect: the booty of John Bargrave and Charles Waterton' in G. Robertson, M. Marsh, L. Tickner, J. Bird, B. Curtis & T. Putnam (eds.), *Travellers' Tales. Narratives of Home and Displacement*, Routledge, London, 155-63.

Bean, G.E. (1978) *Lycian Turkey: an archaeological guide*, John Murray, London.

Becker, M.J. & Betancourt, P.P. (1997) *Richard Berry Seager*, University of Pennsylvania, Pennsylvania.

Bell, A. & Macfarquhar, C. (& Smellie, W.) (eds.) (1771) *Encyclopaedia Britannica, etc.*, Edinburgh.

Bennet, J. (2002) 'Millennial Ambiguities' in Y. Hamilakis (ed.) *Labyrinth Revisited: rethinking Minoan Archaeology*, Oxbow Books, Oxford, 214-25.

Bennet, J. & Voutsaki, S. (1991) 'A Synopsis and Analysis of Travelers' Account of Keos (to 1821)' in J.F. Cherry, J.L. Davis, E. Mantzourani (eds.) *Landscape Archaeology as Long-Term History, etc.*, Monumenta Archaeologica, Vol. 16, California University, Los Angles, 365-82.

Bennett, J.H. (1855) *Memoir of the late Professor Edward Forbes*, Southerland & Fox, Edinburgh.

Bertuch, F. (1821) *Bilderbuch Fur Kinder*, Weimar, Vol. X, No. 30, Landes-Industrie-Comptoirs.

Biers, W.R. (1996) *The Archaeology of Greece: An Introduction*, Cornel University Press, New York.

Bickford-Smith, R.A.H. (1898) *Cretan Sketches*, Richard Bentley and Son, London.

Black, J. (2003) *Italy and the Grand Tour*, Yale University Press, New Haven, Connecticut.

Blackman, D.J. & Branigan, K. (1975) 'An archaeological survey on the south coast of Crete, between the Ayiofarango and Chrisostomas', *Annual of the British School at Athens* 70: 17-36.

Blegen, C.W. (1995) *Troy and the Trojans*, Barnes & Noble, New York.

Boardman, J. (1961) *The Cretan Collection in Oxford: The Dictaean Cave and Iron Age Crete*, Clarendon Press, Oxford.

Borlase, W. (1769) *Antiquities Historical and Monumental of the County of Cornwall*, S. Baker, G. Leigh, T. Payne, B. White, London.

Bosanquet, R.C. (1901/02). 'Excavations at Praesos', *Annual of the British School at Athens* 8: 231-81.

Bosanquet, R.C. (1901/02). 'Excavations at Petras', *Annual of the British School at Athens* 88: 282-5.

Bosanquet, R.C. (1901/02). 'Excavations at Palaikastro', *Annual of the British School at Athens* 8: 286-316.

Bowman, J. (1974) *The Travellers' Guide to Crete*, Jonathan Cape, London.

Boyd Hawes, H. (*et al.*) (1908) *Gournia...etc.*, The American Exploration Society, Free Museum of Science and Art, Philadelphia.

Branigan, K. (1970) *The Foundations of Palatial Crete: A Survey of Crete in the Early Bronze Age*, Routledge & Kegan Paul, London.

Broodbank, C. (2008) 'Long After Hippos, Well Before Palaces: A Commentary on the Cultures and Contexts of Neolithic Crete' in Issakidou, V. & Tomkins, P. (eds.), *Escaping the Labyrinth: The Cretan Neolithic in Context*, Oxbow Books, Oxford, 273-90.

Brown, A. (1986) 'I propose to begin at Gnossos', *Annual of the British School at Athens* 82: 38-44.

Brown, A. (1993) *Before Knossos...Arthur Evans's travels in the Balkans and Crete*, Ashmolean Museum, Oxford.

Brown, A. (2000) 'Evans in Crete before 1900' in D. Huxley (ed.), *Cretan Quests*, British School at Athens, 9-14.

Brown, A. (2001) *Arthur Evans's Travels in Crete, 1894-1899*, BAR International Series 1000, Oxford.

Budde, L. & Nicholls, R. (1964) *A Catalogue of the Greek and Roman Sculpture in the Fitzwilliam Museum Cambridge*, Cambridge University Press, Cambridge.

Burch, O. (1989) *Under Mount Ida: A Journey into Crete*, Ashford, Southampton.

Burrows, R.M. (1907) *The Discoveries in Crete: and their bearing on the history of Ancient Civilisation*, John Murray, London.

Cadogan, G. (2000) 'The Pioneers: 1900-1914' in D. Huxley (ed.), *Cretan Quests*, British School at Athens, 15-27.

Cameron, P. (2003) *Blue Guide: Crete*, A&C Black, London; W.W. Norton, New York.

Castleden, R. (1990) *The Knossos Labyrinth: A new view of the 'Palace of Minos'*, Routledge, London and New York.

Chadwick, J. (2000) *The Decipherment of Linear B*, Cambridge University Press, Cambridge.

Chadwick, J. (2001) *Reading the Past: Linear B and Related Scripts*, British Museum Press, London.

Chapman, W.R. (1989) 'Toward an Institutional History of Archaeology: British Archaeologists and Allied Interests in the 1860s' in A.L. Christenson, *Tracing archaeology's past: the historiography of archaeology*, Southern Illinois University Press, Carbondale, 151-62.

Cheesman, C. (2004) ''The curse of Babel': the Enlightenment and the study of writing' in K. Sloan (ed.) *Enlightenment: Discovering the world in the eighteenth century*, British Museum Press, London, 202-11.

Chitty, S. (1989) *That Singular Person Called Lear*, Atheneum, New York.

Clark W.G. (1858) *Peloponnesus: Notes of Study and Travel*, John W. Parker, London.

Cockerell, C.R. (1903) *Travels in Southern Europe and the Levant 1810-1817*, Routledge, Oxford (1999 reprint).

Cook, B.F. (1998) 'British Archaeologists in the Aegean' in V. Brand (ed.) *The Study of the Past in the Victorian Age*, Oxford Monograph 73.

Cook, J.M. (1950) 'Archaeology in Greece 1948-1949' *Journal of Hellenic Studies* 70, 1-15.

Copplestone, T. (ed.) (1966) *World Architecture*, Paul Hamlyn, London.

Cramer, J.A. (1828) *A Geographical and Historical Description of Ancient Greece*, 3 vols., Oxford University Press, Oxford.

Curthoys, M.C. (2004) 'Cramer, John Antony (1793–1848)', *Oxford Dictionary of National Biography*, Oxford University Press, Oxford.

Damiani, A. (1979) *Enlightened Travellers: British Travellers to the Near East 1715-1850*, American University of Beirut.

Daniel, G. (1967) *The Origins and Growth of Archaeology*, Pelican, Middlesex.

Dapper, O. (1688) *Description excate des iles de l'archipel*, translated from Flemish, George Gallett, Amsterdam, 1703.

Darwin, C. (1859) *On the Origin of Species, etc.*, John Murray, London.

Darwin, C. (1871) *The Descent of Man, etc.*, John Murray, London.

Dawson, L.S. (ed.) (1885) *Memoirs of Hydrography*, Henry Keay, The 'Imperial Library', Eastbourne (Sussex).

Davaras, C. (1976) *Guide to Cretan Antiquities*, Eptalofos, Athens.

Davidson, C. (undated) 'Bucolics (Eclogues)' *The Works of Virgil*, T. Werner Laurie, London.

Davis, R.B. (1955) *George Sandys, poet-adventurer: a study in Anglo-American culture in the seventeenth century*, Bodley Head, London.

Dawkins, R.M. (1903-4) 'Excavations at Palaikastro', *Annual of the British School at Athens* 10, 192-231.

Dawkins, R.M. (1930) 'Presidential Address: Folk-Memory in Crete' *Folklore* Vol. 41, No. 1, Mar, 11-42.

Deacon, M. (1978) *Vice–Admiral TAB Spratt and the Development of Oceanography in the Mediterranean 1841-1873*, Maritime Monographs and Reports, No. 37, National Maritime Museum, Woolwich.

Delheim, C.R. (1979) *Medievalism in Modernity: the Victorian's Encounter with their own Inheritance*, PhD thesis, Yale University, unpublished.

Dermitzakis, M. (1973) 'Recent Tectonic Movement and Old Strandlines along the Coasts of Crete', *Bulletin of the Geological Society*, 10, 48-64.

Díaz-Andreu, M. (2007) *A world history of nineteenth century archaeology: nationalism, colonialism and the past*, Oxford University Press, Oxford.

Dickinson, O. (1999) *The Aegean Bronze Age*, Cambridge University Press, Cambridge.

Dodwell, E. (1834) *Views and Descriptions of Cyclopian, or, Pelasgic Remains, in Greece and Italy; etc.*, Adolphus Richter, London.

Dolan, B. (2000) *Exploring European Frontiers: British Travellers in the Age of Enlightenment*, MacMillan Press, London.

E.S. (1878) 'A Levantine Picnic', *Lippincott's Magazine of Popular Literature and Science*, Vol. 22, July.

Easton, D.F. (1981) 'Schliemann's discovery of 'Priam's Treasure': two enigmas', *Antiquity* 55: 179-83.

Easton, D.F. (1985) 'Has the Trojan War been found?', *Antiquity* 59, 188-96.

Edwardes, C. (1887) *Letters from Crete*, Richard Bentley, London.

Eisner, R. (1993) *Travelers to an Antique Land*, Michigan University Press, Michigan.

Ellison, J. (2004) 'Sandys, George (1578–1644)', *Oxford Dictionary of National Biography*, Oxford University Press, Oxford.

Evans, A.J. (1896a) 'Explorations in Eastern Crete. II. A Town of Castles', *Academy* 1259, June 20, 512-13.

Evans, A.J. (1896b) 'Archaeological News – Explorations in Eastern Krete', *American Journal of Archaeology and the History of the Fine Arts*, Vol. 11, No 3, 449-67.

Evans, A.J. (1899-1900) 'Knossos. Summary report of the excavations in 1900, I: the palace', *Annual of the British School at Athens* 6, 3-70.

Evans, A.J. (1901) 'The Palace of Minos' *The Monthly Review*, March, 115-32.

Evans, A.J. (1909) *Scripta Minoa: The Written Documents of Minoan Crete with Special Reference to the Archives of Knossos, Volume I. The Hieroglyphic and Primitive Linear Classes*, Clarendon Press, Oxford.

Evans, A.J. (1921, 1928, 1930, 1935) *The Palace of Minos*, 4 vols. in 7 books, Macmillan, London.

Evans, J.D. (1971) 'Neolithic Knossos: Growth of a Settlement', *Proceedings of the Prehistoric Society* 37: 95-117.

Evans, J. (1891) 'The progress of archaeology: an address delivered to the Antiquarian Section of the Royal Archaeological Institute, at its Congress in Edinburgh', Virtue & Co., London.

Evans, J. (1943) *Time and Chance*, Longmans, London

Falkener, E. (1854) *Theatres and Other Remains in Crete*, (supplement to his *Museum of Classical Antiquities*), Trubner, London.

Farnoux, A. (1996) *Knossos: Unearthing a Legend*, Thames and Hudson, London.

Fedden, R. (1958) *English Travellers in the Near East*, Longmans, Green & Co., London.

Fellows, C. (1839) *A Journal written during an Excursion in Asia Minor*, John Murray, London.

Finley, M.I. (1991) *Aspects of Antiquity: Discoveries and Controversies*, Penguin, Middlesex.

Fisher, S. (1989) 'Aegean Seas through the English eyes: the British Naval Aegean Survey, 1825-1863', *Paper read at the Symposium of IMCOS and Society for Hellenic Cartography*, Athens, October (from Hydrographic Office, Taunton).

Fisher, J. & Garvey, G. (2004) *The Rough Guide to Crete*, Rough Guides, London.

Fitton, J.L. (1995) *The Discovery of the Greek Bronze Age*, The British Museum Press, London.

Fitton, J.L. (2002) *Minoans*, British Museum Press, London.

Flemming, N. (1978) 'Holocene Eustatic Changes and the Coastal Tectonics in the Northeast Mediterranean: Implications for Models of Crystal Consumption', *Philosophical Transactions of the Royal Society of London*, A 289, 405-58.

Forsdyke, E.J. (1927) 'The Mavro Spelio Cemetery at Knossos', *Annual of the British School at Athens* 28: 243-96.

Fowler, R. (ed.) (1984) *Edward Lear: The Cretan Journal*, Denis Harvey, Athens-Dedham (Essex).

Frazer, J.G. (1898) *Pausanias' Description of Greece*, Vol. III, MacMillan, London

Frere, J. (1800) 'An Account of Flint Weapons Discovered at Hoxne, in Suffolk', *Archaeologia* 13, 204-5.

Frost, F.J and Hadjiaki, E. (1990) 'Excavations at the harbour of Phalasarna in Crete: The 1988 Season', *Hesperia*, Vol. 59, No 33 (July – Sept 1990), 513-27.

Gavrilaki, I (ed.) (undated) *Gerontospilios in Melidoni*, pamphlet – 25th Ephorate of Prehistoric and Classical Antiquities.

Gell, W. (1810) *The Itinerary of Greece with a commentary on Pausanias and Strabo etc.*, T. Payne, London.

Gell, W. (1823) *Narrative of a Journey in the Morea*, Longman, Hurst, Rees, Orme and Brown, London.

Gere, C. (2006) *The Tomb of Agamemnon*, Profile Books, London.

German, S.C. (2005) 'Photography and Fiction: The Publication of the exactions at the Palace of Minos at Knossos', *Journal of Mediterranean Archaeology*, 18: 209-30.

Gladstone, W.E. (1858) *Studies on Homer and the Homeric Age*, 3 vols., Oxford University Press, Oxford.

Green, K. (1996) *Archaeology: An Introduction*, Routledge, Oxford.

Grote, G. (1846-56) *A History of Greece*, 12 vols., John Murray, London.

Grundon, I. (2007) *The Rash Adventurer: A Life of John Pendlebury*, Libri, London.

Hadijaki, E. (1988) 'Preliminary Report of Excavations at the Harbour of Phalasarna in West Crete',

American Journal of Archaeology Vol. 92, No. 4, 463-79.

Hakluyt, R. (1598) *The Principal Navigations Voyages Traffiques & Discoveries of the English Nation etc.*, J.M. Dent and Sons; E.P. Dutton (1927 edition, 8 vols.).

Halstead, P. (1997) 'Storage and States on Prehistoric Crete: A Reply to Strasser (JMA 10 [1997] 73-100)' *Journal of Mediterranean Archaeology*, 10, No 1, 103-7.

Hamilakis, Y. (2002) 'What future for the Minoan Past? Re-thinking Minoan archaeology' in Y. Hamilakis (ed.), *Labyrinth Revisited: rethinking Minoan Archaeology*, Oxbow Books, Oxford, 2-28.

Hatzaki, E. (2005) 'Crete & Knossos' in E. Calligas & J. Whitely (eds.), *On Site: British Archaeologists in Greece*, British School at Athens.

Hall, E. (1909) 'Explorations in Crete', *The National Geographic Magazine*, September.

Hegarty, M. (1989) 'Dr Richard Pococke', *Decies: Journal of the Waterford Archaeological & Historical Society*, 42, 27-32.

Hitchcock, L. & Koudounaris, P. (2002) 'Virtual Discourse' in Y. Hamilakis (ed.), *Labyrinth Revisited: rethinking Minoan Archaeology*, Oxbow Books, Oxford, 40-58.

Hodgkin, T. (1891) 'Opening Address of the Historical Section at the meeting of the Archaeological Institute at Edinburgh' *Archaeological Journal* XLVIII, 253-73.

Hoeck, K. (1823-9) *Kreta: Ein Versuch zur Aufhellung der Mythologie und Geschichte, der Religion und Verfassung dieser Insel, von den ältesten Zeiten bis auf die Römer-Herrschaft*, C. E. Rosenbusch, Göttingen.

Hogarth, D.G. (1889) *Authority and Archaeology: Sacred and profane. Essays on the relation of monuments to biblical and classical literature*, John Murray, London.

Hogarth, D.G. (ed.) (1899) *Authority and Archaeology, Sacred and Profane*, John Murray, London.

Hogarth, D.G. (1899-1900) 'Knossos: Early Town and Cemeteries', *Annual of the British School at Athens* VI, 70-85.

Hogarth, D.G. (1910) *Accidents of an Antiquary's Life*, John Murray, London.

Holworth, H. (1892) 'Old and New Methods in Writing History, being the Opening Address of the Historical Section at the Dorchester Meeting', *Archaeological Journal* LV, 122-44.

Hood, S. (1971) *The Minoans: Crete in the Bronze Age*, Thames & Hudson, London.

Hood, S. & Smyth, D. (1981) *Archaeological Survey of the Knossos Area*, Supplementary Vol. 14, British School at Athens.

Hood, S., Warren, P. & Cadogan, G. (1964) 'Travels in Crete, 1962', *Annual of the British School at Athens* 59, 50-99.

Hopkins, A. (1977) *Crete: Its Past, Present and People*, Faber & Faber, London.

Horwitz, S.L. (1981) *The Find of a Lifetime: Sir Arthur Evans & the Discovery of Knossos*, Weidenfeld & Nicolson, London.

Hutchinson, R.W. (1968) *Prehistoric Crete*, Penguin, Middlesex.

Huxley, D. (2000) 'Cretan Chronology' in D. Huxley (ed.), *Cretan Quests*, British School at Athens, xxi.

Issakidou, V. & Tomkins, P. (eds.) (2008) *Escaping The Labyrinth: The Cretan Neolithic in Context*, Oxbow Books, Oxford.

Jameson, M. H. (1965) 'Book Reviews: *The Earth, the Temple, and the Gods* by Vincent Scully', *Classical Philology* Vol. 60, No. 3, July.

Jenkins, I. (2004) 'Ideas of antiquity: classical and other ancient civilizations in the age of Enlightenment' in K. Sloan (ed.) *Enlightenment: Discovering the world in the eighteenth century*, British Museum Press, London, 168-177.

Jones, E.A. (1924) *American Members of the Inns of Court*, xii, 191-2, The Saint Catherine press, London.

Jones, I. (2004) 'Philosophical time travellers', *Antiquity* 66: 744-57.

Karetsou, A. (1981) 'The Peak Sanctuary of Mt. Juktas' in R. Hagg & S. Marinatos (eds.), *Sanctuaries and Cults in the Aegean Bronze Age – proceedings of the first international symposium at the Swedish institute in Athens*, Stockholm, 137-53.

Kemp, D.W. (ed.) (1887) *Tours in Scotland, 1747, 1750, 1760, by Richard Pococke*, Edinburgh University Press, Edinburgh (reprint by Heritage Books, Maryland, USA, 2003).

Lattimore, S. (trans.) (1998) *Thucydides' The Peloponnesian War*, Hackett, Indianapolis.

Leake, W.M. (1814) *Researches in Greece*, J. Booth, London.

Leake, W.M. (1830) *Travels in Morea*, Vols. I & II, John Murray, London.

Leake, W.M. (1835) *Travels in Northern Greece*, J. Rodwell, London.

Leake, W.M. (1841) *The Topography of Athens, and The Demi of Attica*, Vol. I, J. Rodwell, London.

Leake, W.M. (1846) *Peloponnesiaca: a supplement to Travels in Morea*, J. Rodwell, London.

Leatham, J. & Hood, S. (1958-9) 'Submarine exploration in Crete, 1955', *Annual of the British School at Athens* 53-54, 263-80.

Lehmann, J. (1977) *Edward Lear and his world*, Thames and Hudson, London.

Levi, P. (1995) *Edward Lear: A Biography*, Scribner, New York.

Levine, P. (2002) *The Amateur and the Professional*, Cambridge University Press, Cambridge.

Lithgow, W. (1632) *The Totall Discourse of the Rare Adventures, and painefull Peregrinations, etc.*, Nicholas Okes, London (see Phelps, below, for reprint).

Lloyd, S. (1947) *Foundations in the Dust: A Story of Mesopotamian Exploration*, Geoffrey Cumberlege, London.

Loader, N.C. (1998) *Building in Cyclopean Masonry: with Special Reference to the Mycenaean Fortifications on Mainland Greece*, Paul Åstrőns Főrlag, Goteborg (Sweden).

Lyell, C. (1830) *Principles of Geology*, John Murray, London.

McArthur, J.K. (1993) *Place-Names in the Knossos Tablets: Identification and Location*, Ediciones Universidad de Salamanca (Spain).

McConnell, A. (2004) 'Morritt, John Bacon Sawrey (1771–1843)', *Oxford Dictionary of National Biography*, Oxford University Press, Oxford

Macdonald, C.F. (2005) *Knossos*, The Folio Society, London.

MacGillivray, J.A. (2000) *Minotaur: Sir Arthur Evans and the Archaeology of the Minoan Myth*, Jonathan Cape, London.

MacGillivray, J.A., Sackett, L.M., Driesen, J. & Smyth, D. (1986) 'Excavations at Palaikastro', *Annual of the British School at Athens* 82, 135-54.

MacEnroe. J.C. (2001) 'Cretan Questions: Politics and Archaeology' in Y. Hamilakis (ed.), *Labyrinth Revisited: Rethinking 'Minoan' Archaeology*, Oxbow Books, Oxford.

Maempel, G.Z. (1986) 'T.A.B. Spratt (1811-88) and his contribution to Maltese Geology', *Melita Historica*, 9, 271-308.

Mallet, A.M. (1683) *Description de L'Univers,* Vol. 4, Denys Thierry, Paris.

Manning, S.W. (2008) 'Formation of the Palaces' in C.W. Shelmerdine (ed.), *The Aegean Bronze Age*, Cambridge University Press, Cambridge, 105-20.

Manning, S.W. (1996) 'Archaeology and the World of Homer: Introduction to a Past and Present Discipline' in C. Emlyn-Jones, L. Hardwick & J. Purkis (eds.), *Homer: Readings and Images*, Duckworth, London, 116-42.

Manning, S.W. (1999a) *A Test of Time: The Volcano of Thera and the chronologyand history of the Aegean and east Mediterranean in the mid-second millennium BC,* Oxbow Books, Oxford.

Manning, S.W. (1999b) 'Knossos and the limits of settlement growth' in P.P. Betancourt (ed.) *MELETEMATA: Studies in Aegean Archaeology presented to Malcolm H. Weiner as he enters his 65th year, AEGAEUM* 20, 469-80.

Manning, S.W., Ramsey, C.B., Kutschera, W., Higham, T., Fromer, B., Steier, P., & Wild, E.M. (2006) 'Chronology for the Aegean Late Bronze Age 1700-1400 BC' *Science*, Vol. 312, issue 5773, 565-9.

Marindin, G.E. (1985) (ed.) *A Grand Tour: Letters and Journey 1794-96 (John Morritt)*, Century Publishing, Idaho.

Martin, R. (1988) *Greek Architecture*, Faber & Faber, London.

Matthews, W.H. (1922) *Mazes and Labyrinths: Their History and Development*, Dover Publications, New York (1970 reprint).

Mavor, W. (1803) *An historical account of the most celebrated voyages, travels, and discoveries from the time of Columbus to the present period*, Vol. XIII, Samuel F. Bradford, Philadelphia.

Mee, C. (1982) *Rhodes in the Bronze Age: An Archaeological Survey*, Aris & Phillips, Warminster (Wiltshire).

Michaelis, A. (1882) *Ancient Marbles in Great Britain*, Cambridge University Press, Cambridge.

Miller, W. (1925-26) 'Finley's History of the Insurrection in Crete', *Annual of the British School at Athens* 27, 92-112.

Milles, I. (1721) *An account of the life and conversation of the reverend and worthy Mr. Isaac Milles etc.*, W. & J. Innys, London.

Momigliano, N. (1999) *Duncan Mackenzie: A cautious canny Highlander & the Palace of Minos at Knossos*, Institute of Classical Studies, London University, London.

Moryson, F. (1617) *An Itinerary written by Fynes Moryson...containing his ten yeeres travel etc.*, John Beale, London.

Moss, W.S. (1950) *Ill Met by Moonlight*, Cassell, London (reprinted 2004).

Murray J. (ed.) (1854) *Handbook for Travellers to Greece*, John Murray, London.

Murray, T. (ed.) (2001) *Encyclopaedia of archaeology: Histories and Discoveries*, Santa Barbara, California, Los Angeles.

Myers, J.W., Myers, E.E. & Cadogan, G. (eds.) (1992) *The Aerial Atlas of Ancient Crete*, Thames and Hudson, London.

Newton, C. (1851) 'On the Study of Archaeology', *Archaeological Journal* VIII, 1-26.

Niemeier, W.-D. & Niemeier, B. (1999) 'The Minoans of Miletus' in P.P. Betancourt (*et al.*) (eds.) *MELETEMATA: Studies in Aegean Archaeology presented to Malcolm H. Wiener as he enters his 65th year, AEGAEUM* 20, 543-54.

Noakes, V. (1979) *Edward Lear*, Fontana/Collins, London.

Nowicki, K. (ed.) (2000) *Defensible Sites in Crete c1200-800 BC (LMIIIB/IIIC through early Geometric)*, AEGAEUM 21, University de Liege, Wallonia (Belgium).

Palmer, L.R. (1963) *The Interpretation of Mycenaean Greek Texts*, Oxford University Press, Oxford.

Papadopoulos, J.K. (2005) 'Inventing the Minoans: Archaeology, Modernity and the Quest for European Identity', *Journal of Mediterranean Archaeology*, 18.1, 87-149.

Papadakis, N.P. (1986) *Ierapetra: Bride of the Lybian Sea*, Ireapetra Town Council (Crete).

Pashley, R. (1837) *Travels in Crete*, 2 vols., John Murray, London.

Patroudakis, G. (2004) 'The Secrets of the Labyrinth', *Cretan Panorama*, May-June, 43-81.

Pendlebury, J.D.S. (1939) *The Archaeology of Crete: An Introduction*, Methuen, London.

Pendlebury, J.D.S. (1948) *John Pendlebury in Crete*, Cambridge University Press, Cambridge.

Pendlebury, J.D.S., Eccles, E. & Money-Coutts, M.B. (1932/33) 'Journeys in Crete', *Annual of the British School at Athens* 33, 80-101.

Phelps, G. (ed.) (1974) *The Rare Adventures and Painful Peregrinations of William Lithgow*, The Folio Society, London (reprint of Lithgow's book).

Piggott, S. (1989) *Ancient Britons and the antiquarian imagination: ideas from the Renaissance to the Regency*, Thames & Hudson, London.

Pitt Rivers, A.H.L.F. (1887) 'Inaugural Address to the Annual Meeting of the Institute held at Salisbury. Delivered 2 August 1887', *Archaeological Journal* XLIV, 261-77.

Pitt Rivers, A.H.L.F. (1898) *Excavations in Cranbourne Chase*, London.

Platon, N. (1971) *Zakros: The Discovery of a Lost Palace of Ancient Crete*, Scribner, New York.

Plouviez, C. (2001) 'Straddling the Aegean: William Gell 1811-1813' in S. Searight & M. Wagstaff (eds.), *Travellers in the Levant: Voyagers and Visionaries*, ASTENE.

Pococke, R. (1745) *A description of the East and some other countries*, Vol. II, Bowyer, London.

Pope, M. (1975) *The Story of Decipherment: From Egyptian Hieroglyphic to Linear B*, Thames and Hudson, London.

Postlethwaite, E. (1868) *A Tour in Crete*, John Camden, London.

Quane, M. (1950) 'Pococke School, Kilkenny', *Journal of the Royal Society of Antiquaries of Ireland*, 80, 36-72.

Rackham, O. & Moody, J. (1996) *The making of the Cretan landscape*, Manchester University Press, Manchester.

Rehak, P. & Younger, J.G. (1993) 'New Linear A Inscription from Pyrgos in Crete', *American School of Classical Studies at Athens Newsletter* 32. 2.

Rehak, P. & Younger, J.G. (1995) 'A Minoan Roundel from Pyrgos, Southeastern Crete' *Kadmos* 34.2, 81-102.

Renfrew, C. (1972) *The Emergence of Civilization: the Cyclades and the Aegean in the 3rd Millennium*, Methuen, London.

Renfrew, C. & Bahn, P.G. (1996) *Archaeology: Theories, Methods, and Practice*, Thames and Hudson, London.

Rice, W.G. (1933) 'Early English Travelers to Greece and the Levant' in A. Arbor, *Essays and Studies in English and Comparative Literature*, Michigan University Press, Michigan.

Robinson, A. (2002) *The man who deciphered Linear B: the story of Michael Ventris*, Thames & Hudson, London.

Robinson, H.S. (1969) 'Chiron at Corinth' *American Journal of Archaeology*, 73, 193-7.

Rowley-Conwy, P. (2007) *From Genesis to Prehistory. The archaeology Three Age System and its contested reception in Denmark, Britain and Ireland*, Oxford University Press, Oxford.

Rutkowski, B (1986) *The Cult Places of the Aegean*, Yale University Press, New Haven, Connecticut.

Sackett, L.H., Popham, M.R. & Warren, P.M. (1965) 'Excavations at Palaikastro', *Annual of the British School at Athens* 60, 269-314.

Sakellarakis, Y. & Sakellarakis, E. (1997) *Archanes: Minoan Crete in a new light*, 2 vols., Athens: Emmos.

Sandys, G. (1615) *A Relation of a Journey Begun An. Dom 1610...etc.*, John Sweting, London (5th edition, 1652).

Sayce, A.H. (1923) *Reminiscences*, Macmillan, London.

Schäfer, J. (1991) 'Amnisos - Harbour town of Minos?' in R. Laffineur & L. Basch (eds.), *Thalassa: l'égée prehistorique et la mer*, Aegaeum 7. 111-7, Université de Liège.

Schliemann, H. (1875) *Troy and its Remains*, John Murray, London.

Schliemann, H. (1878) *A narrative of researches and discoveries at Mycenae and Tiryns*, John Murray, London.

Schnapp, A. (1996) *The Discovery of the Past: The Origins of Archaeology*, British Museum Press, London.

Schnapp, A. (2002) 'Between antiquarians and archaeologists – continuities and ruptures', *Antiquity* 96, 134-40.

Scott, C.R. (1837) *Rambles in Egypt and Candia... etc.*, Henry Colburn, London.

Scully, V. (1962) *The Earth, the Temple, and the Gods*, Yale University Press, New Haven, Connecticut.

Seager, R.B. (1912) *Explorations in the Island of Mochlos*, Boston, New York; American School of Classical Studies at Athens.

Searight, S. & Wagstaff, M. (eds.) (2001) *Travellers in the Levant*, ASTENE.

Shaw, J.W. (2006) *Kommos: a Minoan Harbour Town and Greek Sanctuary in Southern Crete*, The American School of Classical Studies at Athens.

Shelmerdine, C.W. (2008) 'Background, Sources and Methods' in C.W. Shelmerdine (ed.), *The Aegean Bronze Age*, Cambridge University Press, Cambridge, 1-18.

Sherratt, S. (1996) 'With us but not of us: The role of Crete in Homeric Epic' in D. Evely, I.S. Lemos & S. Sherratt (eds.), *Minotaur and Centaur: Studies in the archaeology of Crete and Euboea presented to Mervyn Popham*, BAR International Series 638, 87-99.

Sherratt, A. & Sherratt, S. (2008) 'The Neolithic of Crete, as Seen from the Outside' in V. Issakidou, & P. Tomkins, (eds.), *Escaping the*

Labyrinth: The Cretan Neolithic in Context, Oxbow Books, Oxford, 291-302.

Sieber, F.W. (1823) *Travels in the Island of Crete in the year 1817*, Sir Richard Phillips, London.

Skelton, R.A. (1952) *Decorative Printed Maps of the 15th to 18th Centuries*, Staples Press, London.

Skinner, J.E.H. (1868) *Roughing it in Crete*, Richard Bentley, London.

Smith, M.L. (1973) *The Great Island: A Study of Crete*, Allen Lane, Penguin, Middlesex.

Soles, J.S (1992) 'The Prepalatial Cemeteries at Mochlos and Gournia and the House Tombs of Bronze Age Crete', *Hesperia: Supplement XXIV*, American School of Classical Studies at Athens, Princeton University Press, New Jersey.

Spanakis, S.G. (undated, c.1960) *Crete, A Guide to Travel, History and Archaeology*, Vangelis Sfakianakis, Iraklion (Crete).

Spratt, T.A.B. & Forbes, E. (1847) *Travels in Lycia, Milyas, and the Cibyratis, in company with the late Rev. E. T. Daniell*, 2 vols., John Van Voorst, London.

Spratt, T.A.B. (1860) *Description of Crete* Hydrographic Office, Taunton, ref. C36, 684

Spratt, T.A.B. (1865) *Travels and Researches in Crete*, 2 vols., John Van Voorst, London.

Spratt, T.A.B. (1879) *Proceedings of the Society of Antiquaries*, May 1st, 118-23.

Sphyroeras, V., Avramea, A. & Asdrahas, S. (eds.) (1985) *Maps and Map-Makers of the Aegean*, Olkos Ltd, Athens.

St. John, J.A. (1835) *The Lives of Celebrated Travellers*, Vol. II, Harper & Brothers, New York.

Stampolidis, N. C. (ed.) (2004) *Eleutherna*, Athens.

Stephens, J.L. (1840) *Incidents of Travel in Greece, Turkey, Russia & Poland*, Walker & Co, London.

Stevenson, E.L. (1991) *Claudius Ptolemy: The Geography*, Dover, London.

Stillwell, R. (ed.) (1976) *The Princeton Encyclopaedia of Classical Sites*, Princeton University Press, New Jersey.

Strasser, T. (1997) 'Storage and States on Prehistoric Crete: The Function of the Koulouras in the First Minoan Palaces' *Journal of Mediterranean Archaeology*, 10, No. 1, 73-100.

Stukeley, W. (1740) *Stonehenge: A temple restored to the British Druids*, Innys & Manby, London

Taylor, B. (1859) *Travels in Greece and Russia with an excursion to Crete*, G.P. Putman, New York.

Thompson, J. (1992) *Sir Gardner Wilkinson and His Circle*, Texas University Press, Texas.

Thomsen, C.J. (1837) *Leitfaden zur nordischen Alterthumskunde, etc.*, De Gesellshaft, Copenhagen.

Thorne, C. (1992) *Between the Seas: a Quiet Walk Through Crete*, Sinclair-Stevenson, London.

Tournefort, J.P. de (1717) *Relation d'un Voyage du Levant*, Paris.

Toynbee, J.M.C. & Major H.D.A. (2004) 'Gardner, Percy (1846–1937)', Rev. John Boardman, *Oxford Dictionary of National Biography*, Oxford University, Oxford.

Traill, D (1983) 'Schliemann's discovery of 'Priam's Treasure', *Antiquity* 57: 181-6.

Traill, D. (1995) *Schliemann of Troy: Treasure and Deceit*, John Murray, London.

Trease, G. (1967) *The Grand Tour*, Heinemann, London.

Trevor-Battye, A. (1913) *Camping in Crete*, Witherby & Co., London.

Trevor-Battye, A. (1919) 'Crete: Its scenery and natural features', *The Geographical Journal* Vol. LVI, No. 3, 137-57.

Trigger, B.G. (1999) *A history of archaeological thought*, Cambridge University Press, Cambridge.

Tsigakou, F.-M. (1981) *The Rediscovery of Greece: Travellers and Painters of the Romantic Era*, Caratzas Bros, New York.

Tsipopoulou, M., (2003) 'The Minoan Palace at Petras, Siteia', *Athena Review*, Vol. 3, No. 3: 44-51.

Tsountas, C. & Mannat, J.I. (1897) *The Mycenaean Age: a study of the monuments and culture of pre-Homeric Greece*, Macmillan and Co., London.

Vasilakis, A. (undated) *The Great Inscription of the Law Code of Gortyn*, Mystis, Herakleion (Crete).

Vasilakis, A. (1999) *Minoan Crete: From Myth to History,* Adam Editions, Athens.

Vasilakis, A. (2000) *the 147 Cities of Ancient Crete*, Kairatos Editions, Herakleion (Crete).

Ventris, M. & Chadwick, J. (1959) *Documents in Mycenaean Greek*, Cambridge University Press, Cambridge.

Wace, A. (1949) *Mycenae: An Archaeological History and Guide*, Princeton University Press, New Jersey.

Walker, S. (1984) 'Marble Origins by Isotopic Analysis', *World Archaeology*, Vol. 16, No 2, Oct, 204-21.

Warren, P.M. (1972a) '16th, 17th and 18th century British Travellers to Crete', *Kretica Chronica*, 65-92.

Warren, P.M (1972b) *Myrtos: An Early Bronze settlement in Crete*, British School at Athens Supplementary Series, Thames & Hudson.

Warren, P.M. (1996) 'Early Irish and British Travellers to the Island of Crete', *Anglo Hellenic Review* 14, 15.

Warren, P.M. (2000) 'Early British Travellers from Britain and Ireland' in D. Huxley (ed.), *Cretan Quests: British Explorers, Excavators and Historians*, British School at Athens.

Weber, S.H. (1953) *Voyages and Travels: in Greece, the Near East and adjacent regions made previous to the Year 1801*, American School of Classical Studies at Athens, Princeton University Press, New Jersey (facsimile: Martino Publishing, 2002).

Weinberg, G.D. (1960) 'Excavations at Tarrha', *Hesperia*, Vol. 29, No. 1, 90-108.

Weller, C.H. (1906) 'The Extent of Strabo's Travels in Greece', *Classical Philology* Vol. I, No. 4, 339-56.

Whitelaw, T.M., Day, P.M., Kiriatzi, E., Kilikoglou, V. & Wilson, D.E. (1997) 'Ceramic traditions at EM IIB Myrtos, Fournou Korifi' in R. Laffineur & P.P. Betancourt (eds.), *TEXNH. Craftsmen, Craftswomen and Craftsmanship in the Aegean Bronze Age* (*Aegaeum* 16, Liege/Austin), 265-74.

Whitely, A.J.M. (1992) 'Praesos' in J.W. Myers, E.E. Myers & G. Cadogan (eds.), *The Aerial Atlas of Ancient Crete*, Thames and Hudson, London.

Whitely, A.J.M. (1998) 'From Minoan to Eteocretans: The Praisos Region 1200-500 BC' in W.G. Cavanagh & M. Curtis (eds.), *Post Minoan Crete*, 27-39.

Whitely, A.J.M., O'Connor, K. & Mason, H. (1995) 'Praesos: a Report on the Architectural Survey undertaken in 1992', *Annual of the British School at Athens* 90, 405-28.

Wilson, D. (2008) 'Early Prepalatial Crete' in C.W. Shelmerdine (ed.), *The Aegean Bronze Age*, Cambridge University Press, Cambridge, 77-104.

Wilson, G. & Geikie, A. (1861) *Memoir of Edward Forbes, FRS, late professor of Natural History in the University of Edinburgh*, Macmillan, London; Edmonston & Douglas, Edinburgh.

Woodward, A.M. (1949) 'The Gortyn "Labyrinth" and its visitors in the fifteenth century', *Annual of the British School at Athens* XLIV, 324-5.

Wright, T. (1875) *The Celt, the Roman and the Saxon*, Trubner, London.

Younger, J.G. & Rehak, P. (2008) 'The Material Culture of Neopalatial Crete' in C.W. Shelmerdine (ed.), *The Aegean Bronze Age*, Cambridge University Press, Cambridge, 140-64.

Zohany, D. & Hopf, M. (1998) *Domestication of plants in the Old World: the origins and spread of cultivated plants in West Asia, Europe and the Nile valley*, Oxford University Press, Oxford.